Western Political Thought

About the Author

Deepan Das did his M.A. in Political Science from Dibrugarh University. He has also completed his M.Phil in the same department from the same University. He is now pursuing Ph.D. programme in the department of Political Science of Dibrugarh University. He has co-authored books on "Pashatyar Rajnaitik Chintadhara", "Bharatiya Sarkar Aru Rajneeti", "Antrojak Ain", "Antorastriya Samparka", "Rajnaitik Tatwa" Tulanamulak Sarkar, "Uttar Pub Bharator Rajneeti" and "Lok Prashashan" (All these are in Assamese Medium). He has also presented a number of research papers at various conferences. Presently, he is serving as an Assistant Professor in the Department of Political Science R.G. Baruah College, Guwahati. His areas of interest are Government and Politics, Rural Development, Political Theory and Politics of Northeast India.

WESTERN
Political Thought

Deepan Das

CONCEPT PUBLISHING COMPANY PVT. LTD.
NEW DELHI-110059

Western Political Thought: A text book of Political Science written by **Dr. Deepan Das**, Astt. Prof., Deptt. of Political Science, R.G. Baruah College, Guwahati, as per the new Semester System of Degree Course of Dibrugarh University, Guwahati University and North Eastern Hill University

---

BOOK CODE - ENG. - 1

ISBN-13: 978-93-88937-04-7 (HB)

ISBN-13: 978-93-88937-05-4 (PB)

First Published in 2019

Published and Printed by

Concept
Since 1974

Concept Publishing Company Pvt. Ltd.
A/15-16, Commercial Block, Mohan Garden
New Delhi-110059 (India)
Phones : 25351460, 25351794
Email : publishing@conceptpub.com,
Website: www.conceptpub.com

Preface

This book on Western Political thought has been designed primarily to meet the requirements of the students of Political Science for B.A. First Semester (Major) of Dibrugarh University. While writing this book the author has consulted the various standard works on the subject and tried to present the material in a simple and lucid form. The book shall be found useful by the students as well as teachers.

I am grateful to the publisher M/s Concept Publishing Company Pvt. Ltd. for bringing out this book with remarkable speed. Suggestions for further improvement of the book are welcomed and shall be gratefully acknowledged.

SYLLABUS

DIBRUGARH UNIVERSITY

POLITICAL SCIENCE

TOC (Major) (Ist Semester)

PAPER - 10100 PSCM : **WESTERN POLITICAL THOUGHT**

Total Marks - 100

(80 Marks for Final Examination and 20 Marks for Internal Assessment)

Objectives: The course is designed to Introduce the students to the contribution of the main traditions of Western Political Thinkers to Political Thought.

UNIT-I : Greek Political Thought
Plato, Aristotle (Lectures-12 & Marks-16)

UNIT-II : Medieval Political Thought
St. Augustine, St. Thomas Aquinas (Lectures-12 & Marks-16)

UNIT-III : Secular Political Thought
Marsiglio of Padua, Niccolo Machiavelli(Lectures-12 & Marks-16)

UNIT-IV : Contractual Political Thought
Thomas Hobbes, John Locke. (Lectures-12 & Marks-16)

UNIT-V : Enlightenment Political Thought
J.J. Rousseau, J.S. Mill (Lectures-12 & Marks-16)

Contents

Unit-I
The Greek Political Thought

The Greek political philosophy is one of those most ancient political philosophies of the world which has carefully been preserved and passed on from one generation to the other generation. It will, however, be a futile attempt to trace the origin of this political philosophy and also identify the state in which its seeds were first sown. Some European political historians have in vain tried to establish that political philosophy in the West began with the Greek. It is accepted throughout the world that ancient Indian, Babylonian, Roman and Egyptian too had their own political philosophies which were as old as the ancient Greek political philosophy. It is also an undisputed fact that during their own times these civilizations and their political philosophies were studied with keen interest all over the world. For example Ernest Barker says "political thought begins with the Greek. Its origin is connected with the calm and clear rationalism of the Greek mind." In this respect ideas of Maxey appear to be more sound when he says, "The closer and fuller acquaintance with the civilization of remote millennium which we now enjoy reveals an astonishing abundance of the political ideas among the people of those vanished areas and show how both in thought and practice they anticipated, paralleled and to some extent laid the foundations for ideas which subsequently appeared in European political consciousness."

In fact political philosophy of the Greek was a reaction to the developing civilization in other parts of the world. There were definitely varied and various factors which were responsible for the development of political philosophy of ancient Greece which cannot better be described than in the words of Professor Bowles when he said that "For the development of political thought the emergence of Greek city state is of cardinal importance. The heavy routine of Near Eastern Empire, the bureaucracy of Egypt and Mesopotamia, the reckless irresponsibilities of Iron Age, tyrants of Old Testament, gave place to something new. The free play of speculative intelligence, the brilliant formulation of vocabulary of thought in language expressive of the stable shades of meaning, the purposive coherence of Greek ideals—all these things mark the greatest step forward the political speculation has ever made."

Features of Greek Political Thought

The Greek political thought possessed certain distinct features, which deserve our consideration.

1. Exclusively Political Character of Treatise

In the first place, the ancient Greek political thought of other ancient countries like Egypt, Babylonia, Syria, Persia, India, China etc. in so far as it produced treatise of purely political nature. On the other hand in other ancient civilizations the political ideas were intermixed with mythology and religious literature. The Greek political thought is characterized by the presence of a number of independent treatises which are exclusively devoted to the study of political problems.

2. Main Concentration on Nature of State

Another notable feature of the ancient Greek political thought is that it concerned itself mainly with the nature of the state and the concept that man is a political animal. The Greek writers did not concern themselves with the problems relating to the relations between the state and the church, or state and industry which formed a part of the political thought of the later thinkers. As they conceived man as a social animal they naturally did not conceive him in relation to the social whole, viz. the state. Naturally the state became the centre of the Greek political thinkers. They discussed the origin as well as the end of the state and distinguished amongst various forms of state such Monarchy, Aristocracy, Oligarchy, Democracy, Tyranny etc.

3. Social Nature of Man

The Greek thinkers were the first to lay stress on the social nature of man and emphasis that an individual could not be stayed as an isolated and independent unit. They could attain perfection only in a healthy state. Hence, they considered the state necessary both for the sake of happiness as well as good life.

4. The City State

Another notable feature of the Greek political thought was that it centred around the city states, in which the community of men shared a common life and purpose. It was a complete social organization in which the citizens continuously participated. In fact the Greek political thinkers did not distinguish between the state and the society.

5. Importance of Education

Greek thinkers attached great importance to education and emphasized its importance in bringing the people at par with the spirit of the constitution. They emphasized on practical system of education which could be held in promoting modesty, self-control, patriotism, sociability and other similar qualities. The state was responsible for the promotion of education among the citizens and hence considered not only a moral and political institution but also an educational institution. In other words the Greek thinkers laid emphasis on state controlled system of education.

6. Rationalism

Greek thinkers assigned a significant position to rationalism in their thought. They believed that reason is the quintessence of the providence and a man was free only as long as he had freedom of reasoning. Reason enabled the man to identify himself with the corporate life, abandon his personal and selfish interests and leap into the realm of wider views and higher purposes. Naturally the Greek thinkers assigned privileged position to persons possessing rational faculty and relegated those persons who did not possess reason, too much inferior status. In short, we can say that the Greek political thinkers attached great importance to reason and were against acceptance of a thing which was not justified on the grounds of reason.

7. Concept of Law

The Greek concept of law was intimately linked with their belief in reason. They considered law as the life-breath of the state because it represented the acme of the rational being. As the law givers were inspired by divine power it was also the manifestation of God. The Greek thinkers considered Law and Justice as two sides of the same coin and asserted that justice is that which is according to law. However, this did not mean that to them all the laws were just and could not be improved upon.

8. Views on Justice

Justice occupies an important position in the ancient Greek political thought. The Greek thinkers considered justice as an important virtue which enabled a citizen to discharge of proper duties and contributed towards the development of human faculties. Justice was also implied to mean willing obedience to laws of the state. According to Plato, "Justice was the virtue of soul and injustice its vice."

9. Views on Citizenship

To the Greek thinkers citizenship did not merely imply payment of taxes and a vote. It meant direct participation in the management of the state as a soldier, as a judge, as a legislator in person, not through a Deputy. Thus, the Greek clearly ruled out the concept of representative government. Again, the Greeks did not extend citizenship rights to the slaves because they felt that the slaves could not discharge their obligations towards the state. As citizenship required active participation in the affairs of the state only the classes which enjoyed leisure and owned lands, and were hence free from economic worries, were given the citizenship rights. Thus in the Greek political thought the concept of citizenship was quite restricted.

10. Belief in Inequality

The Greeks considered equality as impracticable, unnatural and undesirable and argued that just as the individual was subordinate to the whole, the majority of the individuals who were intrinsically inferior, indolent, unfit, for education could be sacrificed at the altar of the minority of the excellent and the wise. They considered inequality in natural resources and permitted the dominance of the Greeks over barbarians; of the freeman over the slave; of the gentleman over the artisans etc. However, the Greeks permitted equality within a class. This equality was also to be proportional rather than arithmetical. The Greek thinkers emphasized that equality as such was not an ideal thing; on the contrary it was something unnatural and hence impracticable and undesirable.

Impact of the Greek Political Philosophy on European Political Philosophy

Barker has in vain tried to establish that political philosophy began with the Greek because that is not historically well founded. There is now sufficient evidence to prove that the Greek political philosophy was only one of those political philosophies which flourished in the ancient past. The Greek philosophy has survived throughout these ages because it could be made available to us one treatise or the other. Since it could be preserved, therefore, it was widely studied and borrowed by others, including the Europeans. There is no denial, however, that the impact of Greek political philosophy today is deep, as compared with all other political philosophies on European political thinkers and philosophers.

European philosophers are indebted to Greek political philosophy in many ways which can briefly be summed up as under:

1. Source of Inspiration and Information

European political philosophers quite freely and frequently borrowed from Greek political philosophy. Thus, their political philosophy became the main spring-head and European political thinkers to discuss their own political institutions and try to develop their own political philosophy and ideology, which in turn was seriously studied all over the world.

2. Idea of Limited Monarchy

Europe was usually in favour of monarchy and most of the European countries adhered to this form of government. It was from the Greek philosophy that Europe got the idea of democracy which was otherwise practically unknown to them. The concept of limited monarchy, as it prevails today, is the result of healthy blending of monarchy of Europe and democracy of the Greek.

3. Idea of Religious Toleration

With the Greek religion had no importance. They believed in religious toleration. But on the other hand, history is a witness that Europe in the past was the arena for religious struggles. Religious interrelation was the order of the day for centuries in many parts of Europe. Religious strikes were a fashion and the ruler was always obliged to patronize either one religion or the other. From the Greek they got the idea of religious toleration.

4. Importance of Education

Most of the European states had no idea about the importance of education. In fact, it was ignored to the extent that the state undertook no responsibility whatsoever about educating in its citizens. On the other hand, the Greek laid maximum stress on imparting education to the citizens through the agency of the state. For them it was an instrument for producing good citizens who ultimately make good state. Gradual undertaking of responsibility by the state in the field of education has direct influence of Greek thought. Many European states then took upon themselves the responsibility of spreading education.

5. Views about Justice

European states in the past had not developed any clear concept of Justice. The monarch was fountain head of justice and his authority was unquestionable. His interpretation was binding and no court could entertain any appeal against his decision. The Greeks had clear concept of justice which meant to them "Virtue in Action." This idea was borrowed by the European political philosophers who embodied them in their philosophies and subsequently tried to achieve that. They laid stress on the impartiality of judiciary and qualities of the judges.

In the context of these Greek political thoughts, we have made a detailed discussion about the two famous thinkers Plato and Aristotle.

PLATO (427B.C.-347 B.C.)

Early Life

Plato was born in 427 B.C. in a noble family in Athens and claimed to have royal blood in his veins. He traced his origin to Greek God Poseidon and that of his mother with the family of Great Athenian, lawgiver Solon. The period of his birth and that of death was historically important because hardly a year or so before his birth got entangled in Peloponnesian wars in which his own native city had to suffer immense humiliations. It was during his life period that he saw that Macedonian militarism was sweeping away almost everything. From his life to his death he saw Greek legal system in trouble. He also saw the defeat of Athens in wars against Spartans and the establishment of tyrannical rule of reactionaries. He also saw the execution of his master Socrates at the hands of these reactionaries. The result of all these events was that he greatly felt perturbed and wanted to establish that the rule of a philosopher king was the only remedy to remove all these troubles. He also wanted to establish that law-abiding and noble citizens had no place in the tyrannical state. He felt that remedy to Athenian state problems was not in producing ordinary citizens but noble and brilliant sons, like Socrates. The execution of Socrates particularly filled his heart with scorn for democracy and mob. He left his native state and spent most of the time paying visits to Greece, Egypt and Italy. He returned to Athens in 386 B.C. and set up an Academy, which is often described as the first university of the ancient world. In this Academy long discourses and discussions of purely argumentative nature took place and an effort was made to find out the causes of human discontent and political instability. This Academy continued to flourish and Plato spent most of his time guiding and inspiring *his* disciples.

Works of Plato

In the entire history of political thought no thinker evoked the admiration, reverence and criticism that Plato (427-347 B.C.) did. This outstanding

Greek philosopher has left behind many important works, out of which these three, *the Republic* (386 B.C.), *the Statesman* (360 B.C.) and *the Laws* (347 B.C.), were of perennial interest to all those interested in the history of political ideas. Plato has been generally regarded as the founder of philosophical idealism by virtue of his conviction that there is a universal idea in the world of eternal reality beyond the world of the senses. He was the first to formulate and define political ideas within a larger framework of a philosophical idea of Good. Plato perceived political philosophy as an architectonic science of society, and like Socrates (469-399 B.C.) and the Sophists, distinguished the political from the other dimension of life. Within the European intellectual tradition he conceptualized the disorders and crises of the actual world and presented to his readers a vision of a desirable political order, which till today has fascinated his admirers and detractors. He has been described as a poet of ideas, a philosopher of beauty and the true founder of the cult of harmonious living.

The Republic

It was written in 386 B.C. This book may be regarded not only as a philosophical work, but as a treatise on social and political reform. It is written in the spirit of a man not merely reflecting on human life but intensely anxious to reform and revolutionized it. It is the master piece of Plato. The treatise consists of 10 books out of which Books V-VII are very important. Book I deals with "justice and humanity", Books II, III, and IV have been devoted to 'system of education' and subjects like 'reason', 'spirit', 'appetite'. Books V, VI and VII are concerned with such subjects as 'ideal state' and the definition of good and bad. In Books VIII and IX Plato reviews the working of the state and the individuals. It is in Book X that Plato deals with the relation of philosophy with art and human soul.

The Statesman

It was written in 360 B.C. when Plato was about 67 years. It deals with politics. Here Plato is a practical idealist while dealing with the subjects like the role of individual in politics. He has also tried to discuss as to how the people should be governed. According to him, a true politician should try to educate the citizens and aim at promoting virtue and justice. He strongly felt that it was in the fullest development of these faculties alone that the state could best promote their interests and also achieve collective welfare of the citizens in a state. The treatise also depicts a remarkable departure from 'Republic' in the sense that here the author has lost much of his idealism and has also become considerably practical in his approach to the problems of life and politics and state administration.

The Laws

It was written in 347 B.C. The treatise came out at the mature age of 80. In this, Plato has tried to be more practical. Now he has begun to realize that the laws are necessary even for the guidance of the philosopher king. Here he has confessed that since it is difficult to find out a philosopher king, it is essential that the ruler should not be kept above the laws. He too has correctly assessed human nature and even given up the idea of communism of wives and property. On the other hand he felt that human nature requires institutions like property and family without which no human being can have perfect life. He, however, still favours a sort of state control, and censorship over marriages.

Thus, Plato started as an idealist and as he gained more and more experience he became practical idealist in his thoughts. His Republic depicts him as 'Ideal' and his 'Statesman, and 'Laws' as practical idealist. His writings have left a lasting influence on the posterity and provide a guideline for political thinkers who subsequently followed him. In the words of Maxey, "The writings of Plato touch every phase of the thought of his time, and constitute an imposing compendium of Greek learning and culture."

Plato's Theory of Justice

Plato was a great Greek political philosopher. Out of his publications, the most important one is 'The Republic'. Plato attaches great importance to the concept of justice is the evident from the fact that he subtitled his book *Republic* as 'Concerning Justice'. In fact the discovery of the nature and habitation of justice is the fundamental issue of Republic. Justice is the main theme of the Republic round which all other subjects find their due place. But, Plato white discussing his concept of justice, he studied the writings of some contemporary philosophers regarding their views on justice. He studied the Traditional theories of Justice of Cephalous and Polemarchus, Radicalist theory of Thrasyachus and Pragmatic theory of Glaucon.

Traditional Theory of Justice

The traditional theory was propounded by Cephalus and his son Polemarchus.

Views of Cephalus

Cephalus was the believer of the traditional theory of justice. According to him, justice means speaking the truth. It also means implies the payment of loan due to others. One should not tell a lie. Telling a lie is not justice. He also believed that justice is an art. But, Plato did not accept his views on justice.

Views of Polemarchus

Polemarchus was the son of Cephalus. He was also the supporter of Traditional theory of justice. According to him, justice means speaking the truth and paying what is due to God and man. It also implies that justice should be administered in such a way so that good done to the friends and harm to the enemies. But, the traditional theory of justice is not free from defects. Plato has not accepted the views of the traditional theory of justice on the following grounds.

But, Plato rejects this concept of justice on the following grounds. Firstly, according to the supporter of this theory, justice implies doing good to friends and harm to enemies. But the distinction between friends and foes is impossible. Secondly, justice can never be the interest of the stronger. It is meant for all irrespective of strong or weak. Thirdly, justice is universal. It cannot be different from man to man. Fourthly, justice is neither conventional ncr artificial. It is not the product of a social contract. But, it is something internal. Fifthly, justice cannot be considered as an art. If it considered as an art then it may lead to misuse of power.

Radicalist Theory of Justice

The radicalist theory associated with Sophists and propounded by Thrasyachus treated justice as the interest of the stronger.

Views of Thrasyachus

Thrasyachus was the supporter of the Radicalist Theory of Justice. According to him, justice means the protection of rights of the stronger people. In fact, he believed in the principle of might is right. In a government, the ruler should make law to serve their own interest and not for the interest of the people. The duty of the people to seek the interest of the ruler rather their own interest. To him, "Injustice is better than justice and unjust man is wiser than just."

But, Plato did not accept this view on the following grounds. Firstly, justice is universal. It is not meant only to serve the interest of the stronger. His interest should be to serve interest of all subjects. Secondly, generally a just man is wiser, stronger and happier than the unjust man. As such justice is always better than injustice. Thirdly, individual is not a part of unit, but it is a part of order. Fourthly, there cannot be two types of justice—one for the ruler and another for the subjects. Justice is uniform. It is applicable to all. Fifthly, Thrasyachus in his theory of justice lays emphasis on individualism. "But such extreme individualism will reduce the society to pieces."

Pragmatic Theory of Justice

The pragmatic theory of justice is stated by Glaucan.

Views of Glaucan

According to Glaucon, justice is an artificial thing. It is the product of social customs and conventions. Justice is the child of fear and oppression. In the state of nature, there was no justice. People had to live at the mercy of the strong man. To Glaucon, justice implies the protection of interest of weaker section of the society than the stronger section.

But Plato did not accept Glaucon's theory of justice and criticized the theory on several grounds.

Firstly, justice is not the product of any convention. It is not an artificial thing. It is not an external matter. Justice is concerned with human mind. Secondly, justice is not the result of fear. But it is the result of virtue. Thirdly, it is also not the product of any social contract concluded with the weaker sections of the community.

Thus, Plato has rejected all the theories of justice of his contemporary political philosophers. After rejecting all the theories of justice, Plato has developed the theory of justice in his own way.

Plato's View on Justice

Plato in his master-piece '*The Republic*' attaches a great importance to justice. The word 'justice' is derived from a Greek word 'Dikaiosume'. The word 'Dikaiosume' is used in a wider sense in comparison with the general term justice. Plato has developed his theory of justice in a wider sense.

To Plato justice is something internal. It exists in the state and also in the individual. The theory of state culminates in the conception of justice. In other words, Plato defines justice with the help of his ideal state. Plato's conception of justice is synonymous with the English word 'morality'.

Justice is simply the will to fulfil the duties of each individual according to his capacities. Plato thinks that justice is the only remedy against the social and political ills of Greek city state. Justice resides in the ideally constructed community which exhibits four different virtues, viz. wisdom, courage, self-control and justice.

Wisdom

Wisdom is essential for the administration of an ideal state. But all cannot possess the virtue of wisdom. Such virtue can only be possessed by philosopher kings as well as guardians. They should know how to carry on the administration of the state in an efficient manner. They should also know how to maintain internal and external relation with the different classes of people. But in Plato's theory of justice, the philosopher king is the only wise man. As such the administration of the ideal state should be carried on by the philosopher king.

Courage

Another virtue of an ideal state is courage. There should be a class of persons who can protect the security and stability of the state from external attacks. The soldier class represents the virtue of courage. The soldiers may be able to meet any situation that threatens the security and integrity of the state. The courage of a citizen differs from that of a slave. The courage of a slave is concerned with production. On the other hand the element of courage that represents the citizens as well as soldiers is the product of a well planned system of education.

Self-control

The third virtue is self-control or temperance which means that one must be a master of himself. The best element must control the worst. The naturally superior must overcome all passions and emotions. The naturally inferiors should render obedience to naturally superiors. This virtue represents the producing class. As they are naturally inferiors, they should render their obedience to the higher two classes. Moreover, it implies that the naturally superior should rule over the naturally inferiors.

Justice

Another virtue is justice. Plato says that justice is the virtue which remains in the state when the other virtues of self-control, wisdom and courage are abstracted, and is the ultimate cause and condition of the existence of all of them. The existence of other virtues is dependent on justice. Justice only resides in a state where all the three classes of people, viz., the philosopher ruler, soldier class and the producing class perform their own duties properly.

Justice to Plato means the will to concentrate on one's own sphere of duty and task, not interfering in the activities of others. Justice of the state depends upon the sense of duty of the individuals. Plato says that justice is a necessary condition for the realization of other virtues.

Platonic justice is associated with the social justice. Social justice has been defined as a principle of society consisting of different types of classes—the ruling class, the military class and producing class have joined together under the impulse of their need for the promotion of common good. And by their combination in one society and by concentration on their separate functions, they can bring into existence of a state which is just. A state is called wise if the ruling class displays wisdom in the management of its affairs. It is known as brave if the military personnel display courage both in peace and war. And the state will be self-controlled if there is harmony among the different classes born of devotion to the end in all. It follows that the individual is not an isolated self. He is a part of the state with a definite function in it. Since individual is just, the state is just.

Plato says that the justice of the state depends upon the justice of the individual. And the justice of the individual demands that the essential elements of human soul must keep within their proper bounds. These elements are—reason, spirit and appetite. Justice in the individual is just like justice in the state. The individual is just when the elements of reason, spirit and appetite are just. Platonic justice pleads for the division of the society into three classes which should represent the elements of reason, spirit and appetite. It also demands functions of specialization, a state regulated system of education, the rule of philosopher-king and a system of communism. Justice is a principle of specialization, a principle of non-interference and a principle of harmony.

Plato's justice is both social and personal. It is the quality which makes man social and makes them good. Justice is the bond which holds the society together. Justice is both public and private virtue because the highest good of both the state and its member is hereby observer.

Features of Plato's Theory of Justice

There are a number of features in Plato's Theory of Justice. These are as follows—

1. Functional Specialization

Plato believed in a system of complete functional specialization. He did not like that each and everybody should go on performing functions of the type which were not suited to his temperament and test. He was of the firm view that everyone should perform functions assigned to him and should not try to go beyond them. Thus, the king should rule and let the soldiers fight alone on the battle field. But he wished that everybody should be completely devoted to the task assigned to him and should try to attain perfection in that field.

2. Rule of Philosopher King

According to Plato, there should be the rule of philosopher king to realize justice. The philosopher kings should be the passionless person and seeker of truth and wisdom. He was above all types of prejudices and symbol of human wisdom. By his actions he commanded respect from all. He possessed high qualities of head and heart and could not be corrupted by concentration of power in his hands. He combined in himself virtue and knowledge. He was bound by no law. Such a king alone was in a position to look after the welfare of all.

3. Equal Treatment of Men and Women

In Plato's concept of justice, women are given equal position with men. Both should be brought up as useful citizens, as both were an integral part of the state and as such there should be no distinction between the two.

4. State Controlled Education

According to Plato, state should have full and final control over education. According to him, it was the only agency which could produce philosopher kings and train the minds and thoughts of the people in right and proper direction.

5. Communism of Wives and Property

He believed that if the ruling class was to progress and master then it was essential that there should be communism of wives and property. As long as rulers were not free from the bondage of family life and rose above narrow interests of possessing maximum of private property they shall never be in a position to solely devote themselves to the state.

6. Anti-individualism

Plato's theory of justice is anti-individualism. Individual has no separate identity without the state. It is through the state the individual can develop his personality.

7. Social Welfare

Plato's conception of justice lays emphasis on social welfare. Individual welfare is based on social welfare. Man should not be selfish. They should work for social welfare instead of selfish interest.

Criticism

1. Plato's justice has no legal sanction behind it. It has been conceived in moral and not legal terms. Plato has confused in distinguishing the moral duty and legal obligation.
2. Platonic justice is static and passive in character. It envisages a dull uniformity and harmony of social life. It is not justice the real sense of the term.
3. Plato's Conception of justice is inapplicable in a modern state. In modern times, state is so populous that it is not possible to divide the entire population into different groups and fixed their respective functions.
4. Plato's theory of justice is based on a system of communism. It goes against the essential elements of human psychology. Plato's justice is inadequate; it does not give us a full account of the human mind.
5. Plato's conception of justice gives a monopoly of power to the philosopher kings. The despotic rule of the philosopher-rulers seems to be destructive for the freedom and liberties of the individual. It denies the principle of equality. It is totally undemocratic and it leads to totalitarianism.
6. Platonic justice emphasizes the whole duties of man and not merely his legal duties. It is a justice concerned not with the rights but with the duties of individuals. Plato's justice is too subjective. It has no connection with the objective law for the guidance of the people.

Plato's Theory of Education

Among the Greek philosopher Plato was the first person to formulate a theory of 'Education' provided by the state. Book-II and Book-III of 'the Republic' deals with Platonic education. It has been described as the greatest work on education ever written.

Platonic education is the direct outcome of his conception of justice. Plato observes that communism and education are the two great institutions for the realization of justice. However, Plato places his main reliance upon education. According to him, education is a great thing. It is a social process by which the units of a society become instinct which develops social consciousness and learn to fulfil the social demands. Plato describes the state as an educational institution. For him, education is the most important function of the state.

Aims of Plato's Education

Plato's education has certain aims and objectives—

- The aim of education is self-realization.
- Creation of philosopher rulers for the state.
- Education should not be private. It should be imparted under the supervision of the state.
- Education is meant both for the mental and physical development.
- Education is meant for the realization of the idea of good. It is concerned with the reaction of the soul and environment.
- It wants to make man socially and politically fit to discharge his function properly.

The aim of Plato's education is the creation of philosopher rulers. It is the positive means by which the rulers mould the character of individuals. The permanent stability of the state can be assured through education. Education helps people to secure the power of self-governance. It changes the whole outlook of life. It touches evils at its very roots. Plato insists upon a system of state regulated education. For him, it can best create the spirit of devotion in the discharge of public works which is the demand of every individual. Again, Plato believes that the education system means for bringing of the soul into proper environment for its development.

Platonic education is systematic and progressive. It imparts knowledge. It promotes justice and right action. Vice can be cured by education. It may be said that Plato emphasizes the social aspect of education. It is a process by which the individual is adjusted to society and realize the truth.

Platonic education combines the curriculum of Athens and organization of Sparta. In Athens the scheme of education was not controlled by the state. It was fully private. The parents were responsible for the training of their children. They could send their children to the educational institutions at their discretion. So, the family regulated education in Athens might be against needs and character of the state. In Athens, education was not compulsory except the military training for a period of three years only. In Sparta, on the other hand, the parents could not control and regulate the education of their children. The Spartan Constitution provides for the system of state-controlled compulsory education to all. Spartan education was intended to develop the military spirit and intellectual faculties of the youth. Plato, therefore, seeks to combine the elements of both the Spartan and Athenian system of education and to create a harmonious balance between them.

In the Republic, Plato does not provide for the education of the citizen in general. Platonic scheme of state controlled compulsory education for both men and women may be divided into two stages, viz. elementary education which means the training of the youth up to the age of 20 years and higher education, which includes the proper training of the guardians extending from the age of 20 to 35 years. The distinction between the two stages of education rests on difference of ages and classes.

Elementary Education

Plato observes that education must begin in early childhood. To him, soul must be surrounded with the ideas which are helpful for the development of it. The youth persons should be thought up in happy surroundings. A perfect and healthy atmosphere help in the growth and development of the youth. So far as the elementary education is concerned, Plato divides the curriculum into two parts, viz. music and gymnastics. Music is essential for the training of the mind and gymnastics for the training of the body. Music develops the intellectual faculties of youth. It includes literature, poetry, singing and playing the lyric. In the early boyhood (up to the age of 18), the child must be taught simple religious truth and simple moral stories. He is to learn the lessons of good manners and good tests. For this purpose, Plato recommends the state censorship of good and moral stories. Stories of war, falsehood and the lies should not be placed before the youth minds. Literature must be narrative in nature. Plato says the children should not be given any wrong ideas about God. They should be taught that God is the source of good only and that he always governs us to act rightly. The poets should be asked not to write anything about the terrors of hell because such stories will discourage the guardians. The youth should be taught that the death in battle field is better that slavery.

Let us now consider the training in gymnastic. Gymnastic is the training of the body for the sake of physical culture. Its object is to develop the qualities of courage and self control in individual. Gymnastic is a preparation for the vocation of the warrior. Plato says that from 18 to 20 years, there must be exclusive training in gymnastic which is intended for muscular growth and development. Gymnastic means the general care of the body. The guardians must not get drunk and should take fish and boiled meat. There must not be luxury of cooking. Therefore, music and gymnastic intended to serve a moral purpose. Both are essential for the formation of character.

Higher Education

The higher education is meant for members of the guardian classes. Its aim is to train the philosopher kings to become the ruler of the state. The higher education commences at the age of 21 years and lasts for 10 years. At this stage, the guardian acquires knowledge and see the good. The special virtue of philosophic guardian is wisdom. They are to be given scientific education which is comparable to education given in the modern universities. Dialectical power must be developed and military training should be given. To Plato, the curriculum of higher study is mathematics. It has a practical value. It contributes to the increase of human knowledge. Mathematics enables the students to realize the truth.

Plato now discusses the selection of candidates for the training as philosopher guardians. To him, those who have showed keen interest in music and elements of sciences should be selected for further training. During the period of training from 21 years to 30 years, arithmetic, geometry and astronomy should be taught in a formal manner. Plato has no place for grammar and rhetoric. To him, mathematics is the proper introduction to philosophy. The man of war should know mathematics for the arrangement of the troops. But, it is necessary whether the candidate show the faculties for dialectics.

During the 4th stage (31years to 35 years) the philosophic guardians will have to study dialectics. Plato lays emphasis on dialectics. It teaches man how to put and answer questions. Dialectics is the instrument by which knowledge of pure ideas is attended. Dialectics helps one to reach perfect truth. It is above mathematics. From 35 years to 50 years, the philosophic guardians undergo an apprentice course. They should be given some public services of serious nature and they will have to acquire some practical knowledge. At the age of 50, the perfect guardians will be declared as the philosopher ruler if they can show aptitude for public services. They occupy positions of authority in the states. From the age of 50, the philosopher kings should labour for the sake of humanity. They will be the supreme council in the state dividing their times between theoretical study of the good and practical Government. It has been rightly remarked that the scheme of higher education is the most original as well as the most characteristic proposal in the Republic.

Hence, the aim of Plato's theory of Education is the creation of philosopher guardians. The philosopher guardians must be properly trained.

Criticism

Platonic Education has been criticized on the following grounds—

- Plato's system of education is anti-democratic. For him, theory of education is meant for the guardians only. It does not provide for the producing class, the labourers and the slaves which represent the majority part of the population of the state.

- Platonic education has been criticized for advocating state censorship of poems, literature, arts, comedies etc. Such a control is destructive to the principles of individual liberty.
- Plato does not allow freedom of expression but it is very essential to individual liberty.
- Plato's education gives much emphasis on mathematics and ignoring the value of literature on the minds of man.
- Plato's education is one sided. The curriculum be prescribed is defective. He does not include the study of law and finance. But the philosopher kings should be taught something about finance and military tactics.
- Plato's theory of education is more theoretical than practical. It will create an ideal philosopher rather than an ideal man of action. Plato cannot realize that education should be relative to the character of the individual.

However, it may be said in favour of Plato that his scheme of education anticipates many modern theories of education. It is intended to promote the harmonious development of the individual and of the society.

Plato's Theory of Rule of Philosopher King

Book V and VI of Plato's '*The Republic*' deals with philosopher kings. The conception of the rule by the philosopher king is regarded as the most profound as well as the most original concept in the entire political theory of Plato. The rule of philosophy is an important feature of the Republic.

According to Plato, the perfection of the ideal state depends upon those persons who possess supreme wisdom, virtue and courage. Therefore, the Government in the ideal state should be entrusted to a few highly trained experts. Society can rightly be ordered, if philosophers are kings and kings are philosophers. In this way, the community expresses its real will. The rule by philosopher kings embodies the true will of the many. The philosophers should not self-seeking. They are competent and efficient to become the rulers for the states. They have a vision. It may be possible for the philosopher kings to give an expression to what all desire. They should not have any love for power. Further they can understand the pros and cons of everything.

Plato says that the government of the ideal state must be associated with knowledge. True knowledge is philosophy. Plato advocates rule of philosophy, because it is the only means by which the political incompetence and political selfishness can be stopped. Hence, the Government must be controlled by the philosophers.

To Plato, a philosopher is the person who has knowledge. He is a great statesman. He must have a vision. To a philosopher monarchy is the best form of Government. A philosopher is a passionate seeker of truth. He has the noblest gifts of nature and makes the highest use of them. He rules for the welfare of the people.

The philosopher king is the logical outcome of the conception upon which Plato builds up his ideal state. His ideal state is based on ideocracy that is the rule of the intellect. To Plato, justice is the corner stone of the ideal state. It is the knowledge in action and the philosopher kings alone represent this knowledge in action. He embodies in himself the highest and the greatest of all political virtues. Plato's philosopher king is the guardian of truth. He possesses goodness and divine wisdom.

The rule of philosopher king is absolute. He is not bound by trammels of written law. People have no share in the Government. They cannot determine the politics of the state. They simply carry out the orders of the philosopher king who is not responsible to them. Plato's citizens are in a state of servitude. However, the rule of philosopher king is not tyrannical. It is not an unqualified absolutism.

The philosopher king must respect the fundamental articles of the Constitution. He cannot change the basic principles related to—

1. The system of Education.
2. The regulation of wealth in the state.
3. The size of the state.
4. The rule of justice.

The philosopher kings possess some qualification. *Firstly,* the philosopher kings should understand the guiding principle by which the state is to be administered. They have some definite knowledge of these principles. *Secondly,* philosophers must have courage. They should not afraid of life and death. They must not influenced by any emotion and passion. *Thirdly,* philosophers must be the lover of intrinsic beauty. They must have the curiosity for new knowledge and experience. *Fourthly,* they must have strong memory power. They must have the capacity to learn and remember everything. *Fifthly,* they must have a well balanced mind. They must be self controlled.

It is possible to realize the ideal state, provided the philosophers are kings and they know the art of ruling. The rule of philosopher king was actually realized in Sparta. Platonic philosopher king is genius. He possesses highest wisdom and other qualities and which make him a great statesman.

Features of Plato's Rule of Philosopher King

The conception of the rule by the philosopher king, which is described by Prof. Foster as the "the most profoundly original conception in the entire political thought of Plato" has some distinct features, which are as follows—

1. Plato did not favour democratic features democratic system of government in which every citizen had the right to participate in the affairs of the state. He denounced it as a government of the ignorant.
2. The philosopher king being a lover of wisdom and passionate seeker of truth is in better position to determine what is in the interest of the community than an ordinary person.
3. The interest of the philosopher king and those of the state are identical and there is no clash between the two.
4. Plato's philosopher rulers are the product of comprehensive and rigorous training and education spread over the period of thirty-five years.
5. The philosopher rulers are assigned absolute power by Plato and the rulers are not accountable to public opinion or not bound by customs or written laws.

Criticism

Several criticisms have been made against the Platonic conception of Philosopher King or rule of philosophy. These are as follows—

1. The rule by Philosopher King goes against the spirit of democracy, liberty and quality. The Philosopher kings are not democratically elected.
2. Plato assigns the monopoly of political power to a few trained persons. In other words, the government will be in the hands of some self-perpetuating minority of experts.
3. Plato's philosopher kings are the permanent rulers of the government. Such a government breeds discontent among the general people.
4. The conception of a philosopher guardian is unrealistic and impracticable. He has given more importance to contemplation than to action.
5. Power corrupts man, and absolute power corrupts man absolutely. Platonic philosopher kings cannot be exempted from this rule. They are liable to be corrupted by exercising their absolute power. They may abuse their power for their private interest.

Plato's Theory of Communism of Property

Platonic communism of property is the logical outcome of his conception of justice. Without it, there may be a conflict between reason and appetite. Private property distracts man's attention from his duties to the society. To Plato, community is everything. The individual is an urgent part of it. He is nothing apart from the community. He shall have to render the greatest possible service to the state. Therefore, individual is not entitled to collect and hold private property in order to bringing about perfect harmony in the state. It is a material and economic corollary of the spiritual reformation of the ideal state. Communism of property destroys self as an isolated unit and pleads for a self as an integral part of a social whole.

Plato in 'the Republic' supports the abolition of private property for the rulers and warriors. His communism does not affect the producers of economic goods. Thus, Plato advocates communism of property for the guardian that is the ruler of the state, the warriors and the philosophers. Communism of property is essential for the attainment of justice. Plato intends to reform the society by means of communism. He proposes a system of state regulated education to train the guardians for the performance of their duties. Their primary aim is to secure the unity of the state. The material conditions under which the guardians live must not impair their virtue as guardians of tempt to prey upon the other citizens. Plato says that the guardians should not have any property or houses of their own beyond what is absolutely necessary. They should receive from the citizens a fixed rate of pay enough to meet the expenses of the year and no more. They should live in common barracks like soldiers in a camp and this will be their salvation and they will be the saviours of the state. But, if they acquire homes and monies of their own, they will become house keepers and husbandman instead of guardians, enemies and tyrants instead of allies of other citizens. And here lies the practical basis of Plato's communism of property. To Plato guardians with economic power cannot discharge their functions properly and honestly. They can work efficiently only under the system of communism. They should surrender economic power. Plato advocates that the union of economic and political power in the same hands is fatal to political purity and efficiency.

The main source of corruption of the ideal state is due to the union of economic and political power. It may produce disastrous consequences. Such a union can demoralize even the rules of the state. The guardians are sometimes influenced by economic motives and, therefore, they forget the need for wisdom. Again, they utilize the political power for promoting their economic interests. They also exploit the other classes for their own advantages. Hence,

Plato suggests that the political power and economic motive should be separated from one another. Those who exercise political powers should have no economic gains and *vice versa.* Plato has given the guardians the monopoly of political power. So, the guardians should discharge their duties properly. They must abnegate the private property and economic power.

Plato says that superiority in virtue is necessary to perform the business of the government. If all citizens possess property, the person should be selected for political offices on the basis of property and not on the ground of virtue. If private property is abolished, the person may hold position in the ideal state because of their wisdom. Communism of property can remove the hindrances and provide opportunities for the development of spiritual qualities for the guardians.

Platonic communism of property is regarded as half-communism. It does not affect the producing class which is allowed to retain private property and the old individualistic system of production. The producers are free to acquire and hold as much as property as they can. But, it is under the strict supervision and control of the government. So, Plato says that the guardians should be partners in the renunciation and abnegation. They have no house, no land and no property. They will receive a salary paid by the producers. All payments will be regulated as a common property of all and will be consumed on the common table. Platonic communism does not affect the economic structure of the society. It is a political conception which is aristocratic in nature.

Criticism

Several criticisms have been leveled against Plato's communism of property. These are—

1. Communism of property is negative in character. Plato does not furnish a positive system of socialization of all means of production.
2. Platonic communism of property is aristocratic in conception. It is restricted to the upper classes (rulers and warriors) of the community. The producing class, which is the majority section of the society, exempted from his scheme of communism.
3. There may be discontent and dissension in the society. Those who work much but receive little will surely revolt against those who work little and receive a much.
4. Without private property, the guardians cannot understand others who have property. So, men cannot live together in the society.
5. Platonic communism ignores the essentials of human psychology.

Everyman needs a certain amount of private property to develop his individuality. It is in conformity with the nature of human beings. Thus, the abolition of property means the violation of human principle.

6. Platonic communism destroys the richness and variety of life. Unity and harmony cannot be achieved by communism in property.

Plato's Theory of Communism of Wives

Plato's concept of communism of wives is discussed in his book '*the Republic*' which is the logical extension of his scheme of communism of property. Family and property are two inter-related terms, that is why he fully realized that the abolition of the institution of private property without the abolition of the family would result in the failure of his scheme and private property would appear in some different form. He wants to remove particular interest from every share of life.

Objective of the Scheme of Communism of Wives

Plato's communism of wives is rest on two fundamental objectives—(i) Emancipation of women and (ii) Reformation of marriage system.

Arguments in Support of Communism of Wives

Plato has advanced the following arguments in the support of his scheme. His arguments may be classified into three categories : (1) Political (2) Moral and (3) Eugenic Reason.

1. Political Reason

Plato wanted to create unity in the state, but he realized that the family was the most important stumbling block in the way of unity of the state. It was even more than the institution of private property. It will affect the loyalty of the people to the state. Family affection may lead to the division of the society.

2. Moral Reason

Plato also wanted to abolish family on the moral grounds. In Plato's days, the condition of women was very deplorable. They had no equal right with men. They lived at the mercy of men. The main function of women is bringing up children alone. So, Plato wanted to emancipate women by giving a share in the administration of the state. According to him, if the women are given necessary training along with men of same caliber, they can play a significant role in the administration of the state.

3. Eugenic Reason

Plato also advocated the abolition of family on eugenic ground. He wanted to raise better and more intelligent race by introducing a system of temporary marriage. In such state-controlled temporary marriage, the best man and women of certain age limit would be united to give birth children. Such children will be nourished under the guardianship of the state so that they may become good citizens in due course.

Plato supports communism of wives and also wants to abolish family life from amongst the warriors and rulers. Private property has already been abolished. Family cannot be maintained without it. Like property, family is a source of all evils and dis-unity in the state. It is the centre of self-interest. Plato, therefore, condemns the private household. Women may be emancipated from the drudgery of home and set free for the service of the state.

It is said that the abolition of family is an attack on individual liberty. But, Plato says that the abolition of private household is necessary for the emancipation of women and the reformation of marriage. Seclusion of women in house means that the state is derived from the service of the women who constitutes nearly one-half of the total population. Women should be enlisted and utilized for the service of the community. He wants to convert the whole guardian class—man and woman into one family. He rules out the individual family for the guardians. There is no such thing as father, mother and children. It will promote brotherhood among men. Common parentage establishes unity and harmony.

Plato wants to abolish wives and family on eugenic ground because of the better and healthy children for the future guardian. The state must combine good man with good woman at proper age and at proper season for producing requisite number of children. Children born of such unions will be brought up by the state so that no parents will know their children. All the children are regarded the common sons and daughters of all. In other words they are the children of the state. In this way perfect unity will be realized. Undesirable children are to be destroyed. Communism in women also facilities the growth of population.

Plato prescribes the age for procreation on eugenic grounds. To him, 25 to 50 years for men and 20 to 45 years for women is the proper time for marriage. Beyond this age, no marriage should be held. There should no permanent marriage system in the ruling class. This is called the Plato's Scheme of State Control Marriages. We are to note that men and women do not come together merely for the purpose of procreating children. They are bound together by common interest for the welfare of all. It will pave the way for the real unity of the community.

Criticisms

Plato's theory of communism of wives has been criticized on the following grounds—

1. It is said that Platonic scheme is incompatible with the growth of the state. Family is the source of the state. It is also the centre of unity.
2. It destroys a time honoured institution of marriage. Influence of heredity, and of family environment have no place in platonic system.
3. Plato fails to realize that the stability of the state depends largely on the integrity of the family. Abolition of family must weakened the internal feeling of the community. It is an absurd idea that the family man is the worst citizen.
4. It is an anti-social idea that in a community no child will know its parentage and no parents will know their children. It is against the rule of civilized society.
5. Marriage is a permanent and spiritual relationship between a man and a woman. This traditional ritual of the society cannot be replaced by a temporary male-female relation who is prescribed only for procreating a healthy child for the sake of the state only.
6. Plato lays a special emphasis on the equality of women with man for the service of the state. But the women are characterized by sensibility, grace and gentleness. All these qualities do not and cannot fit them for hard work of the community.

Plato's Theory of Ideal State

In his '*the Republic*' Plato has tried to portray the picture of an ideal state, which is more or less utopian. Plato was deeply moved at the political situation and functioning of the governments of the Greek city states of Athens and Sparta of his time. So, he wanted to reform the existing system of governments of his days. According to him, the citizens can be at their best only in ideal state. While depicting the picture of such a state, he was attempted to show as to what an ideal state ought to be, without caring whether that was practicable or not.

But, Plato while depicting his ideal state, he was not aware of the fact that whether it could be set up anywhere or not. In fact he did not bother for the functioning of such type of state. What he wanted to do was to set an ideal for all times to come. In his '*The Republic*', he remarks, "Ideal state exists in idea only, for I do not believe that such one is anywhere on earth. In heaven there is laid up a pattern of it. But, whether such one exists or ever will exist in fact is no matter."

Sabine, explaining further, pointed out that Plato made two fundamental assumptions which were interrelated. These were: (a) that government ought to be an art depending on exact knowledge; and (b) that society existed for the mutual satisfaction of needs by persons whose capacities supplement one another. While the first was intrinsic to human personality, the second referred to education and experience. In view of these two assumptions, Plato was convinced that if ruling was entrusted to the experts who could be trained, then governance would be above mediocrity and expediency. Political leadership was both an art and a science. Good governance would confer a dynasty of political rulers who could meet every contingency, rather than have occasional premiers of the people. It would eliminate factionalism and petty groupism in politics. Ruling, for Plato, had to be in accordance with the true dictates of moulding and transforming the state and individuals in light of an absolute standard. Political philosophy had to prevent incompetence and knavery in public life. The philosophers' vision of the Forms and Good was a moralizing experience, and that explained their commitment to the Ideal State of which they were the architects. For Plato, every individual had a social side. Besides ensuring his own good, a philosopher must also be useful to society, for it was only within a society that an individual realized his true self. The philosopher ruled in order to prevent victimization at the hands of inferior rulers.

The ideal state is composed of philosopher kings, soldiers, peasant and artisans. Besides, there are systems of communism of property, communism of family, a state regulated system of education and a conception of justice.

According to Plato, the state is the product of human soul. The human soul is consisted of three elements—Reason, Spirit and Appetite. These three elements of mind represent three classes of men in the state. The element of reason represents the philosopher king. It leads man how to learn and how to love. A man without reason cannot know anything fully and also cannot love properly. The function of the state is based on reasons. The spirit represents the soldiers' class. This element makes man courageous. Courageous man can fight against enemy. They can fight injustice. Another element of mind is appetite. This element may be found only in ordinary man. Appetite represents the producing class. The individual is just when the elements of reason, spirit and appetite are just. However, spirit and appetite are subordinate to reason.

Basic Principles of Ideal State

Plato's ideal state is based upon certain principles and these fundamental principles are (1) the Theory of Functional Specialization (2) the Philosopher King (3) the Military Factors in the State (4) Proper Administration of Justice.

1. Functional Specialization

Plato believed in a system of complete functional specialization. He did not like that each and everybody should go on performing functions of the type which were not suited to his temperament and test. He was of the firm view that everyone should perform functions assigned to him and should not try to go beyond them. Thus, the king should rule and let the soldiers fight alone on the battle field. But he wished that everybody should be completely devoted to the task assigned to him and should try to attain perfection in that field.

2. Rule of Philosopher King

According to Plato, there should be the rule of philosopher king to realize justice. The philosopher kings should be the passionless person and seeker of truth and wisdom. He was above all types of prejudices and symbol of human wisdom. By his actions he commanded respect from all. He possessed high qualities of head and heart and could not be corrupted by concentration of power in his hands. He combined in himself virtue and knowledge. He was bound by no law. Such a king alone was in a position to look after the welfare of all.

3. The Military Factor in the State

Plato fully well realized that the defense of the state was most essential for all the states. He, therefore, gave this responsibility to the soldiers. He believed that these people should not be ordinary soldiers but persons specially trained for the purpose. Maxey says that Plato believed that these soldiers should be "specially trained for their task and of the very highest physical and mental fitness."

4. Proper Administration of Justice

According to Plato, justice was an essential and integral part of a state and it kept various organs and individuals in close harmony with each other. Therefore, he pleaded that justice should be properly administered. His conception of justice was something different from that of a modern one. It was not something to be measured in terms of courts of law. It was not a legal conception but something quite different from it. It was something in which there was functional specialization and everybody was required to remain within his limits. Under it there was perfect harmony among various sections of society and none was to encroach upon the rights of others.

5. State Controlled Education

According to Plato state should have full and final control over education. According to him, it was the only agency which could produce philosopher kings and train the minds and thoughts of the people in right and proper direction. Education had both social and individual aspects in his philosophy. In society, education should promote social welfare while individually it should bring soul closer to reality.

6. Communism of Wives and Property

He believed that if the ruling class was to progress and master it was essential that there should be communism of wives and property. As long as rulers were not free from the bondage of family life and rose above narrow interests of possessing maximum of private property they shall never be in a position to solely devote themselves to the state. Without such a communism there was every possibility of their becoming corrupt and selfish.

7. Absence of Discrimination

In Plato's ideal state, there is no discrimination between man and woman. Both are integral part of the state. Hence, he has given same status to men and women in his ideal state. If the woman is not given the same status, the principle of justice will be defeated. Moreover, the state will loss the services of the half of the population of the state.

8. Nourishment of Children

Plato made special provision for the nourishment of children in his ideal state. He considered them as the property of the state. In his scheme of education, he provided all sorts of education and training for them so, that they could develop their personality in all sphere. Children were nourished under the supervision of the state since the day of their births.

Criticism

Plato's conception of ideal state is not free from criticism. Some of the arguments advanced against this concept are:

1. Non-development of Human Personality

If, at all Platonic ideal state materializes, it is very much doubtful whether proper development of human personality shall be possible in such a state. Plato has preached functional specialization which implies devotion to one's duty and perfection in a particular direction. Such perfection can only be achieved when other aspects are either absolutely ignored or are not properly developed.

2. Anti-Democratic

Plato's ideal state is anti-democratic. Here all powers and functions are concentrated in the hand of few rulers. The people cannot take part in the administration of the state. The philosopher rulers are not responsible to anybody. Moreover, the properly trained rulers can rule the ideal state. The rulers are also not bound by any law and customs.

3. Lack of Individual Freedom

Another defect is that there is no individual freedom in the ideal state. Individuals have to live under the complete control of the state. The state is an end in itself and it is not a mean to an end.

4. Defective Education System

Plato's scheme of education is defective and that is why the product of his education system, the philosopher kings are also defective. The philosopher king has no practical knowledge of administration because Plato did not include the necessary subjects like public administration, law, finance etc in his education scheme.

5. Utopian State

Plato's ideal state may be called as an utopian state. Such state cannot be realized in practice. His conception of philosopher king, state controlled lengthy education scheme, communism of property and wives are anti-human. The whole arrangement is more or less ideal rather than real. Such institutions are neither desirable nor possible for proper functioning of the state.

6. It can Result in Anarchy

Another criticism advanced against Plato's concept of ideal state is that it can degenerate into bureaucracy of the worst order. There is every danger that this class might try to identify its interests with the masses and thus, ultimately create confusion and disorder.

7. Ignorance of Producing Classes

Like a true aristocrat Plato has ignored the role of working and producing classes. The very idea of ignoring the majority class of the society is undesirable and unwanted and does not fall in line with the philosophy of perfect or an ideal state. In fact in modern set-up no advanced state can afford to ignore the welfare of a particular class at the cost of other classes.

8. Wrong Analogy between Individual and State

Plato has drawn far-fetched analogies between the individual and the state. His analogy between the three organs of the state, namely the Appetite, Reason and Spirit with those of individual, namely, the rulers, the soldiers, and the producers, is rather too much far-fetched and is likely to lead to confusion.

The Comparison of Platonic Communism with Modern Communism

There are fundamental points of similarity and differences between Plato's communism and modern communism. The Points of Similarities are as follows—

1. Like Platonic communism, modern communism also emphasizes the unity of the state and the promotion of the common good of the state.
2. In Platonic system, rulers and subjects are united together by mutual regard and mutual gratitude. Likewise modern communism aims at the establishment of the unity and the removal of selfishness.
3. Again, Plato's communism and modern communism lay emphasis on the supremacy of the state. They ignore the individuality of the citizens. Both the schemes of communism is based on justice and human instincts.
4. Further modern communism like Platonic communism pleads for the elimination of unregulated economic competition. Again, in both the schemes, individuals can secure their interests best by securing the common interests.

5. Moreover, both Platonic communism and modern communism are against private property. Both the schemes are not practicable if they are applied on a larger scale.

The Points of Differences are as follows:

1. Platonic communism of property is applicable only to the rulers and the warriors of the state. It does not affect the producing class of the state. Therefore, the individualistic system of production and the economic structure of the state remain entirely unchanged. Modern communism on the other hand stands for the complete abolition of the private ownership of the means of production. It seeks to change the economic pattern of the society. Unlike Plato's scheme, modern communism wants to put an end to the exploitation of the workers by the capitalists.
2. Modern communism is economic in character. It wants the worker to control the life of the state. But Platonic communism is political in nature. For it emphasizes the unity of the state. It does not look after the equal distribution of wealth. In Plato's communism, inequalities of wealth must remain so far as the producers are concerned.
3. Plato's scheme of communism has two aspects—communism of property, and communism of wives. But modern communism is concerned only with property and no family and children.
4. Platonic communism is negative in character. Modern communism is positive. It involves socialization of property and just distribution of good among the member of the state.
5. Platonic communism is described as half communism. It touches a small part of the total population of the state and ignores the major part of the population. On the other hand, modern communism is universal. For it effects the whole population.
6. Plato's communism seems to be totalitarian. But, modern communism is democratic. Further, Platonic communism is idealistic in nature. On the other hand, modern communism is scientific and practical.
7. Platonic communism prevails the concentration of political and economic power in the same hands. Modern communism on the other hand, gives political power to the producing classes. Thus, Plato's communism is basically spiritual-cum-political. Modern communism is based on economic materialism. It aims at material welfare of the state.

ARISTOTLE (384 B.C.-322 B.C.)

After Plato came Aristotle, who significantly contributed to political philosophy and even now is studied seriously all over the world. History is much indebted to him for giving mature ideas to world political philosophy.

Life Sketch

Aristotle, the ablest of Plato's disciples, whose name means "the best purpose", was born in Stagira, Chalcidice, in 384 BC, about 55 km (34 mi) east of modern-day Thessaloniki. His father Nicomachus was the personal physician to King Amyntas of Macedon. Aristotle was trained and educated as a member of the aristocracy. At about the age of eighteen, he went to Athens to continue his education at Plato's Academy. Aristotle remained at the academy for nearly twenty years before quitting Athens in 348/47 BC. The traditional story about his departure reports that he was disappointed with the direction the academy took after control passed to Plato's nephew Speusippus upon his death, although it is possible that he feared anti-Macedonian sentiments and left before Plato had died. He then traveled with Xenocrates to the court of his friend Hermias of Atarneus in Asia Minor. While in Asia, Aristotle traveled with Theophrastus to the island of Lesbos, where together they researched the botany and zoology of the island. Aristotle married Hermias's adoptive daughter (or niece) Pythias. She bore him a daughter, whom they named Pythias. Soon after Hermias' death, Aristotle was invited by Philip II of Macedon to become the tutor to his son Alexander the Great in 343 BC.

Aristotle was appointed as the head of the royal academy of Macedon. During that time he gave lessons not only to Alexander, but also to two other future kings: Ptolemy and Cassander. In his Politics, Aristotle states that only one thing could justify monarchy, and that was if the virtue of the king and his family were greater than the virtue of the rest of the citizens put together. Tactfully, he included the young prince and his father in that category. Aristotle encouraged Alexanders towards eastern conquest, and his attitude towards Persia was unabashedly ethnocentric. In one famous example, he counsels Alexander to be "a leader to the Greeks and a despot to the barbarians, to look after the former as after friends and relatives, and to deal with the latter as with beasts or plants."

By 335 BC he had returned to Athens, establishing his own school there known as the Lyceum. Aristotle conducted courses at the school for the next twelve years. While in Athens, his wife Pythias died and Aristotle became involved with Herpyllis of Stagira, who bore him a son whom he named after his father, Nicomachus. According to the Suda, he also had an eromenos, Palaephatus of Abydus.

Establishing a New School

It was in 335 B.C. that Aristotle decided to set-up a new school to preach his own ideas, thoughts and philosophies. An institution known as 'Lyceum', sprang-up with the patronage and backing of his pupil Alexandra. For 12 years he personally headed this institution and produced many research scholars and pupils who politically carried his image. Since he himself was embodiment of human knowledge in all walks of human life, he made errors to systematize the whole body of human knowledge. He even stressed on the study of comparatively less known subjects as logic and astronomy.

Works of Aristotle

It is during this period in Athens from 335 to 323 BC when Aristotle is believed to have composed many of his works. Aristotle wrote many dialogues, only fragments of which survived. The works that have survived are in treatise form and were not, for the most part, intended for widespread publication, as they are generally thought to be lecture aids for his students. His most important treatises include *Physics*, *Metaphysics*, *Nicomachean Ethics*, *Politics*, *De Anima (On the Soul)* and *Poetics*.

Aristotle not only studied almost every subject possible at the time, but made significant contributions to most of them. In physical science, Aristotle studied anatomy, astronomy, embryology, geography, geology, meteorology, physics and zoology. In philosophy, he wrote on aesthetics, ethics, government, metaphysics, politics, economics, psychology, rhetoric and theology. He also studied education, foreign customs, literature and poetry. His combined works constitute a virtual encyclopaedia of Greek knowledge. It has been suggested that Aristotle was probably the last person to know everything there was to be known in his own time.

Though Aristotle wrote extensively on subjects like metaphysics, psychology, rhetoric, poetry, biology, moral science, politics etc., but we are primarily concerned with his political writings. In this regard also we are greatly handicapped in so far most of the works produced by Aristotle in the early part of his life have since perished. The only important work of Aristotle which has come down to us and provides valuable information about his political philosophy is *Politics*. This work is also not available in complete form. Further there is difference of opinion among scholars as to who composed *Politics*. According to one view the work was edited by his students at his school. According to yet another view it is merely a collection of notes taken by his students. Whether the book was written by Aristotle or is a collection of his notes, it represents his views.

Arrangement of Politics

The treatise consists of 8 Books which can conveniently be divided into three parts. The first three books form the basis and provide material for the ideas developed in Books IV, V and VI, which form another part of the treatise and deal with nature of constitutions and their similarities and dis-similarities with each other. Books VII and VIII deal with the constitution of an ideal state most suited to a city state which is Platonic in nature. Thus briefly speaking each book deals as under:

Book I: It was perhaps written last of all. It deals with slavery and introduces the treatise.

Book II: It deals with Plato's ideal state.

Book III: It deals with citizenship, normal and perverted forms of constitution and also with monarchy.

Book IV: It deals with various form of government.

Books V and VI: These deal with oligarchy and democracy.

Book VII: It discusses the constitution of an ideal state.

Book VIII: It develops the point discussed in Book VII.

Aristotle's View on State

Aristotle's claim that the state is the highest, most developed form of social organisation is at the centre of one of his major works, 'The Politics'. His theory focuses mainly on the state as a natural progression, and draws upon two central themes—'the good life' and human beings as 'political animals'. Whilst Aristotle does raise many valid points, he does not convince us that the state is the pinnacle of social organisation.

Aristotle's '*The Politics*' encompasses many themes and topics, some of which provide the basis for the state being the highest form of social organization. Written during the fourth century BC, Aristotle's work forms the basis for many arguments concerning philosophy and is still extensively used today. Aristotle claims that the state is a natural process, and in order to understand its complexity it is necessary to study the state in its "first growth and origin." It is natural for human beings to live within the state and natural for humans to reach their potential within it. Furthermore, Aristotle also places a strong emphasis on good and evil in his work. The state is a natural process, and therefore, it has a natural end, anything that disrupts this process is evil. Perfection is also important in Aristotle's work, which can be achieved by man within the state. Aristotle's teleological approach is highly important to his argument and reaffirms many of the points he raises.

The first argument put forward by Aristotle is one of the most valuable analysis of the state in the whole realm of political speculation. In order to find the natural origin of the state he analyses it into its parts and studies it in its beginning. There are two primary natural instincts which compel human beings to associate themselves together—the reproductive instinct which brings man and woman together and the instinct of self-preservation which brings together master and slave. Thus, we get the first natural society of three persons—the family which is the association established by nature for the supply of everyday wants. The next stage is the village, which is a union of several families for the supply of something more than everyday wants. The village, he adds, is formed almost naturally by the union of families by common consent. Such is Aristotle's first argument to prove that State is a natural institution.

The second argument and the most typical of Aristotle is that "the nature of a thing is its end." This is the argument based on his teleology. His view of the world is teleological; everywhere things are regarded as determined towards their end. Everything realizes its true nature when it reaches its end. The apple fruit shows the true nature of the apple seed. The state shows the real nature of man. Man can get perfect development of his nature in the state only. Beyond the state he is no longer a human being. Man is not at all animal but his true nature is rational. The possession of the faculty of Reason is what distinguishes him from an animal. And it is only in the State that an individual gets the opportunity for the development of his rational nature. The family and the village prove inadequate not only because they do not adequately supply the needs of man's animal nature but also because they do not supply the needs of man's rational nature. Since the end of all human development is to realize its rational nature, the latter is realized in the state only. Since "the nature of a thing is its end; where thing is when fully developed, we cal its nature; hence the man by nature is a political animal." This is how Aristotle proves through his teleology that the state is a natural institution and that man is by nature a political animal.

The third argument which Aristotle gives in order to prove that the state is a natural institution is that the state is an organism which has developed and grown. The state is a whole of which the individuals are the parts. He is the father of all organism theories of State. "According to him, the state is a natural community; and organism with all the attributes of a living being."

It is clear from the preceding account of the state, the end or fulfillment of earlier forms of human associations like the family and village that Aristotle views it as a growing or developing thing.

Aristotle justified the natural character of the state with the help of theological arguments. He asserted that the true nature of man could be realized only in the state. And since the man was a rational being, the state was a rational institution. In the words of Prof. Foster "The lower forms of society, the village, for example prove inadequate not only because they do not supply the needs of man's animal nature, but also because they do not adequately supply the needs of his rational nature. These latter can be supplied only in a political, as distinct, for example, from a purely economic society; and man's rational nature finds its proper development only in political, as distinct from an economic activity."

Aristotle emphasized the organic nature of the state and asserts that a man finds his true meaning and significance of his life only in and through relation to the state. In the words of Ebenstein, Aristotle held that "the state is a natural community: an organism with all the attributes of a living being." Just an organ cannot be separated from the organism; similarly an individual cannot be separated from the state. The individual and the other associations draw all their importance from the state and without it they would stagnate and die. No person can attain his fullness outside the state.

Aristotle considers the state as a supreme association because it is the highest of all the association. It is a supreme association because it is the culmination of social evolution and also because man realizes his highest moral perfection in the state. Whereas family and village exist essentially for the preservation of life and the comforts of companionship, the state exists for the sake of a good life and not for the sake of life only, and political society exists for the sake of noble actions and of mere partnership.

Functions of State

As already pointed out the main objective of the state is to promote perfect and self-sufficient life, by which Aristotle meant a happy and honourable life. For this purpose he wanted the state to create essential conditions for mental, moral and physical development of the people. He did not want to restrict the functions of the state to mere preservation of the rights of the members against infringements by others or preservation of life and property of the members. On the other hand he assigns to the state most positive function of promoting the good. It should give proper education to the members for proper performance of their functions. It should train young minds in the way of righteousness and make the life of the citizens supreme and moral. He considered the state like a mother to its citizens and its actions could legitimately extend to all affairs of the individual. In short, Aristotle considers state as a supreme association whose chief function is to make men moral.

Aristotle's Theory of Citizenship

Free citizenship is the most important feature of Greek society. Each man has a share in the common life of state. Citizens are the part of the state. To, Plato, there is no distinction between a citizen and a slave. All the three classes of individuals, viz. man of reason, man of spirit and man of appetite are the citizens with the respective rights and duties. They are inter-dependent and they live in harmony.

Aristotle's idea of citizenship is more comprehensive than that of Plato. His conception of citizenship is laid down in Book-III of the 'Politics'. Aristotle defines the term 'citizen' in this book. He first discusses the concept of citizenship negatively. To Aristotle, citizenship cannot be defined in terms of residence, enjoyment of legal right or of birth. For aliens and slaves resides in the state along with the citizens. Foreigners also enjoy legal rights. Therefore, citizenship should be defined in terms of function.

Aristotle things that participation in judicial and deliberative power and public offices marks off a citizen from an alien. A citizen is one who participates in the administration of justice and in legislation as a member of the governing body and who holds public offices for an indefinite period. Therefore, citizenship means participation in the exercise of sovereignty. The essence of citizenship lies in the employment of rights and duties. So, the naturalized persons are also citizen since they have the right to hold public offices in the state. Aristotle's definition of citizenship is applicable to democracy only. Democracy grants citizenship to a larger group. In oligarchy, all citizens cannot take part in legislation and serve as jurors. Hence, oligarchy restricts the rights of citizenship to a few persons only. To Aristotle, women, children, slave, mechanic and labourer cannot be recognized as citizens. They are inferior in moral and intellectual capacities to citizens. They lack the capacity of ruling. To Aristotle, citizen is an active agent capable of practical speculation and actively take part in the public affair.

Let us now discuss whether the virtue of good citizen is identical with that of the good man. The virtue of a good man is uniform and changeless. It is same everywhere and in all governments. A good man endowed with justice, courage and moral wisdom. But, the virtues of citizens differ from one another. They perform different function though all of them desire to protect the safety of the state. The virtues of good citizens are relative to the constitution of a Government to which he belongs. He cannot possess the absolute and perfect virtue of a good man. A good citizen must know how to rule and be ruled.

According to Aristotle, citizens have the rights to hold offices. The rule required practical wisdom. It can be acquired if every citizen is given opportunities to participate in the affairs of the state. Again, all citizens should be treated equally. Equal treatment means the proper distribution of honours and officers according to the capacity. Then only justice can be possible. A state ceases to be a state which does not observe the principle of justice. According to Dr. V. Venkata Rao "Aristotle is not an ideal of equalitarian democracy. To Aristotle equal treatment should be given to those who are equal in virtue. It is applicable to the citizens only. Women, slave or aliens cannot perform the functions of the citizens."

Aristotle says that a citizen must have recreation and leisure. Leisure is not relaxation. It is a kind of activity undertaking for its own shake. It is non-economic in nature. Activities of leisure include political activities of ruling. Welfare and public services, persuade of science and philosophy etc. Leisure activities concede the activities of good life for the promotion of which the state exist.

Criticism

Aristotle's conception of citizenship though democratic in form but aristocratic in essence. Only a few persons have the power and privilege to participate in the deliberate and judicial functions of the state. The producing classes are excluded from the body of a citizen although they are 9/10 of the total population.

To Aristotle, citizenship was applicable to small city state of his time where direct democracy prevailed. It cannot be applied to a modern state with representative Government.

According to Aristotle, to be a citizen is to be a direct part of the active sovereignty. It is not merely as it is with us to be a part of the sovereignty behind the screen which determined and controls the visible sovereignty. Modern concept of citizenship is passive. Citizen may or may not exercise their right to vote during an election.

Aristotle's analytical definition of citizenship divides the state into two unequal groups. Aristotle took upon the larger groups as a means to the welfare of the smaller ones.

Aristotelian citizenship is not liberal. We know that the end of the state is to promote the greatest good of the greatest number. Citizenship should not be confined to a few people based on wealth and/or birth. If this is shown, the ruling class may identify its private self-interest with the public interest of the state.

Aristotle is realist. His conception of citizenship through the flood of a light upon the deficiency of modern citizenship. Today, citizens cannot actively participate in the function of the state unless they enjoy economic security and leisure.

Aristotle on Slavery

Aristotle discussed at length the relationship between the master and the slave. He tried to explain the relevance and use of slavery, an institution that was universal. Greece was no exception. Unlike Plato, who ignored the institution, Aristotle defended slavery both from the point of view of the slave and the master, the householder. Many feel that Aristotle endorsed and systematized Plato's views on slavery. Plato protested against the enslavement of Greeks by Greeks in the fifth book of *the Republic.* In *the Laws*, he recognized the need for legislation for slaves. He clubbed them with children, for having imperfectly developed minds. Personally, Aristotle recommended less harshness towards slaves. He also rejected the enslavement of the Greeks, but thought it proper for barbarians who were by "nature" slaves.

Aristotle as a realist justified the institution of slavery and considered it essential for the proper functioning of the family. He considered the slaves as the living possession of the family which was as vital for its proper functioning as the lifeless possession of property. But such property is only fit for work and not for production. The slave has no separate identity of his own. Though he has sufficient power to understand and follow reason, but he has no reasoning power. Since slaves have lower capacity they should obey those possessing higher capacities. In all sphere of his life, he is guided by his master. Slaves are also essential to develop his moral and intellectual excellence. But, the development of such qualities, it requires leisure for the masters as well as the citizens and such leisure can be provided by slaves.

Aristotle believed that it was essential that household should be properly maintained and for that the institution of slavery and property were most essential. The slaves are animate institutions whereas property is the inanimate weapon for running a household. He did not agree with the Sophists that it was not a natural institution but had come to stay by convention alone. He also did not agree with the idea that since slavery was unnatural.

Aristotle classified the slaves into two classes—Slaves by nature and Slave by law. But Aristotle was sympathetic only to slaves by nature and not slave by law. He does not support slave by law because of the fact that the motive of such slave is not honest. They want to engage themselves in war. However, Aristotle considered the Greeks as a superior race and as such they should not be enslaved even if they become the prisoners of war.

Classification of Slaves

Aristotle classified the slaves into two classes—(1) Slave by nature (2) Slave by law.

1. Slave by Nature

According to Aristotle men by nature are not equal. Some men have knowledge and intelligence. They may be mentally strong. It is due to their wisdom and intelligence, they guide others. They are the masters. On the other hand there are some people who may be physically strong but they are lacking in wisdom and intelligence. They may not have superior reasoning capacity or less power of understanding. They may not be able to lead their life without the help of others and they like to live under the guidance of the others. Aristotle called this class of people as slaves.

2. Slave by Law

Another class of slave is known as slave by law. This kind of slaves means the prisoners of war. If a group of people is defeated in the war, then this group of people as prisoners of war has to serve under the victors. According to Aristotle such kind of persons are called as slaves by law.

Of course sometimes the wise, virtues, intelligent group of persons may be defeated in war. In such an eventuality, they should not be treated as slaves. In this connection, Aristotle has pointed out the Greeks. This is superior to other race and as such they should not be treated as slaves by law even if they are defeated in war. But in case of people of other race, if they are defeated in war they may be enslaved by law. But he was not sympathetic to this class of slaves.

Justification for Slavery

Aristotle has justified slavery on many grounds, namely:

(i) It is a natural phenomenon that the inferior must be subordinated to the superior. As soul rules over the body or reason over appetite, similarly those who have more reasoning capacity should rule over those who have no superior reasoning capacity or less power of understanding. The former are naturally masters and latter slaves. The masters have superiority in wisdom and the slaves in physical strength. As a musician cannot live without musical instrument so a family cannot live without a slave.

(ii) Slavery is necessary because it will provide leisure for the virtuous which is most essential for the welfare of the state.

(iii) Since a slave does not possess rational faculty and cannot regulate appetite by reason, it is good for him and is in his own interest to be a slave because then alone he will be in a position to share in the virtues of his master and will thus be elevated.

(iv) Slavery is essential for the master because that will enable him to lead a good and happy life which is essential for productive and creative work.

(v) He justified slavery on the ground that in case the system was denounced whole Greek social system would collapse resulting in social disorder and chaos in the Greek life.

(vi) Slavery is manifestation of will of nature which is clearly indicated from birth and wisdom of people which is always of varying degrees.

(vii) According to him since family is social unit it has two natural instincts, namely sex and appetite. The relationship on the one hand is between the master and slave and on the other between husband and wife.

(viii) According to him, it is with slavery that perfection can be attained. Slaves and the masters are just complementary and not contradictory to each other. The institution of slavery is thus, a social necessity.

Conditions Essential for Slavery

Aristotle, however, did not give unqualified support to the institution of slavery. He justified it only under certain specific conditions, namely:

(i) Only those who are mentally deficient and virtuously not so superior as others should be treated as slaves. All prisoners of war should not be enslaved.

(ii) Slaves should not be harshly treated but be given human treatment. Those who violate this established principle should be legally punished.

(iii) There should be provision for emancipation for those slaves who show good conduct and develop capacity for reasoning and virtue.

(iv) Slavery is essential for all-round development, thus, an integral point of growth. Master has no right to misuse his power and authority. Slave is not subordinate but only assistant.

(v) He was opposed to the idea of using force for slavery. Only those should be enslaved who were inferior in understanding and virtue.

Criticism of Aristotle's Views on Slavery

Aristotle's views on slavery have met with severe criticism at the hands of critics. In the main they have highlighted the following defects in his theory:

Firstly, Aristotle wrongly assumes that some are born to rule because they are intelligent and virtuous. This is contrary to the modern notions of equality which assumes that all are born equal and some develop the faculties which equip them to rule over others.

Secondly, even if we accept Aristotle's conception that nature has ordained that the superior should rule over the inferior, there shall be a number of classes in the society each superior to one and inferior to others. On the other hand, Aristotle presumes the existence of only two classes—the masters and slaves.

Thirdly, his theory of slavery is largely the development of his basic notion that the Greeks are superior to the non-Greeks or barbarians. He believes in the racial superiority of the Greeks and would not permit their enslavement.

Fourthly, Aristotle lays emphasis on the principle of heredity. Once a slave is always a slave. But, there is no justification to this view.

Fifthly, it goes against the notion of social justice. On the one hand Aristotle advocates that slaves are essential for the leisure of their masters and on the other hand, he has not recognized the importance of services of the slaves.

Sixthly, it is anti-democratic in nature. In democracy all can enjoy equal rights. But, Aristotle has not given the same status to the slaves as like the other persons of the society.

Aristotle's Theory of Revolution

The theory of revolution presented in Books V of Aristotle's *Politics* and is largely based on his study of the working of 158 constitutions of the Greek city-states. Aristotle undertook this study because of the frequent changes in the governments of city-states during his times.

He argues that despite important differences of emphasis, rhetoric, and tone, there is a surprising degree of similarity to the theory of revolution familiar to Amcricans from John Locke's Second Treatise of Government. Aristotle and Locke share the views that governments must avoid oppressing their subjects if they are to avoid being overthrown, that revolution against oppressive rulers is inevitable, that security for property would have a central place in the avoidance of oppression, and that the succumbing to the temptations of power on the part of ruling groups is the fundamental provocation of revolution. This aspect of Aristotle's political thought has been little noticed, but is an important dimension of it. Moreover, it provides a certain depth of insight into that side of Locke's thought that most sharply contrasts with Hobbes's thought, namely Locke's distrust of the corrupting force of political power.

According to Aristotle, Revolution Conveys Two-fold Meaning–

(a) A major or minor change in the constitution means a revolution to Aristotle. If the constitution has changed from Monarchy to Aristocracy, revolution has taken place. Any small or big change in the constitution meant revolution to him. Even if oligarchy has become less oligarchic or democracy less democratic a revolution is deemed to have taken place. The example of big change can be: if oligarchic rule is overthrown by democrats or if, otherwise, the democratic rule is overthrown by oligarchs.

(b) Even if the constitution remains the same and the ruling power has been transferred from one man to another, revolution is supposed to have taken place, e.g. if one tyrant is replaced by another or one monarch is substituted by the other.

We know already any change in the constitution had far reaching importance. It meant a change in the social and moral rules of the state. The ruling power had great part to play in the cultivation of virtue. Hence, he does not restrict the meaning of revolution of political conception.

Causes of Revolution

Aristotle has broadly classified the causes of revolution into three classes.

(a) General cause.
(b) Particular cause.
(c) Revolution causes in particular state.

(a) General Causes of Revolution—

The general causes of revolution may be discussed as follows—

Demand for Equality

Revolution may be caused if there is no equality among the different sections of people of the state. There should not be vast difference between the ruler and the ruled. All people are equal by birth and if the demand of the common people for equality along with the privileged class is not fulfilled, this may lead to revolution. In the same way, the aristocrat people also may demand more privilege than the common man and if their demand is not fulfilled, they may resort to revolution.

Demand for Justice

Another general cause of revolution is the demand for justice. According to Aristotle injustice to the people is the major cause of revolution. The ruled should not be made to feel that they are deprived of justice due to rulers. In other words if a substantial section of people of the society feels that justice is not being done to them, this may lead to revolution.

(b) Particular Causes of Revolution:

The particular causes of revolution according to Aristotle are:

(i) The possession of the absolute powers by one or a few individuals so as to excite fear in the minds of the public.

(ii) The disproportionate increase of any part (territorial, social, economic or otherwise) of the state.

(iii) Grant of undue prominence to some people is resented by the people and they mobilize the public opinion which poses a serious threat to the unity and solidarity of the state.

(iv) Misuse of authority by those in power and attitude of defame and disgrace adopted towards the opponents is resented and is likely to promote the spirit of revolution.

(v) The use of unscrupulous methods in elections for capture of power leaves bitter taste and the people are bound to retaliate at the earliest available opportunity for the fraud played on them.

(vi) Careless admission of corrupt and disloyal officers to civil and military posts can generate revolution.

(vii) The rivalry among the members of various races living in a state leads to irreconcilable interests and is bound to have serious repercussions.

(viii) The neglect of minor changes can sometimes assume serious dimensions and culminate in revolution.

(ix) Free flow of immigrants can also lead to revolution.
(x) The conquest of one nation by another nation also contains seeds of revolution.

(c) Revolution in a Particular Kind of State

Finally, Aristotle also discusses the cause of revolution in particular types of state, viz. democracies, oligarchies, aristocracies and polities. According to him, in democracies revolutions are caused due to excessive use of powers and unwarranted condemnation of the rich by the demagogues. In oligarchies revolutions take place either due to rivalry and dissensions among the ruling oligarchies or due to oppressive and dictatorial nature of their rule. In Aristocracy, the revolutions are spearheaded by those who are denied honours which are conferred only on the few. In Polity the revolution is caused due to defective balance of the different elements in the constitution. In other words the revolutions in polity are due to mal-admixture of the oligarchic and democratic elements. Revolts in Monarchy and Tyranny are caused by two factors, viz. hatred and contempt generated in the minds of the people due to insolent and oppressive behaviour of the rulers; personal insult inflicted by the ruler on some notable persons; or influence of the foreign state of opposite character.

Preventions of Revolutions

Aristotle's account of the preventions of revolutions is again indicative of his penetrating knowledge of the then constitutions. In addition to laying down some general means of preventing revolutions or making the state stable, he touches upon particular remedies for particular diseases to be found in particular constitutions.

Methods for Prevention of Revolution

According to Aristotle, the methods for the prevention of revolution may be broadly classified into two—

1. General method and
2. Particular method.

General Methods for Prevention of Revolution

1. People should obey law. They should not violate law even for a trifle matter.
2. There should be no sudden promotion to any political posts. It should be gradual as far as possible.

3. The outsiders should not be given any responsible post, because they may not think for the welfare of the local people. They may work to serve their selfish interest.
4. The general population should be properly educated. They should have knowledge about the constitution.
5. There should be close co-operation between the rulers and the people. The rulers should try to take the people into confidence so that they feel oneness with the government.
6. The higher officers of the government should not be selected from a particular community. The virtuous persons should be elected for the higher posts of the government so that they can take interest for the welfare of all classes of people.
7. No particular group of people should be allowed to grow more powerful.
8. The state should be free from corruption.
9. In case of defensive matter, the state must be very strong so that it can prevent foreign aggression.
10. The tenure of the government offices should not be long. The tenure of the higher officers should be very short.
11. The rulers should not try to be cunning. They should not try to deceive the people. People should not be kept in dark in case of the policies and working procedures of the rulers.
12. When the ruler introduces any change, they should carefully observe the reaction of the people. Those who exploit the situation, they should be tactfully handled.

Particular Methods for Prevention of Revolution

After suggesting general method for the prevention of revolution, Aristotle also suggested certain other means for the prevention of revolution in the different forms of governments. Revolution may be caused in different constitution due to different factors and it means for avoiding such revolution in such state should also be different.

1. In democracy, the rich should be made to feel that their property shall not be redistributed. They would be allowed to take part in the administration of the state.
2. In Monarchy, the monarch should undertake welfare activities for the people. The ruler should try to fulfil the desire of the people. They should not be made to feel that the government is not doing anything for their welfare.

3. In Oligarchy, the poor should be allowed to take part in the administration along with the rich people. The people should be treated with fairness. No person should be allowed to become more powerful.
4. In Aristocracy, efforts should be made to distribute offices on democratic lines. People of lower classes should be treated with fairness.
5. In Polity, revolution may be avoided by proper blending of the democratic and oligarchic elements.
6. In case of Tyrannical form of government, Aristotle has suggested a number of measures for avoiding revolution and these measures are discussed below—
   - There should be espionage system to detect the offenders. In this regard he should appoint female spies.
   - The ruler should follow the policy of aggression and expansion.
   - He should make the people always feel the threat of foreign attack from powerful enemy.
   - The criminals should be given heavy punishment.
   - He should not allow the development of intellectual life of the citizens.
   - The city should be made impressive for the outsiders.
   - The rulers should not be impartial. He should try to control his passion under all circumstances.
   - Those who can do good works, they should be promptly honoured. This will inspire the people to do good works.
   - He should not allow the people to form any club.
   - He should always keep the people busy.
   - He should always increase the material well being of the people.
   - The ruler should lead a simple life so that the people respect him.

Criticisms

Aristotle's theory of revolution is subjected to severe criticism from different points of view.

1. Aristotle in his theory of revolution has mentioned that the major cause of revolution is the political injustice. But political injustice cannot be the only cause of revolution. Revolution may be caused due to economic factor as well.

2. Aristotle's theory of revolution has failed to give any explanation of the revolutions of the modern world. One cannot explain the French Revolution or Russian Revolution with the help of Aristotle's conception of revolution.
3. The change or amendment to a constitution of a particular state cannot be termed as revolution as Aristotle defined. Revolution may be occurred against the imperialist rule.
4. According to Aristotle, revolution cannot be initiated by the middle class. But this view is also not correct.
5. An elected government may pass law against public opinion. But Aristotle is also silent on this issue.
6. Aristotle also failed to mention the role of religion, caste and language as the factors of revolution.

Aristotle's Classification of Constitution

According to Aristotle, a constitution is not only a basic law determining structure of its government and allocation of powers between the different branches within a government, but it also reflected a way of life. A constitution gives an identity to a state, which meant that a change in the constitution brought about a change in the state.

A political community, like all other communities, involved concerted actions and joint activity working towards a common purpose. It could be distinguished from other associations by the fact that it had a supreme authority. A constitution could be described as "an organization of offices in a state, by which the method of their distribution is fixed, the sovereign authority is determined, and the nature of the end to be pursued by the association and all its members is prescribed."

According to Aristotle, every constitution contains three elements, namely deliberative, official or magisterial, and the judicial. The deliberative has four functions:

1. It is responsible for the most important decisions in foreign policy, matters of war and peace, and making and breaking of alliances.
2. Making and interpreting laws.
3. Administration of severe penalties, such as death, exile and confiscation of property.
4. Election of magistrates and their examination on completion of their term.

Aristotle analyzes and compares 158 constitutions, thereby uniting the empirical and speculative modes of enquiry. He builds on Plato's classification of constitution in the *Statesman* by taking into account the ends of a constitution and the number who wield political power. Constitutions promoting general well-being of the governed are true or good, whereas those that fettered the interests of the ruled are bad or perverted. A government ruled by one, few or many in the general interest of the community are monarchy, aristocracy and polity respectively. Conversely, a government ruled by one, few or many in the self-interest of the ruler are tyranny, oligarchy and democracy respectively. Aristotle emphasizes that the state changes its identity when the constitution changes. According to Aristotle, no constitution in the world is either absolutely good or bad it is only comparatively good or bad.

Classification of Constitutions or States

Aristotle followed two principles for the classification of constitution. These two principles are quantitative and qualitative. In other words he followed the principle of number and purpose or end of the state. According to the first principle whether the supreme power of the state is to be exercised by one, few or many. Aristotle's second principle of classification of state is concerned with the ends of the state. If the purpose or the end of the state is concerned with the welfare of the community, he called it to be normal but when it is used for the selfish ends then that type of government is called perverted.

Thus, Aristotle classified government into six classes, out of these classes monarchy, aristocracy and polity are normal whereas tyranny, oligarchy and democracy are perverted forms of government. Aristotle's classification of constitutions can be shown as follows:

Number of persons upon whom power is vested	*Normal Form*	*Perverted Form*
One	Monarchy	Tyranny
Few	Aristocracy	Oligarchy
Many	Polity	Democracy

According to Aristotle, the Polity was the best and the most practicable form of government because it possessed a healthy combination of liberty and wealth. He held that the best constitution was the one which was practicable. He was even willing to have a monarchy provided the Monarchy was enlightened. However, he asserts that monarchy and aristocracy have a tendency to degenerate and do not possess the quality of moderation and stability which is a characteristic feature of Polity.

Aristotle says that no form of government or constitution is permanent or everlasting and the different forms of government keep on changing. This change, according to Aristotle, takes place in a circle. The Monarchy, which is a normal government, gets degenerated in course of time and is replaced by Tyranny. Similarly Aristocracy degenerates into Oligarchy and Polity into Democracy. But democracy is also not the ultimate solution and is replaced by Monarchy. In this way the process of change continues. This process of change envisaged by Aristotle is popularly known as Aristotle's Cycle of Change.

Aristotle's Classification of State has been subjected to Criticism on the following grounds:

First, it is said that his classification is not applicable to the present times in so far as it does not cover a number of governments which exist at present, viz. parliamentary, presidential, unitary, federal etc.

Secondly, Aristotle considers democracy as a perverted form of government in which the government is run by many poor people. However, this notion of Aristotle is difficult to accept because the majority of people in a given society may be prosperous. In modern times democracy makes no reference to the qualification of poverty of the people and simply insists on the principle of equality and we consider it as the best form of government.

Thirdly, Aristotle has failed to point out the difference between the state and the government. But in reality it cannot be used in the same sense.

Fourthly, his classification is not based on scientific principles. According to the critics, his classification is quantitative rather qualitative.

Fifthly, he has not given any place to theocracy.

Sixthly, Aristotle's classification is not an original concept. He had borrowed the main ideas from Plato's theory.

Aristotle's Ideal State

Aristotle's political thought combines the elements of Political Ideals and Political Actualities. Books II, III, and VIII of his Politics deal with the Political ideas while in Books IV, V and VI deals with the political actualities. Again in Books VII and VIII, he tries to describe the physical, mental and geographical conditions which are essential for the existence of the Ideal State. All these conditions are derived from Plato's "Law." And as we know, in the laws, Plato depicts his Second Best State. Hence, it is very correct to say that "what Aristotle calls the Ideal State is always Plato's second best state." Therefore, it is desirable to discuss Aristotle's Ideal State as well as the best Practicable State.

At its heart, Aristotle's ideal state, whatever its specific form of government, maintains its legitimacy by serving the good life for the people as a whole. Aristotle's description of the state as an association of free men aligns him with democratic theory, though he expresses distaste for democracy at a certain level and finds that there are certain classes in society that should not be given the right to participate because they are not worthy. Aristotle calls his version of democracy by the name "polity" and describes its constitution as assuring political control to be exercised by the mass of the populace in the common interest, and he analyzes the nature of the polis, the city-state, and its workings in his Politics, a work which actually addresses issue of ethics and morality more than politics as we mean it today. It is a book of politics because it acknowledges that to achieve a moral and so happy life, the attempt must be made in terms of a civil society embodied in the city-state of the time.

Before we come to the depiction of conditions essential for Aristotle's Ideal State two facts of great importance are to be noted:

First, Aristotle is not an absolutist like Plato. He is a relativist by nature. Plato prescribes that his Ideal State in the Republic is good for all communities for all times to come. But according to Aristotle, we cannot pronounce which is the best government for a particular people without taking into account the special nature of that people.

Second, Aristotle's normal preference goes in for Monarchy as the Ideal State, since transcendent virtue is more likely to be found in one man than in any large number. And according to Aristotle, in any good state the law must be the ultimate sovereign and not any person whatsoever. And if this be taken seriously, Monarchy is ruled out as the Ideal State.

Features of Aristotle's Ideal State

Aristotle's views regarding his Ideal State are scattered here and there. Some views are in Book III, others in Book VII and VIII. As noted earlier, Aristotle's Ideal State is a government by men of high and enlightened virtue, in which no one is admitted to citizenship who is not qualified, and in which all citizens rule and are ruled in turn. Now this Ideal State as depicted by Aristotle is an ideal according to him, which is pitched too high for human nature and is unrealizable. But at present we are concerned with the features of Aristotle's Ideal State whether realizable or not.

The following are the features of Aristotle's Ideal State:

1. The Ideal State of Aristotle is the small city-state consisting of small and intimate group of citizens whose social life overlaps the interests of family, of religion and of friendly personal intercourse.

2. In his Ideal State, the law occupies a predominant position. He does not favour the personal and despotic rule of even the most virtuous person and favours impersonal rule of law, which according to him represents the wisdom of the community since the ages.
3. The Ideal state of Aristotle is an ethical institution which means to bring about moral improvement amongst the citizens. He holds that state alone can provide the conditions under which the individual can achieve the highest type of moral development.
4. In the Ideal State of Aristotle education plays an important role in making the citizens virtuous. He insists on compulsory state regulated education to cultivate good habits among the citizens and to make members perfect.
5. In the Ideal State of Aristotle, right to private property is conceded because he considered private property as a natural institution which must be preserved. He pleads for equal distribution of land among the citizens.
6. The division of labour is another essential feature of Aristotle's ideal state. Thus, he assigns agriculture to the slaves, commerce and trade to the resident-aliens and political functions to the citizens. He justifies the institution of slavery and insists that only the leisured classes should actively participate in the exercise of the sovereignty.
7. Aristotle's ideal state is neither too small nor too big. However, Aristotle does not prescribe any maximum or minimum number of citizens to constitute an ideal state. He simply insists that the population should be manageable. He is certainly against large population and argues that ideal conditions cannot exist if the population is large.
8. The Ideal State is self-sufficient in all possible respects. It is never aggressive. It does not attack any foreign country as it is self-sufficient.
9. The population of the Ideal State is divided into many classes, i.e. (i) husband-men (agriculturalist) (ii) artisans (iii) a war-like class (iv) a well-to-do leisured class (v) priests (vi) administrators. Of all these classes, only the last four form the constituent parts of the state, i.e. only they are the citizens. The first two classes are non-citizens.
10. It should be located at such a place whose climate is temperate, i.e. neither too cold nor too hot, it is congenial to both mental and physical activity.

11. The situation of the Ideal State should be such that it should have ample access to sea in order to have necessary imports.
12. In addition to these important features of the Ideal State, Aristotle discusses many minor features regarding the internal ordering of the city, i.e. arrangement of water supply and of streets. He is also keen to make necessary arrangements for defense against foreign attack, i.e. fortification, both of walls and citadel, training in the use of the latest war-like weapons.

Prof. Maxey criticizes Aristotle's middle-class state on the ground that "middle-class mediocrity is no shining ideal for the foundation of a state." However, this criticism seems to be misplaced because Aristotle himself says that Polity is not the best Ideal State, rather it is the best on the average. It is the best practicable. Further, even the actual experience of the working of various political societies confirms the contention of Aristotle that most of the stable, durable and well-administered states have been under the control of the middle class. Viewed in this context his concept of middle-class rule is one of the most important contributions to the political thought.

Aristotle's Theory of Justice

Aristotle attached great importance to the conception of justice. The Greek political thinks felt that it was one of the most outstanding and important features of the state. It was virtue in action and worked on the basis of mutual cp-operation in which each and every member of the society should try to discharge his duties towards the community as a whole. It was of general excellence and depicted moral development. It was moral virtue in social relationship.

Though Greek political thinkers might differ in details about the conception of justice, yet its fundamental importance remained unshaken throughout the Greek period. According to Plato, justice was in proper performance of duties. He felt that the philosophers, soldiers and the peasants, who had been allotted a particular job, should perform that property and honestly. The philosophers should rule, soldiers fight and the peasants serve the community as a whole with emotion and honesty.

Types of Justice

Aristotle makes a reference to two types of justice, viz. complete justice and particular justice. The former was a moral virtue concerned with the regulations of the public and social relations. This implied complete obedience to law and was possible only in an ideal state. On the other hand the particular was concerned with the distribution of offices and observance of rules of proportionate equality. It also implied distribution of wealth, honour and goods.

Distributive Justice

Aristotle further divides particular justice into two groups, distributive justice and corrective justice. Distributive justice lays emphasis on proportionate allocation of office according to the worth of the individual and is mainly concerned with political privileges. According to Aristotle, distributive justice was the most powerful instrument for the prevention of revolution, because it ensures to each person what is due to him as a member of society and keeps him satisfied. According to Aristotle, each type of political organization has its own distributive justice.

Corrective Justice

Aristotle also mentions about corrective justice. According to him, it is a type of justice which prevents people from encroaching upon the rights of his fellowmen. He believed that, "It relates to voluntary and commercial transactions like hire, sale and furnishing of security etc. and with involuntary actions involving aggression of life, property, honour and freedom."

Criticism

Aristotle's concept of justice suffers from numerous defects. In the first place he insists that the virtuous should rule because he can contribute most to the discreet and cannot be accepted as a standard or measuring rod.

Secondly, there is a clear contribution in the views of Aristotle. On the one hand he pleads that the cultivation of virtue should be the criteria for the distribution of office, but on the other hand he insists that the masses should not be ignored. He pleads for the sharing of honour by all because collective wisdom was superior to the wisdom of the few virtuous.

Thirdly, Aristotle's conception of justice, particularly his views on particular and distributive justice, do not fit in well with the modern notions. It is indeed difficult to contemplate how offices can be distributed to all the citizens. Again, in our times distributive justice is taken as payment of due taxes to the state rather than distribution of offices.

In conclusion we can say that in comparison the Plato's view on justice, which hold good even today, Aristotle's views have not found favour in modern times and treated as outdated.

Contribution of Aristotle to Political Theory

Aristotle's thought has exercised profound influence on the political thinkers of subsequent centuries and left a deep impact on the development of political thought. In view of his valuable contributions to the science of politics he is rightly treated as the father of Political Science. He was the first pragmatic thinker who based his conclusions on data, facts, figures etc. and imparted a scientific outlook to the study of the subject. Some of the important principles of universal nature, which are accepted even today, contained in the thought of Aristotle, are as follows:

1. His Idea About Liberty and Authority

He tried to reconcile the concepts of liberty and authority. What should be the relation between the two and how should these be adjusted with each other is a problem which requires solution even today. Credit goes to him for his making a sincere attempt to solve this problem which, no doubt, is his great contribution to modern political thought. He perhaps rightly felt that liberty meant subjection to constitutional authority and obedience to right type of laws. Without obedience to the laws stability of state was in danger.

2. Command of Law

Aristotle was the first political thinker who established the supremacy of law and felt than in an ideal state law should be above over every individual irrespective of his status because it is always impartial and dispassionate. This supremacy of law is adhered to and respected even in modern times.

3. Respect for Public Opinion

Aristotle's another feature of universalism is his respect for public opinion. He feels that the multitude of people has always better knowledge and judgement than a single or few individuals. He wants to vest power in the hands of the masses rather than the monarch or the few oligarchies.

4. Natural Origin of State

His another contribution is that he has expounded the idea that the state is of natural origin and that man's joining the state is absolutely natural which cannot be avoided. In order words, according to him, joining of state is not an optional matter but a compulsion and that each and every individual must join the state. This idea also holds good even in modern times.

5. Forerunner of Utilitarian Philosophy

He has given utilitarian outlook to the functions of the state. By saying that state came into being for the sake of life and continues for the sake of good life, he has became forerunner of the utilitarian philosophy which believes that the sole aim of the state is to give maximum happiness to the maximum number of people.

6. Assigning Positive Functions of the State

He has assigned direct and positive functions of the state with some specific aims and objects. It is the duty of the state to promote moral development of the citizens. It should be the aim of the state to make the citizens virtuous and happy.

7. Forerunner of Theory of Separation of Powers

He is the forerunner of the theory of separation of powers. According to him, state should be divided into various classes and each class should confine itself to the duties allotted to it. He has also divided the functions as deliberative, judicial and legislative and has pleaded that each function should be performed by a particular class.

8. Establishing Relationship Between Politics and Economics

Aristotle emphasized the close relationship between politics and economics and asserted that the economic activities were bound to influence the political organizations as well as actions. This is evident from his assertion that where there was concentration of wealth or power, political stability could not be possible. He says that political stability is possible only in a state where there are no extremes of wealth or poverty.

9. Use of Comparative Method

Aristotle also laid the foundations of the comparative method of study of political institutions. His views were mainly based on the study of 158 constitutions of the Greek city-states.

10. Father of Individualism

Aristotle is called the father of individualism as well. He was the first political scientist who rejects Plato's concept that the individual was merely a means to an end. He asserts that the sole aim of the state is to exist for the sake of good life and considers state as a means for the development of the individual.

11. Separation of Ethics from Politics

His important contribution is that he makes the political philosophy an independent character. He applied scientific methods for the study of Political Science and also tried to separate ethics from politics. His idea was further developed by Machiavelli and Hobbes.

12. Father of Realism

Aristotle was the father of realism. He took note of the things as they were rather than concentrating on the things as they should be. Therefore, he moved from the particular to the general. He completely rejected the ideal state of Plato and accepted his second best state as his ideal because it was practicable and attainable.

13. Supporter of Private Property

Aristotle offered most effective justification for the institution of private property and made a strong plea for its retention. According to him, private property is very much essential for the development of personalities of individuals and for the welfare of the communities. His arguments for the retention of private property are used by the supporters of private property even today.

14. Supporter of Middle Classes

Aristotle was the first to emphasize the importance of the middle-class as a balancing force for the preservation of the political institutions. He considered Polity as the best and practicable state because it was a middle-class state.

15. Father of Modern Conservatism

Aristotle is considered as the godfather of modern conservatives. He was the first to insist that the existing institutions must be preserved because they represented the collective wisdom of generations. He argued that since these institutions have existed for such a long time, it was by itself sufficient proof of their utility.

Estimate of Aristotle's Philosophy

There is no denial that Aristotle is one of the most outstanding figures of political philosophy. His idea of preaching what is the best practice in the existing circumstances is his greatest quality. He does not follow blindly his teacher and arrives at the decisions after studying the problem analytically with a great insight and by following deductive methods. By his systematic treatment of the subject he has given politics the character of a science. In addition to this, he has given pride place to politics over ethics.

His glory also lies in the fact that he became the first individualist and constitutionalist who established supremacy of law. His theories put forth clear-cut dogmas with rational conclusions. His estimate can well be expressed in the words of Zellen when he says that "The Politics of Aristotle is the richest treasure that has come down to us from antiquity it is the greatest contribution to the field of political science that we possess."

Unit-II
Medieval Political Thought

Introduction

This study seeks to interpret the history of the political ideas of medieval Western that is Latin, Europe and covers the period between the early fourth and the mid-fifteenth century. This starting-point, still within late antiquity, has been chosen because it marks the public acceptance and then dominance of Christianity, a development which was to provide the fundamental context for the political ideas of the Middle Ages proper. The concluding date is more problematical, because it can well be argued that the period from the thirteenth to the mid-seventeenth century forms a coherent whole in terms of political thought. The problem is that there is no clear end to the Middle Ages because of the diversity of cultural development in different parts of Europe and the survival of medieval ideas and attitudes well into the seventeenth century. It would, however, prove far too unwieldy to prolong this book to 1650 or thereabout. A division in about the middle of the fifteenth century has been accepted because it reflects the effective end of the medieval papacy and the beginnings of early modern territorial monarchies, and because the development of Renaissance humanism increasingly created a new world of political discourse.

The first and fundamental problem, however, in treating medieval European political thought is to define clearly the nature of the subject. In this study a broad definition will be used: ideas concerning the nature, organisation, government and ends of society. This wide approach is dictated by the characteristics of medieval political thought and of the sources from which the historian may reconstruct it. The most obvious omission from this definition is any mention of the state, which would have to be included in any examination of post-medieval political ideas.

The reason for this absence helps characterise a large part of the Middle Ages: although the term 'state', being in content historically fluid, can have medieval as distinct from a variety of modern connotations, it is difficult to see that it can be meaningfully employed to describe aspects of politically organised society in the medieval west before the twelfth century. The whole question of the state in the middle Ages is, however, a very vexed one: there are, for instance, scholars who would locate an idea of the state in as early a period as the Carolingian. The disagreements hinge around the degree of rigour employed in the application of the term 'state' and illustrate a profound difficulty concerning the interpretation of western medieval political thought: so much of its content does not fit into modern preconceptions about what comprises political thought.

This difficulty is also apparent in the nature of the sources for this enquiry. Medieval political thought cannot be adequately treated by considering the works of a string of political thinkers: such writings were largely lacking in the Middle Ages, and in so far as they existed, were products only of the period from the twelfth century onwards. Most medieval writers relevant to this study were primarily theologians, philosophers or jurists: political ideas formed only a minor part of their concerns. The basic intellectual orientation of these thinkers must be borne in mind when interpreting them. Similarly, the works of publicists involved in the disputes between the papacy and secular rulers have to be understood within the context of each conflict and according to the intentions of the writer: such men were not professedly political thinkers. The importance of legal, and especially juristic, sources was paramount, and because of the role of the church, ecclesiological questions assumed a political significance which they would have lacked in a more secular age. Furthermore, throughout the medieval period, and certainly in its earlier part, a range of other kinds of source has to be considered: coronation orders, for instance, and histories. The sources of medieval political thought, therefore, consist both of writings directly or indirectly concerned with political matters, and other forms of material which permit the elucidation of political assumptions, attitudes and mentalities.

Such considerations lead the student of medieval political thought to treat it within its historical context. This method will be followed here, because the historical meaning of the whole range of medieval political ideas can only be discerned, when the sources, in all their variety, are viewed against the background of the societies, institutions, conflicts and intellectual milieux in which they were produced and with which they were concerned. This is in any case very much a historian's attitude, and of course it is perfectly possible to approach, where relevant, the sources of medieval political thought from a purely philosophical or jurisprudential stand-point. Differing kinds of meaning would thereby be gleaned from the material, but not that which was originally contained in the source, or which, in the case of a writer, he sought to express.

Given the nature of the sources to be considered and the method to be followed, it has seemed best to combine in this book a thematic with a chronological approach, thereby enabling the integrity of every historical stage to be preserved and the longer-term connections to be made. The focus is on the West; Byzantine political thought is only considered for purposes of comparison and in so far as it affected the West, because the Byzantine empire had a very different history: there the state endured as a continuation of the Roman empire of antiquity, and the position of the church in relation to the secular power increasingly diverged from that existing in the West, where ecclesiastical claims to independence developed to an extent unknown in the East. Although the church and secular rulers normally worked in harmony throughout the Middle Ages in the west, the opportunity for conflict was ever-present from the mid-eleventh century onwards, when the papacy substantially enlarged its jurisdictional claims. There was thereafter an underlying tension between secular and ecclesiastical power, which on occasion broke out into full-scale conflicts. The existence of such disputes in the west and their virtual absence in the more static East had the most profound long-term implications for the political ideas of both parts of Christendom. The conflicts between the church and secular power, reflecting the divided loyalties of those involved, provided so much of the dynamism of Western medieval political thought, and prevented the emergence of the idea of a monolithic society. Writers engaged in these disputes radically disagreed about the ordering of society, its government and the public obligations of its members. Fundamental enquiries concerning the nature and purpose of ruler ship were exhaustively pursued precisely because of this disagreement. As a result, profound contributions were made to perennially important political questions, but contributions which were characteristically medieval in content. The modern enquirer into medieval political thought is first struck by the prominence of religious aspects; but, as we shall see, therein lies only part of the story.

The Origin of the Medieval Political Ideas

The political ideas of the ancient world largely conditioned the development of those of the Middle Ages. This process was, however, a highly complex one involving reinterpretation and innovation as these ideas were applied in the context of medieval conditions radically different from those which prevailed in ancient Greece, Rome or Israel. Antiquity provided so much of the intellectual raw material which was worked into peculiarly medieval structures of thought. Furthermore, the history of political ideas reflected the vicissitudes of the classical heritage in the Medieval Latin West. In the early Middle Ages that inheritance was severely attenuated, whereas it was deeply enriched from the late eleventh century by the rediscovery of the whole of Justinian's codification of the Roman law, the Corpus iris civilise, 1 and from the mid-twelfth by the growing body of Aristotelian works available in Latin translations. This is not to suggest, however, that the whole content of medieval political ideas rested on concepts derived from the ancient world. Some areas, such as, for instance, feudal notions, were specifically medieval developments. The rich texture of political ideas in the middle Ages was provided by the way in which the medieval versions of ultimately Graeco-Roman and biblical concepts coexisted and interacted with purely medieval modes of thinking. In the Byzantine empire the integration of classical and biblical ideas into a structure of political thought followed a path markedly different from that which the West pursued, but one which directly influenced the west in certain crucial phases.

The immediate foundations of early medieval political thought lay in the lengthy period of transition between the ancient world and the Middle Ages proper, that is to say between the reign of the Emperor Constantine (306-37) and the early eighth century, which in the West saw the rise to power of the Carolingians and in the east the existence of a thoroughly Greek Byzantine empire. It is necessary to begin our enquiry with this period of transition because it produced ideas basic not only to the whole thought-structure of the early middle Ages but ones which were pervasive throughout the medieval period. A complete survey of intellectual life in these transitional centuries will not be attempted here: only those aspects important for the Middle Ages will be considered.

This period witnessed the conversion of Constantine, his foundation of Constantinople as the first predominantly Christian city and the reception of Christianity as the official religion of the Roman Empire in 380; thus was provided the Christian context fundamental to the development of political ideas in the middle Ages. In the West, Roman life became gradually barbarised with the settlement of Germanic peoples within the frontiers of the empire. With the gradual collapse of Roman administration as barbarian kingdoms emerged in the fifth and sixth centuries, regionalism developed leading ultimately to territorial kingship which became the characteristically medieval form of ruler ship. Yet within these kingdoms, notably in Gaul, Spain and Italy, increasingly diluted elements of Roman civilisation persisted into the seventh century. In the East, the Roman Empire survived and became more and more Greek in outlook.

Although the bases of Byzantine political thought had already been laid down in the fourth century, when the Roman empire remained intact, the eastern empire—despite its continuing universalist claims—had by the second half of the seventh century become clearly Byzantine, possessing control over only a part even of the original eastern portion of the empire: despite the attempted reconquests of Justinian the West had been lost apart from a remnant of power in Italy, and the advance of Islam in the seventh century had conquered Syria, Palestine and North Africa. Indeed it was the seventh century which really marked the end of antiquity and the beginning of the middle Ages. The West in reality was left to its own resources; its regionalism crystallised into kingdoms: the Visigoth in Spain, the Frankish in Gaul, and the Lombard in Italy and the Anglo-Saxon and Celtic ones in the British Isles. Byzantium, despite its grandiloquent universalist claims, turned inwards into its Greek culture and destiny. Much of the future lay with Islam which through its conquests largely destroyed what remained of the unity of Mediterranean civilisation. By 713 Islam had conquered the Visigothic kingdom, and by 720 Septimania in southern France, although its control there proved to be only short lived. Indeed, in 732-33 the Frankish leader Charles Martel halted any further Moslem advance northwards in a battle which took place at Tours or Poitiers. In a western Latin Europe limited, in effect, to Gaul, parts of western Germany, Italy and the British Isles, the stage was set for the Carolingian Renaissance, the flowering of a purely medieval western culture, in which were elaborated concepts of rulership which remained fundamental for the rest of the Middle Ages.

General Features of Medieval Political Thought

It is very difficult to present the ideas of medieval political thought in a logical sequence and establish a link between the various ideas. In this chapter we shall deal with some of the outstanding characteristics of medieval political thought.

1. The Origin of the State

All medieval thinkers usually believed that the state was the result of a convention though it was against the philosophy of Plato and Aristotle which preached that the state was the product of nature or that it was natural. They believed with Romans and church fathers, that it was artificial arrangement—the state being the result of an agreement between the king and the subjects or the result of sins of man. The theory held grounds for considerably long time and was appreciated by our modern thinkers till it was shaken by Montesquieu and Rousseau.

2. Idea of Monarchy

Medieval political philosophy practically believed in the theory of Divine origin of kingship. It was believed that God was overlord of all kings and earthly lordship flowed from the Divine Lordship. Monarchy was considered as the best and normal form of government and political organisation. But as Barker has said, "The popular business and the popular right of critics of monarchy are cardinal tenets of medieval theory." They believed that though the king was representative of God yet the community had a right to control him. Reconciliation between the two might appear paradoxical yet it got reconciled throughout the Middle Ages because of amalgamation of Germanic and Christian ideas. Throughout the Middle Ages monarchy and not the monarch was exalted. The office and not the person were infallible and that the subjects should obey not the individual but the office. Unjust monarch could be disobeyed and resisted. Ruler was not absolute in the exercise of his authority but was bound by certain limitations, namely those of the law of nature and of the community etc. Monarch was supposed to promote peace and justice. He had certain obligations towards community which he could not defy. He should have regard for customs which are the product of wisdom of men. He was not supposed to make laws but promulgate them. They believed that the laws are made by the king.

3. The Idea of Law

The concept of law also occupied an important position in the medieval political thought. However, their concept of law was quite different from the modern concept of law. The medieval conception of law was very wide and includes the positive law, natural law, customary laws etc. The law was considered as superior to the king and even the king was expected to obey it. In other words the government was subordinated to law and not *vice versa.* The concept of law was further widened by Thomas Aquinas. He asserted that law is something much broader in its scope than a means of regulating human relationship. Thus, he tried to extend the law to the human beings as well as animate and inanimate things of universe. However, Aquinas held that no will—whether Divine or human—could be the source of law and that law was essentially an expression of reason.

4. Theory of Sovereignty

The concept of sovereignty was unknown to the medieval political thinkers. They never conceived political authority in absolute terms and considered divine reason and moral orders as serious checks on the political authority.

The Laws of Nature and the Church also acted as a limitation on the authority of the Sovereign. The feudal lords posed still another check on the authority of the king. They were always eager to see that the kings were weak and did not assume power. The community also enjoyed control over the king and could change a tyrant or despotic king. Thus the concept of sovereignty in the sense in which we understand it in our times was conspicuously absent in the medieval political thought. There only existed a concept of limited or constitutional sovereignty.

5. Faith in Universalism

Another notable feature of the medieval political thought was faith in universalism or the existence of a cosmopolitan society. The medieval thinkers held that the church and the state were indivisible parts of the society. These two organisations headed by the Kings and the Pope respectively, worked in complete co-operation for the spiritual salvation of man, which was the sole aim of all human beings.

6. Growth of Papal Power

Middle ages are also known for the organisation of church into a mighty organisation. It was a general conviction that for Heaven's blessings church was essential. The Pope ruled as the deputy of God on earth and he demanded that all Christians should obey him. The monarchs began to invite Pope on their coronation ceremonies to seek his blessings. Gradually it also began to interfere in the temporal affairs as well. Its organisation was gradually strengthened and began to be considered as one of the soundest organisations in the world. As the time passed the state became only its department. The causes for this rapid growth were the destruction of Holy Roman Empire and also the rise of feudalism. The former weakened the temporal authority thereby giving the church an opportunity to exert itself whereas in the latter case it strengthened the hands of Pope against the Emperors, the feudal lords usually clashed with the Emperors. However, it was against the interests of the feudal to have a centralised authority. Their interest was to see a weak king on the throne which could only be influenced through a powerful church.

7. Controversy Over Secular and Spiritual Supremacy

Through the Middle Ages it was believed that the state and the church were two other different organisations. The church should have autonomy and be free from temporal control. It should have an independent character of its own. A conflicts however, ensured because the temporal authority did not wish to part with its traditional power and refused to reconcile to the idea of absolute spiritual autonomy. This resulted in the theory of two words which implied that spiritual and temporal aspects of a man should never be combined. The kingly and priestly duties should be separated from each other and Pope should be obeyed in religious matter and the king in secular affairs. An attempt was made to establish that Pope was superior to the king because the former derived the authority from God. The Pope could check the king either by interdiction or ex-communication. The Secularist on the other hand pleaded that the king was equally representative of God on earth. He exercised both spiritual as well as secular powers before the establishment of the church. The church was thus, a usurper and nothing less than that. In other words, religion and not politics dominated the Middle Ages which made Dunnings remark that Middle Ages were un-political. In addition to this, throughout the Middle Ages no political investigation was carried out which established the idea that age was barren of any new political philosophy.

8. Theory of Representation

The Medieval Ages are known for the system of representation but the representative was considered as a trustee or agent of the people to whom he represented. The representative was elected with the object of promoting the welfare of the people. Leaving aside the question of nature of work which a representative was required to perform, in this arrangement, modern representative system is indebted to this age for this philosophy. The fundamentals of this system shall remain unchanged.

9. Scholasticism

Middle Ages are also known for the medieval scholasticism. It included in its folds persons like Thomas Acquinas and Albortus Magnus. These intelligent Christians—realised the need and necessity of studying pre-Christian civilisation and thus, were not conservatives. According to Foster, it was a representative civilisation and product of "Union of Christianity with the ancient culture of the Graeco-Roman world." These scholars believed that philosophy did not come into conflict, with theology. They assigned foremost importance to theology and as Dunnings says, "Scholasticism was a system of thought in which philosophy in the purely rational sense was subordinated to the established theological doctrines." Hearnshaw says, "Scholasticism of the 13th century is a master key to the understanding of medievalism." Foster had said, "Scholasticism was the representative characteristics of the civilisation of the Middle Ages who arouse from the union of Christianity with the ancient culture of Graeco-Roman world."

10. Feudalism

The medieval thought and institutions were also moulded by the institution of feudalism. As Prof. Sabine has said "Feudal institutions dominated the Middle Ages as completely as the city state dominated antiquity." As a result of the impact of feudal institutions it was argued that the feudal lord held his position not as an agent of the king but on account of his prescriptive rights. The feudal lords did not enjoy the delegated power but their own powers. Under the circumstances the powers of the king depended largely on his ability to limit the feudal lords. As a result the old concept that the state is a community of persons bound together by the bond of law and common interest suffered a setback. This idea got mingled up with the feudal idea that the king has contractual relations with his vassals.

Medieval Feudalism

Feudalism was the dominant form of political organization in medieval Europe. It was a hierarchical system of social relationships wherein a noble lord granted land known as a fief to a free man, who in turn swore fealty to the lord as his vassal and agreed to provide military and other services. A vassal could also be a lord, granting portions of the land he held to other free vassals; this was known as "subinfeudation," and often led all the way up to the king. The land granted to each vassal was inhabited by serfs who worked the land for him, providing him with income to support his military endeavours; in turn, the vassal would protect the serfs from attack and invasion.

Feudalism arose at a time when central governments were weak or non-existent in Europe, and kings used the system to exert control over their subjects and secure military strength throughout their lands. In the absence of a strong monarchy and rule of law, the feudal relationship between the lord and his vassal was the glue that held medieval society together.

Of course, this is an extremely simplified definition, and there are many exceptions and caveats that go along with this model of medieval society, but the same could be said of any model applied to a historical period. Generally, it is fair to say that this is the explanation for feudalism you'll find in most history textbooks of the 20th century, and it is very close to every dictionary definition available.

Feudalism was not the "dominant" form of political organization in medieval Europe. There was no "hierarchical system" of lords and vassals engaged in a structured agreement to provide military defence. There was no "subinfeudation" leading up to the king. The arrangement whereby serfs worked land for a lord in return for protection, known as manorialism or seignorialism, was not part of a "feudal system." Monarchies of the early Middle Ages may have had their challenges and their weaknesses, but kings did not use feudalism to exert control over their subjects, and the feudal relationship was not the "glue that held medieval society together."

In short, feudalism as described above never existed in Medieval Europe.

I know what you are thinking. For decades, even centuries, "feudalism" has characterized our view of medieval society. If it never existed, then why did so many historians say it did for so long? Weren't there entire books written on the subject? Who has the authority to say that all those historians were wrong? And if the current consensus among the "experts" in medieval history is to reject feudalism, why is it still presented as reality in nearly every medieval history textbook?

The best way to answer these questions is to engage in a little historiography. Let's begin with a look at the origin and evolution of the term "feudalism."

Contribution of Christianity and Church Father on Western Civilisation and Thought

There are good numbers of contributions made by the Christianity and Church father on the Western civilization and thought. These are as follows—

1. Primary to all contributions Christianity has made to Western civilization is education. Formal education began in the abbeys and convents of Europe and continued as the New World expanded.
2. Record keeping—the Church is the oldest record keeper on the planet. All of records for the births, deaths and marriages were maintained by the Church, especially since the Church and the governments were the same entity, at one time, that was the basis for taxation.
3. Choral music—was formalized and written down in abbeys and convents for the sake of teaching music and passing the traditions on.
4. The Roman calendar was created by one of the early Popes—Pope Julian—who created the Julian calendar which has been passed down ever since.
5. Along with record keeping, history was also recorded by the local abbeys and convents, since there was no one else to perform this function in the locales where life occurred.
6. The largest organization and the most studied in the world—the

Roman Catholic Church. It is by far, one of the richest and the most historically based organizations that go all the way back to Jesus. It has documents that are one of a kind and have not been seen by humans for centuries!

7. Genetics was the result of studies undertaken in German abbeys where the initial studies were done by Fr. Gregoire Mendel. Studies were originally done with plants and then expanded from there!
8. Holidays—initially the holiday celebrations were founded in the Christian experience so that Christmas and Easter were celebrated as a part of calendar year. Other holidays were also celebrated but are no longer generally celebrated in the secular calendar.
9. Inductive and Deductive thinking—given to us by St. Thomas Aquinas who was one of the greatest minds in the Middle Ages church. Created many ideas that are still held today and increased the awareness of philosophy plays in the minds and hearts of humans.
10. Jesus in the Gospels illustrated that dignity and respect was intended for all people, especially women. This was the first documented indication which humans saw a respect for the gender, and for all people who were sinners, sick, crippled and lame.
11. Art was created in a large measure to illustrate the life of Jesus and his disciples. This was a major contribution of the Middle Ages to our civilization, which is the only means we have today of some of the visual thoughts about Christianity.
12. Charitable giving and hospitals are the work of the early Church where those who had were asked to give to assist those who had not. These are a part of the moral fabric of Western thought as we know it today!

ST. AGUSTINE (430A.D.-354A.D.)

Early Life

St. Augustine considered as the greatest of the Father of Western Church was the son of a pagan father and a Christian Church. He lived between 354 and 430 A.D. and was a witness to the sack of the Roman Empire at the hands of the German barbarians in 410 A.D.

St. Augustine lived in the early part of the 5th century. It is often called the formative period of Christian thought. It was a period of transition from the ancient to the medieval age. The medievalism began with St. Augustine. Europe had gained religious unity after the spread of Christianity in the

Roman Empire. The Church and the state were not hostile to each other. This period was critical for Christianity. The barbarian attacks brought ruin for the empire of Rome. It had been the most stabilising factor for about eight centuries for the civilised world. The fate of civilisation and Catholicism alike hung in the balance. Finally, Rome was sat and plundered by King Alaric and the Goths in 410 A.D.

Rome was the symbol of all that was potent and enduring. Its fall caused a great disturbance and confusion in the minds of Pagans and Christians alike. Pagans were the enemies of the Church. This attributed the fall of Rome to Christianity. They pointed out that so long as the Romans worshipped the old Gods of City State, success followed in their footsteps. Rome grew from a City State to a great world empire. When Romans abandoned the old Gods and adopted Christianity, Rome made its ruin. Thus, Christianity was a source of universal misery. The Christians refuted this contention like the pagans. They were themselves terror stricken that their faith and religion could not save Rome from this disaster. Not only the facts of the empire were the cause of the concern to the thinking people but the state of affairs in the Church was also not less source of anxiety.

De Civitate Dei

De Civitate Dei, (full title: De Civitate Dei contra Paganos), translated in English as *The City of God*, is a book of Christian philosophy written in Latin by Augustine of Hippo in the early 5th century AD. It is one of Augustine's major works, standing alongside his *The Confessions*, *On Christian Doctrine*, and *On the Trinity*. Augustine is considered the most influential Father of the Church in Western Christianity, and The City of God profoundly shaped Western civilization.

Augustine wrote the treatise to explain Christianity's relationship with competing religions and philosophies, as well as its relationship with the Roman government, with which it was increasingly intertwined. It was written soon after Rome was sacked by the Visigoths in 410. This event left Romans in a deep state of shock, and many saw it as punishment for abandoning traditional Roman religion for Catholic Christianity. It was in this atmosphere that Augustine set out to console Christians, writing that, even if the earthly rule of the Empire was imperiled, it was the City of God that would ultimately triumph. Augustine's eyes were fixed on Heaven, a theme of many Christian works of Late Antiquity.

Despite Christianity's designation as the official religion of the Empire, Augustine declared its message to be spiritual rather than political. Christianity, he argued, should be concerned with the mystical, heavenly city, the New Jerusalem–rather than with earthly politics.

The book presents human history as being a conflict between what Augustine calls the City of Man and the City of God, a conflict that is destined to end in victory of the latter. The City of God is marked by people who forgot earthly pleasure to dedicate themselves to the eternal truths of God, now revealed fully in the Christian faith. The City of Man, on the other hand, consists of people who have immersed themselves in the cares and pleasures of the present, passing world.

Augustine provides a brief description of the contents of the work:

> However, this great undertaking was at last completed in twenty-two books. Of these, the first five refute those who fancy that the polytheistic worship is necessary in order to secure worldly prosperity, and that all these overwhelming calamities have befallen us in consequence of its prohibition. In the following five books I address myself to those who admit that such calamities have at all times attended, and will at all times attend, the human race, and that they constantly recur in forms more or less disastrous, varying only in the scenes, occasions, and persons on whom they light, but, while admitting this, maintain that the worship of the gods is advantageous for the life to come. But that no one might have occasion to say, that though I had refuted the tenets of other men, I had omitted to establish my own, I devote to this object the second part of this work, which comprises twelve books, although I have not scrupled, as occasion offered, either to advance my own opinions in the first ten books, or to demolish the arguments of my opponents in the last twelve. Of these twelve books, the first four contain an account of the origin of these two cities—the city of God, and the city of the world. The second four treat of their history or progress; the third and last four, of their deserved destinies.
>
> —Augustine, Retractions

In other words, the City of God can be divided into two parts. Part I, which comprises Books I-X, is polemical in style and is devoted to a critique of Roman cultures and mores (Books I-V) and of pagan philosophy (Books VI-X). Interpreters often take these first ten books to correspond with the Earthly City, in contrast to the City of God discussed in Part II, which comprises the remaining twelve books. Part II is where Augustine shifts from criticism to positing a coherent account of the relationship between the City of God and an Earthly City subordinated to it.

As indicated in the above passage from the Retractions, the City of God can be further subdivided into the following parts:

PART I (Books I-X):

(a) Books I-V: criticism of Rome
(b) Books VI-X: criticism of pagan philosophy

Part II (Books XI-XXII):

(c) Books XI-XIV: the origins of the two cities
(d) Books XV-XVIII: their history or progress
(e) Books XIX-XXII: their deserved destinies

Augustine's Defence of Christianity

St. Augustine took up the defence of Christianity by explaining the cause of the fall of Rome. He started the suppression of heresy and the combat of paganism. He used his philosophical genius to strengthen the Church and for the depiction of its ideals. He wrote voluminously.

Just as an analysis of the use of language begins by using words of some kind, so an exploration of Christian theology begins with assumptions central to that theology. Augustine was conscious of these paradoxes, so Christian Doctrine begins with a dense and subtle book in which he makes his assumptions explicit. Since the purpose of this book is introductory, readers often pass through it briskly to get to the real business at hand, the manual of exegesis in Books 2 and 3, without penetrating the sophistication of thought and expression in this little summa of Christian teaching.

The starting point is deceptively simple and obvious. All teaching consists of two parts: things and signs. Theology makes certain claims, using the signs of language, about the things that make up reality. It begins with the metaphysical claim, to be explored in detail in the later books of Christian Doctrine, that language and reality can be securely related to each other in some way.

In this world, things exist as we encounter them. Augustine thus defines only two classes: the things that we enjoy and the things that we use. This, like the distinction between signs and things, is a purely utilitarian distinction and makes (for the moment) no metaphysical claims. Some things enter our consciousness as instruments by which other things may be obtained or affected—they are there to be used. Other things seem to have more final value, and are objects for which instruments are employed. At first it is unclear whether Augustine intends any absolute distinction between classes of things or merely a distinction in our relations with things. For the most part, the latter seems to obtain. Things to be enjoyed themselves seem to fall into a hierarchy with a single highest good—enjoyed but never used—at the pinnacle.

But this ethical analysis will preoccupy us a little further on, after we have seen the theological use Augustine makes of his distinction. Suffice it to say for the moment that the distinction itself (like the distinction between things and signs) is purely neutral and does not point towards any particular value system. Augustine's purpose in these short opening chapters is to provide himself with a neutral vocabulary with which to describe basic Christian doctrine. Indeed, the whole of the first book is a tour-deforce for the way Augustine can use two simple *a priori* categories as the framework for a full and comprehensive theoretical description of Christian theology.

Two things need to be said about this assumption (some would say arrogation) of authority. First, when he wrote these words, Augustine spoke as a bishop of the Christian church, that is to say, as one of the direct successors of the apostles, with the same authority to preach and teach in the church as they had. He spoke, not out of any personal authority derived from superior wisdom and training, but out of the authority that came to him by virtue of his office. He could say what the church said with no diffidence at all.

Second, in due course he makes clear, as he describes the ways of God's intervention in the world, how it is that this ecclesiastical authority makes sense within the structure of Christian doctrine. But, it must be admitted and emphasized that this work exists only within that structure. Augustine was never concerned with demonstrating the truth of the Christian religion entirely on the basis of principles accessible to the unaided human reason. As Christian Doctrine makes clear, divine revelation, that is to say, intervention in human affairs by a power anterior to all human reasoning, is the necessary condition of Christian theology. Perhaps when that revelation has done its work well, it might be possible to reconstruct the doctrines of Christianity as they would appear if the unaided human reason were in fact capable of devising them, but even in that case, only faith would make it possible to assent to that exercise of the rational faculty.

At any rate, Augustine is clear in stating where he begins: with the trinity. He lived at the end of a century that had worked out the church's basic trinitarian doctrines, at the ecumenical councils of Nicea in 325 AD and Constantinople in 381 AD. Christians, finally, had a universal vocabulary in which to state what they believed about God, Christ, and the Spirit lucidly and concisely without error or imprecision. Simple creeds are important as a foundation for a treatise such as this; when new candidates for church membership were instructed for baptism during the forty days before Easter, two themes predominated: introduction to the creed as a statement of the essentials of belief (all creeds were trinitarian in shape;

what we call the Apostles' Creed was one of the most common) and introduction to the Lord's prayer as the prime medium of spirituality.

In a few chapters, Augustine then states the essentials of Christian belief in God, with a most important preamble: God is ineffable, that is, we can say nothing truly meaningful about one who transcends the categories of human language. Indeed, it is the wisdom of God that gives reasonableness to all things in human life. This feat is accomplished through the incarnation of the Word of God—and suddenly we have moved to the second person of the trinity. The mystery of incarnation is the nexus between God and man, by which, "though God himself is our home, for our sake he made himself the very road that would lead us home." A brief summary of the human life of Christ culminates with the resurrection and ascension (1.6.6-1.15.14).

Here in a dozen pages, then, Augustine has laid out his assumptions. Since they arise from the teaching authority of the church he represented, his statement of them thus resembles in outline one of those simple baptismal creeds. But although he has presented this material in what seems to be a rather abstract and forbidding way, his is in fact a manner precisely suited to the development of his hermeneutical theory and practice in the following books. The second principal section of the first book of Christian Doctrine is devoted to a sketch of the implications of the distinction between use and enjoyment. This outline makes sense when seen as a statement of the way in which members of the church, the body of Christ, are to conduct themselves.

The implications of the Christian idea of love that was preached throughout Europe for over a thousand years deserve to be drawn a little more clearly. First, ordinary self-love is put in its place. Men are part of a whole larger than themselves and their needs and wants cannot dictate values to the whole. They have responsibilities, even to themselves, to recognize that this is so and to refrain from asserting private advantage at the expense of others—and even where others would not be hurt. The seven deadly sins (pride, avarice, lust, envy, gluttony, sloth, and wrath), even if committed in perfect solitude, do harm to the sinner. (A system of this kind takes the individual seriously in a way that one which merely counsels that we refrain from harming others cannot. This quality of the Augustinian system deserves to be called democratic.)

Second, love of fellow man appears in new light. The romantic love that was invented in the middle ages and glorified in the modern world runs a risk of going astray, for when the love of one person for another becomes all-consuming and exclusive, it begins to resemble idolatry (the medieval authors who toyed with the notion we call courtly love still knew this) and becomes a kind of false religion. When the lover's praise of his mistress flirts with hyperbole, it is forgivable, but when the hyperbole begins to be taken seriously, some derangement has occurred.

Third, this view of love is profoundly communitarian. In a system in which every person voluntarily knows and accepts his or her place in the ordered pattern of society and acts for the best interests of every other member of that society and of the society as a whole at all times, a theoretically perfect life is in view. The medieval world could both attempt to establish such a system on earth and yet accept the inevitability of failure through sin; the modern world either tries to establish such a utopian system (under a variety of dictatorial regimes) or else (under more liberal regimes) refuses to believe that such a system is even possible—both systems pervert the democratic ideal by carrying it to excess. True love of neighbour eschews grand schemes that attempt to impose one person's views on others and contents itself with doing what is possible.

Political Principles and Christian Thought

St. Augustine was the 1st Christian intellectual who found a place for political principles in the Christian thought. Sabine says, his writings were a mine of ideas in which both protestant and catholic writers of later times have dug. Augustine aims at saving Christianity and wanted to wipe out the impression that new Gods but divine will was responsible for such a fall. He also wanted to establish that all human history was enfoldment of Divine will. It was the will of God that there should be kingdom of God on earth. There is a pre-planned goal for the establishment of Christian Common Wealth. According to him, there is a constant struggle going on between good and evil in which former is destined to prevail over the latter and there would be spiritual salvation. In other words in his philosophy he paved way for conception of constant struggle which was subsequently picked up by Karl Marx.

Augustine on State

According to St. Augustine, state was the result of gregarious nature of man and result of sin and church provided Divine remedy for all these sins. According to him, it was of Divine origin and inferior only to the city of God. He has not agreed with the Greek that it was based on justice because justice could not prevail in non-Christian state and as such justice was attributed to Church and not of state. The Church was derived from God himself. The state was the kingdom of Devil. It was necessary for the existence of church because it sanctioned for it men, money and material. If the laws of the state are not in violation of morality these must be obeyed because the state has divine sanction. It was remedy for the sins of the people.

Thus, Augustine subordinated the State to the higher authority of the God and asserted that obedience to the laws and authority of the state is justified so long as it does not conflict with the duty towards Gods. In other words he held that men obey the civil laws because they have the sanction of God behind them. Augustine insisted that Emperor should defend the Church and stamp out heresy. However, he did not accord the Emperor any authority over spiritual matters. On the other hand, he insisted that the citizens should not obey the civil authority it seeks to interfere in the spiritual realm. Thus he wanted the state and the church to be mutually helpful to each others and work in complete harmony. In fact he deprecated the position of the state and exalted the position of the Church. He subordinated the state to the Church even in secular matters.

Augustine on Justice

Justice to him was conformity to order and as such prevail in the City of God. It meant respect for duties and obligations but was not something which was absolute but only relative. He interpreted justice in the Platonic sense and described it as "conformity to order and respect for duties arising from this order." However, he assigned to justice a wider meaning than assigned by Plato. Plato held that justice could be realised in the state if all the members whole-hearted accept its orders and carry out their obligations towards it. According to Augustine, a man can be just only to some extent or degree or to a particular extent. He cannot be just both to the family as well as to the state. Absolute justice was possible only in a universal City of God in which universal laws were obeyed. These laws also conform to universal order. A state will not be unjust if it violates universal order. In cases of conflict the individuals are always justified in obeying universal order if secular order is in conflict with it. Justice thus symbolises the City of God as it cannot be in the pagan state. According to Dunnings, "Augustine thus not only deprecates the early state as compared with the state of the future life, but denies to non-Christian earthly states all social virtues. For he early in his works lays down that without justice there is nothing to distinguish a state from a band of brigands." Justice means conformity to order and performance of duties which arise out of that order. Absolute justice can be possible only in absolute order. A state which conforms to universal order can give complete justice. His justice is not bound by time and space.

Augustine on Peace

According to Augustine, peace does not mean negation of conflict but it is relationship in concord. He stood for universal peace based on universal order under a universal law. The peace is the end of struggle of all societies. He considered peace as a cardinal virtue of a good state which could be attained only in the *City of God.* It may be noted that to Augustine peace did not meant the absence of war or social strifes. To him, it was a positive relation to love which embraced all human beings. He considered the peace provided by the state as only a temporary tranquillity and was a relative peace. He held that universal peace was genuine peace which could be achieved only if all acted in accordance with the universal order and in common love to God. In short, Augustine laid emphasis on universal peace in which all men are united with one another by their common love for God. It was quite different from mere absence of war or peace produced by a system of legal relations as in a state.

Both Augustine's political world view and his approach to war incorporate his conception of peace. According to Augustine, God designed all humans to live together in the "bond of peace." However, fallen man lives in society as according to the divine will or as opposing it. Augustine distinguishes the two cities in several important ways, as well as the kind of peace they seek.

There is, in fact, one city of men who choose to live by the standard of the flesh, another of those who choose to live by the standard of the spirit. The citizens of each of these desire their own kind of peace, and when they achieve their aim, that is the kind of peace in which they live. Because the common choice of fallen man is a piece of his own liking—one that selfishly serves his own immediate or foreseeable ends, peace becomes, in practice, merely an interlude between ongoing states of war. Augustine is quick to point out that this life carries with it no guarantee of peace; that blessed state is reserved for the saved in heaven of peace in which they live.

Augustine delineates three kinds of peace: the ultimate and perfect peace which exists exclusively in the City of God, the interior peace enjoyed by the pilgrim citizens of the City of God as they sojourn on earth, and the peace which is common to the two cities. Sadly, Augustine is abundantly clear that temporal peace is rather an anomalous condition in the totality of human history and that perfect peace is altogether unattainable on earth.

Augustine on Slavery

St. Augustine did not believe like Aristotle that man is slave by nature. He defends slavery as a punishment for human sin as a result of original sin. Slavery could not be abolished because it was divine retribution for sin. His theory did not explain the cause of individual slavery. If slavery is caused due to original sin then all must be slaves and not only a few unfortunate persons. As such it may be stated that his justification of slavery was against Christian teaching of fatherhood of God and brotherhood of man. In short, Augustine emphasises that slavery is an external phenomenon which has been ordained by God to cope with the menace of human wickedness. In the words of Carlyle, St. Augustine held that slavery "is the consequence of man's sin" and "also a divine remedy for the sinful nature of man."

Another noteworthy point about Augustine is that he does not deprive the slave of the status of a human being and treats the master and the slave as fellowmen who are bound to each other by the bond of fraternity in the Kingdom of Christ, even if they are unequal in terms of human law He, therefore, advices the slaves to remain near their masters to seek purification because masters were purer than the slave.

The Pauline idea that the relationship between master and slave had to be a relationship of love because we all have only one common Lord through faith, is echoed by Augustine with the following words: "You (the Church) see to it that the masters are mild towards their slaves out of regard for the one God who is master of both, and you dispose them to look after their interests rather than keep them down by force. You teach that love is due to everyone and that it is forbidden to treat human beings unjustly whoever they may be."

Augustine on Property

Augustine supported the institution of private property and felt that its holding was legitimate. It was a conventional and not natural institution but this convention should be preserved. He, however, felt that one should not have more property than what was required by him for his legitimate and reasonable needs. He felt that it was essential for each individual for proper performance of his duties. As Carlyle has observed St. Augustine like other Christian thinkers believed that, "All property is the gift of God and it was his will that the earth which he had created should be common possession of all men and satisfy the needs of all; it was avarice which created rights of private property."

Augustine on War

Augustine tried to reconcile Christian pacifism with the world as it actually was; to bring together the pacifist teachings of Jesus Christ with the obligations of Roman citizens-including Christians-to fight for their country when required to Augustine accepted that there would always be wars. He thought that war was always a sin, and if there had to be a war, it should be waged with sadness.

But Augustine said that war was always the result of sin, and that war was also the remedy for sin. And if war was the remedy for sin, then war could sometimes be justifiable—but only if it was a remedy for sin. Augustine made it clear that individuals and states (or the rulers of states) have different obligations when it came to wàr or violence. He stated that Christians did not have the right to defend themselves from violence; however, they could use violence if it was necessary to defend the innocent against evil. The rulers of states, he said, had an obligation to maintain peace, and this obligation gave them the right to wage war in order to maintain peace. It also gave them the right to wage war in order to ensure justice and even impose punishment-something that would not be accepted now-a-days. This was because injustice was a greater evil than war, and it was proper to carry out a lesser evil if it would prevent a greater evil. But, a war is only just if those waging it do so with the intention of doing well. Punishing the enemy is not a sufficient motive on its own. Augustine was much less concerned with how people should be treated during a war, because to him, physical death was not a particularly important thing.

The Just War

As the Roman Empire collapses around him, Augustine confronted the question of what justifies warfare for a Christian. On the one hand, the wicked are not particularly concerned about just wars. On the other hand, the righteous vainly hope to avoid being affected by wars in this life, and at best they can hope for just wars rather than unjust ones. This is by no means a perfect solution; but then again, this is not a perfect world. If it were, all talk of just wars would be altogether nonsensical. Perfect solutions characterize only the heavenly City of God. Its pilgrim citizens sojourning on earth can do no better than try to cope with the present difficulties and imperfections of the earthly life. Thus, for Augustine, the just war is a coping mechanism for use by the righteous who aspire to citizenship in the City of God. In terms of the traditional notion of *jus ad bellum* (justice of war, that is, the circumstances in which wars can be justly fought), war is a coping mechanism for righteous sovereigns who would ensure that their violent international encounters are minimal, a reflection of the Divine Will to the greatest extent possible, and always justified. In terms of the traditional notion of *jus in bello* (justice in war, or the moral considerations which ought to constrain the use of violence in war), war is a coping mechanism for righteous combatants who, by divine edict, have no choice but to subject themselves to their political masters and seek to ensure that they execute their war-fighting duty as justly as possible. Sometimes that duty might arise in the most trying of circumstances, or under the most wicked of regimes; for Christ's servants, whether they are kings, or princes, or judges, or soldiers, or provincials, whether rich or poor, freemen or slaves, men or women, are bidden, if need be, to endure the wickedness of an utterly corrupt state, and by that endurance to win for themselves a place of glory hereafter in the heavenly City of God.

In sum, why would a man like Augustine, whose eye is fixed upon attainment of citizenship in the heavenly city, find it necessary to delineate what counts as a just war in this lost and fallen world? In general terms, the demands of moral life are so thoroughly interwoven with social life that the individual cannot be separated from citizenship in one or the other city. In more specific terms, the just man who walks by faith needs to understand how to cope with the injustices and contradictions of war as much as he needs to understand how to cope with all other aspects of the present world where he is a stranger and pilgrim. Augustine takes important cues from both Cicero and Ambrose and synthesizes their traditions into a Christianized world view that still retains strong ties to the pre-Christian philosophic past. He resolves the dilemma of just war and pacifist considerations by denying the dilemma: war is simply a part of the human experience that God Himself has ordained or permitted. War arises from, and stands as a clear manifestation of, the nature of fallen man. For adherents to nominal Christianity, the explanatory power of Augustine's thoughts on just war is substantial; his approach enables Christians to understand just war as a coping mechanism for just men who are trying to get along as morally (if not as piously) as they can in an imperfect world.

However, since Augustine seeks to resolve the nature of his ethical tensions, the synthetic character of Augustine's approach to war is important, not merely for adherents to Christianity, but also for others seeking a strictly rational account of the problem. For example, if one were to take a de-theologized view of Augustine's approach and focus simply upon the general theoretical problem of the morality of war, Augustine's attempt fully deserves serious philosophical consideration. His approach explains how a morally upright citizen of a relatively just state could be justified in pursuing warfare, in prosecuting war, and ultimately, although unhappily, in taking human life. In any case, Augustine's just war theory arises from his most deeply rooted philosophical assumptions. Augustine as a Christian philosopher achieves a full synthesis of the Roman and Christian values associated with war in a way that legitimizes war as an instrument of national policy which, although inferior to the perfect ideals of Christianity, is one which Christians cannot altogether avoid and with which they must in some sense make their peace.

Influence or Contribution of Augustine

St. Augustine was the most important political thinker of the medieval Europe. His *'Civitate Dei'* has been characterized as the mine of ideas. He was responsible for moulding the ideas of the rulers like Charlemagne and Otto the Great. It is said that Thomas Acquinas and Dante drew largely from his writings. He also influenced Gregory and Martin Luther. His concept of Christian commonwealth became the basis of Holy Roman Empire to a great extent. His subordination of secular authority to spiritual authority became the basis of ecclesiastical oneness. He gave the idea that political authority was not absolute and that there was also a higher authority over the state. Thus, he shook absolute nature and character of the state from its very basis. He also challenged the established idea that state laws should be obeyed under all circumstances. Both these ideas remained alive throughout the Middle Ages. The concept of universal society, as expounded by him again remained alive in the Middle Ages. His concept of City of God became the basis of all Papalists and both the Protestants and the Roman Catholics equally borrowed from his philosophy. Sabine has characterized him as the most important thinker of his age. Gettell is of the view that his philosophy gave a crystallized body of thought at a very critical period of history. Christopher Morris says that, "He was the father whose authority counted highest with almost every Medieval Thinker."

Augustine was the most influential thinker of middle ages and his philosophy practically remained the foundation of the philosophy of his age. According to Ebenstein "St. Augustine, the greatest of the Church Fathers, stood at the turning point of two words, that of antiquity and Christianity." According to Sabine, "His philosophy was only in a slight degree systematic, but his mind had encompassed almost all the learning of ancient times and through him to a very large extent, it was transmitted to the Middle Ages. His writings were mines of ideas in which, the later writers, Catholic and Protestant have dug." Dr. J.E. Green says, "So inclusive were Augustine's genius and so satisfying were his formulations that he was equally the father of medieval Roman Catholicism and (after St. Paul) the inspiration of Protestant Reformation." His writings, therefore, undoubtedly influenced the thinkers of medieval political thinkers who followed him.

ST. THOMAS ACQUINAS (1225-1274)

St. Thomas Acquinas believed that function of a Government is to make man virtuous for leading a good life and for seeking salvation. As salvation can be achieved through Church so head of Church, i.e. Pope possesses supreme powers. He argues that law is an ordinance of reason for common good. He believes that divine laws consist commands of God and is supreme to man made laws. As divine laws can be enforced by Pope so Church and its Head Pope is supreme.

It was argued spiritual power is supreme so Church which holds spiritual power ought to be considered supreme. Hindus consider Vedas, Muslims Koran and Christians Binle as revelation from God, so propounder of these revelations may be considered supreme but this argument was not accepted by kings who claimed divine origin, so with the rise of powerful national states supremacy of Pope got a death blow and his supremacy became confined to religious matters. In spite of all this according to Foster, "Acquinas was one of the greatest philosophers who brought synthesis" (doctrine of Aristotle, the Stoics, Cicero and of Roman jurists). As such Foster is of the opinion that St. Thomas Acquinas represents, as no medieval author singly does, the totality of medieval thought.

Life

Though the lifetime of Saint Thomas Aquinas was not lengthy in years, he managed to obtain great scholarly and religious authority during his life, and he also composed more than sixty literary works that ranged in classification from theological to philosophical to scriptural. His talent in writing and his leadership qualities in the Roman Catholic Church earned Aquinas the title of the Prince of Scholastics. Although Aquinas would most likely debate the rank of a prince or even saint, there is no doubt that he greatly influenced Italian philosophy and theology with his service and his writing.

In the year 1225, Thomas Aquinas was born into nobility in Roccasecca, into a line of kings and emperors. He was the son of the Count of Aquino and the Countess of Teano. Even from the beginning of his life, religion and theology played a large part in his education and upbringing. During his early years, Aquinas was educated at the Benedictine monastery of Monte Cassino, and when he was eleven, he was sent to continue his education at the University of Naples. In 1243, Aquinas's father died, and though Aquinas was still an undergraduate at the university, he decided to join the Dominican order. However, his mother was completely against his association with the order and subsequently ordered Aquinas to be confined within the family castle until he abandoned what he believed to be his calling. Even after months, Aquinas maintained that his decision was still the same, and finally in 1245 he was released from his confinement. His first act of freedom was to travel to Paris to attempt to continue his scholastic studies.

Aquinas was ordained as a priest some time around 1250 and began two years later to teach at the University of Paris. It was at this time that Aquinas began to explore the depth of his literary ability and began writing works that coordinated with his lectures at the university. Around 1256, Aquinas composed the first of his major works, *Scripta Super Libros Sententiarum*. In that same year, Aquinas was also awarded a doctorate in theology and subsequently given the position of professor of philosophy at the university. In 1259, Aquinas was summoned to Rome by Pope Alexander IV. There he performed duties of an adviser to the papal court. When Aquinas returned to Paris nine years later, he was thrust into one of the most extreme controversies of the time.

For centuries philosophy and theology had been strictly separated and were deemed by most to be incompatible. On one side there were the teachings of Aristotle, which emphasized logic and learning from earthly experience. On the other side there were the teachings of the Roman Catholic Church, which were based on faith and the acquirement of knowledge through revelation. When the teachings of Aristotle became increasingly popular in the early 13th century, members of the Roman Catholic Church felt that these new teachings threatened orthodox religious doctrine. However, Aquinas believed that philosophy and theology were both essential and had their proper place in life. He began teaching that there was knowledge that was gained through revelation and knowledge that was gained through experience, and still further knowledge that was gained through both. He believed that knowledge could be acquired by earthly experience and study, but that the highest of truths could only be learned through revelation and divine thought. He first displayed his thinking in 1270 in the treatise De Unitate Intellectus Contra Averroistas. He continued to teach these beliefs when he left Paris in 1272 and travelled on to Naples. There he organized a new Dominican school and continued in service of the Church. While venturing to the Council of Lyon in 1274, Aquinas became ill. His state worsened until he finally died on March 7, 1274 at the Cistercian monastery of Fossanova.

Saint Thomas Aquinas continued to earn fame even after his death. His teachings that knowledge could serve the purpose of faith inspired many great thinkers around the world from many different religions. In 1567,

Pope Pius V proclaimed Aquinas to be a Doctor of the Church. Even centuries after his death, the teachings of Saint Thomas Aquinas remained strongly influential. In the late 19th century and early 20th century, the philosophy of Aquinas became a foundation of Roman Catholic doctrine. Today, the works of Aquinas are still deemed to be quite revolutionary and his teachings still influence a great deal contemporary thought.

Environment

During the 13th century contest between the Holy Roman Empire and Papacy resulted in the complete victory of the Pope. Spain and Portugal were conquered by Arab invaders. Aristotle and Cicero were revived and through Spain it reached in Europe. The classics translated into Latin reached to Europe and had a profound influence on the political thought of Europe and St. Acquinas. St. Acquinas thought had a strong Aristotelian bias. He gave a new birth to Politics of Aristotle and principally though him it was incorporated in the political thought of Europe. He fused the teachings of Aristotle's Politics with the teachings of St. Augustine's City of God in an amalgam which still remains the essence of catholic society and the state. In his book '*Summa Theological*' containing three parts and about a million words, he embodied a great edifice of thought in which some of the Platonic traditions and the teachings of Aristotle are united with the Roman law, the Bible, the saying of Church fathers and other great theologians. As per Dunning, his doctrine presents the reconciliation of St. Augustine and Aristotle.

His Works

His work was synthetic, architectonic in nature incorporating the best in scholasticism with the best in Hellanism. He agrees with Aristotle that the state is natural to man but he believes that happiness which is the aim of the state can only be achieved through salvation. He agrees that the state is necessary to provide conditions of good life but for eternal good church is necessary. The church is the root of social organization and the rival of the state.

Summa Theological is not a book dealing primarily with politics, but it discusses law, justice, government and topics like sin, incarnation, faith, resurrection etc. In his commentaries on Aristotle, he discusses about law and justice and incomplete work *De Regima Principum*, he deals with the Rule of Princes. His Political philosophy can be gleaned from his books, De *Regima Principum* and *Summa Contra Gentiles* and *Commentaries on Politics of Aristotle* in a modified way.

According to Thomas the whole of Human knowledge makes a unity like a pyramid whose base consists of the various special sciences each of which has its own subject matter and philosophy deals with general reason. As such he and Aristotle are one in their conceptions. While Hellenic philosophers regarded philosophy as the summit theology whose instrument is faith and revelation and not reason. There are things which could not be understood by philosophy or reason and here faith is necessary. He believes, according to Sabine that Theology completes the system of which science and philosophy from the very beginning but never destroys its continuity. Faith is the fulfilment of reason. Together they build the temple of knowledge but nowhere do they conflict or work at cross purpose.

He agrees with Aristotle that in nature everything acts under an inner urge to realize its own nature or perfection and so a man has also a purpose. Aristotle holds this purpose is rational contemplation because his reason is the highest faculty, but Thomas says highest thing is soul and so a man should try to achieve salvation of his soul, which cannot be achieved by reason as such a man should have faith in religion.

His Writings

His works on the whole were synthetic and he followed Aristotle's philosophy that the state was natural to man. It was thus a necessity. In his philosophy general theory of Laws, as expounded by Aristotle, was quite visible. Though he died at premature age of 47, yet he has left much behind him. His important works are:

Summa Theological

It is one of his philosophical works in which he had treated 'ethical' and juristic concepts which lie at the basis of politics and which he has subsequently developed.

De-Regmine Principum (Rule of Princes)

In it he has tried to present political science in a systematic way but could not finish the work as he died before he could do so—a task which he had undertaken upon himself.

Summa Contra Gentiles

This is one of his most important works and gives us his views on problems like the classification of government, laws, state and also relationship of state with the church.

Aquinas on the Origin of the State

Church Fathers usually believed that the state was the result of fall and sins of men and that the Government came into being to punish the people for their sins. Aquinas did not agree with this general belief. He believed that man was a social animal both by nature and necessity and that the state was natural to man.

In his social and political philosophy Thomas states that human society is a system of ends and purposes in which the lower serves the higher and the higher directs and guides the lower and such state is necessary. According to Sabine, he regards state as a mutual exchange of services for the sake of good life to which many calling contribute. He held like Greek thinkers that the state is necessary not only to check evil but without it, an individual could not realize himself fully and as such it has somethings of a natural character. He further agrees that the state is a positive organ of social welfare. He is modern in giving preference to nation state. Community of manners and customs can be found in a nation state than in a heterogeneous empire. He states that state justifies itself by education and by the provisions for the poor. From God legitimate authority to govern passes to the whole society. The people are sovereign and they may delegate authority to any form of government such as monarchy, aristocracy or democracy. According to him, "life in community enables a man ...to live fully, with all that is necessary for its well being."

He believed that the end of state is the realization of good the virtuous life. But the state can only achieve earthly happiness and not salvation. He believes that society and state should be organized with a view to an end beyond earthly happiness and for this, he advocates social legislation as the main function of the state. But salvation and eternal happiness can only be achieved by church so it should be subordinate to church achieve higher end to life. Thus, Acaquins corrects Aristotle by making church the crown of human life and greater than the state. He believes in Christian truth that man has also a supernatural end, namely salvation and further blessedness to which the end of his happiness of life is itself subordinate.

According to him, the state should aim at making the citizen virtuous and moral. It should aim at spreading knowledge. According to him, monarchy was the best suited form of government as no other form could promote unity. In addition to this, it was inevitable law of nature that the superior should rule over the inferior and as such monarch, who was definitely superior should rule over the subjects. It was also in the interest of the inferiors that they should be ruled by the superiors.

Classification of Government

According to St. Thomas Acquinas, man's rule on man may be either result of sin which takes the form of slavery or it may be due to social instinct and may take the form of civil government which may be sacraderoal or royal or political or economic. Of these first headed by the Pope is the best and highest. Form of government did not matter much but what matter is its work.

St. Aquinas followed the Aristotelian principle of classification of governments and divided the governments into normal form and perverted form. He placed monarchy, aristocracy and polity in the category of normal government and tyranny, oligarchy and democracy in the perverted category of governments. However, he considered Monarchy as the best form of Government not only because the scriptures described it so but also on the basis of rational arguments. He said it can establish unity which no other form of government can achieve. He asserted all natural government is by one—the heart rules the body as reason rules the soul. Society is derived from one God. Government is art and art is a reflection of Nature which is ruled by one. He supported Monarchical form of government because it brings unity, regularity, experience and an analogy with divine rule. Tyranny is worst. Monarchy can be prevented from degeneration if it is limited as such limited monarchy is the best. He opposed tyranicide as stated by John of Salisbury because it may be followed by mob rule which is the worst type of tyranny. He, however, held that the elected monarchy may be deposed and he preferred elected monarchy. He believed that state exists for the welfare of individual and not individual for the state.

Functions of Government

A good government, according to him, is only one which performs good functions as there is no other standard for measuring quality of a form of government. It should pave way for pleasure, happiness and a virtuous life. It should also give better administration, justice, civic facilities and ensure defence of the citizens. In other words it should have good system of coinage, maintain population, and look after the needy. He assigned a positive role to the state and assigned it the duty of making the citizens virtuous and moral. He asserted that happiness lies not only in the virtue but also in the availability of adequate material goods. He thus wanted the state to provide order and peace without which virtue was not possible. Paramount functions of the state is to promote moral life of the people. In other words according to him, functions of the state should be: (i) to look after the poor; (ii) to promote unity; (iii) to look after common, instead of individual good and welfare; (iv) to introduce sound system of weights, measure and coinage; (v) to remove hindrances from the from the path for the citizens; (vi) to promote right living and virtuous life; (vii) to keep road safe and free; (viii) to maintain peace and happiness and also to protect the properties of the subjects; and (ix) to avoid undue taxation and provide economic relief to the subjects; and (x) to reward the worthy so that they continue doing good work.

Views on Sovereignty

He has given his idea about sovereignty but only indirectly. He has said sovereignty is derived from the people if taken political viewpoint and from God if studied from theological viewpoint. The sovereignty is indivisible. It is the only source of positive law, the end of which is temporal tranquillity of the state. A positive law therefore, must derive its strength from natural law and aim at common good. It must provide directives for human acts of justice. Aquinas asserted that this positive law must fulfill four requirements: (i) it must be derived from natural law; (ii) it must be ordained for the common good; (iii) it must be framed and promulgated by the government and (iv) it must serve as a directive for human acts of justice. This in simple words meant that Aquinas considered a bad law as *ultra vires* and permitted its disobedience. Another point in this regard emphasized by Aquinas was that a positive law derives its authority not from the divine or natural law but from the enactment by the ruling authority, viz. the law is the command of the sovereignty.

Another notable feature of Aquinas theory of sovereignty is that the sovereignty is derived from the people. Emphasizing this point Aquinas defined law as "an ordinance of reason for common good, promulgated by him who has the care of the community." In this respect his views come very close to Rousseau's views on general will.

Views on Law

According to Aquinas, "Law is an ordinance of reason for the common good." Thomas Aquinas believed that main function of the state to make its citizens morally and to help them to realize the true end. Political authority must be exercised in accordance with law and a ruler who disregards law becomes a tyrant. According to John of Salisbury, the binding character of law follows from its rational or moral character and according to modern concept, law means command of sovereign or will of the sovereign body.

But Thomas Aquinas defined law as an ordinance of reason for the common good prorogated by him who has the care of the community. Thus, according to him, law should be based on reason and it should be for the common good and it should be enacted by the ruler. Modern definitions of law places emphasis on enactment of ruler but Thomas Aquinas puts emphasis on reason of common good also. His definition of law combines the Greek, Roman, Stoic and Christian point of view.

He held that law must be related to reason for command and it should be enacted by public or its representative and it should have obligatory power to force to obey those who are subject to law. He distinguished between four kinds of law (1) eternal (2) natural (3) divine and (4) human. Eternal is ordained by God which governs the whole universe. It governs celestial and territorial spheres, animal and inanimate kingdoms and heavenly bodies such as starts, the sun and the moon etc. In the world where human beings dwell who is, rational, it is interpreted by the reason of rational being and is called natural law. The natural law was written in the heart of man and though his reason enables him to recognize and obey the eternal law. Man understands general principles of conduct due to his reasoning faculty and these general principles make the general law. Neither eternal law nor natural law is positive law because these are not man made laws. Divine law consists of commands of God communicated to man by revelation as through Vedas to Hindus, Bible to Christians and Koran to Muslims.

Positive laws are divine and human laws are man made Divine law consists of direct revelation of divine purpose through the Bible or through the saints. Human law is derived from natural law and is valid if it is not against the natural law to whom it is subordinate. Human law is concrete then man made law but natural law is created in the conscience of man by God. He believed that there can be no clash or conflict between natural and divine law because God can never command unreasonable things. Revelation supplements reason. According to Sabine, "Revelation does not destroy reason; it only supplements it." According to Sabine the structure of Thomas' system is built on reason and faith, but he never doubted that it was one structure. Human law is necessary to supplement natural law. For example, natural law may state that stealing is bad but how this bad act should be punished and who should punish? And in what manner? Comes within the purview of human law.

He is of the opinion that if human law is inconsistent with the natural law it loses his binding force. He states a law made by the ruler against the dictates of reason does not bind a citizen. In short, he holds that in order to have binding force on citizen, Law should be just and virtuous and in conformity with the natural law, otherwise it can be disobeyed. It must aim at common good and must have backing of the community. It should also be in accordance to human consciousness and natural law. Thus, he links up political obedience with the moral obligation. Tilak and Gandhi also refused to follow unjust laws.

St. Thomas Aquinas wanted to improve mankind by bringing about a combination between divine and human knowledge. He tried to compromise divine will and revelation and human reason and knowledge. He interpreted teachings of Plato, Aristotle and Cicero in accordance with Christian teachings. He was individualist and believed that the social and political order existed for the sake of individual. True end of human life is total salvation and in this direction only Church can be of help so Church is greater than the state. As such he gave power of supervision and control to church or the Pope over secular rulers. As such he reconciled Christian ideas with Aristotelian ideas.

Nature of God

Thomas believed that the existence of God is self-evident in itself, but not to us. "Therefore I say that this proposition, "God exists," of itself is self-evident, for the predicate is the same as the subject. Now, because we do not know the essence of God, the proposition is not self-evident to us; but needs to be demonstrated by things that are more known to us, though less known in their nature, namely by effects."

Thomas believed that the existence of God can be proven. In the Summa Theological, he considered in great detail five reasons for the Existence of God. These are widely known as the *quinque viae*, or the "Five Ways."

Notes: (i) For a more in-depth analysis of the five proofs, *see* "Existence of God."

(ii) For the original text of the five proofs, *see* "*quinque viae*."

The Five Ways Aquinas Tried to Prove God's Existence:

1. *Change:* Some things are undoubtedly undergoing change, though cannot cause their own change. Since Thomas believed there can be no infinite chain of causes of change, this leads to the conclusion there must be a first cause of changing that is not itself changed by anything else, and this is what everyone understands by God.

2. *Causation:* Like change, nothing can cause itself, and like change there must be a First Cause, called God.

3. *Existence of necessary and the unnecessary:* Our experience includes things certainly existing but apparently unnecessary. Not everything can be unnecessary, for then once there was nothing and there would still be nothing. Therefore, we are compelled to suppose something that exists necessarily, having this necessity only from itself; in fact itself the cause why other things exist.

4. *Gradation:* If we can notice a gradation in things in the sense that some things are more hot, good etc., there must be a superlative which is the truest and noblest thing, and so most fully existing. This then, we call God—note Thomas does not ascribe actual qualities to God Himself!

5. *Ordered tendencies of nature:* A direction of actions to an end is noticed in all bodies following natural laws. Anything without awareness tends to a goal under the guidance of one who is aware. This we call God—Note that even when we guide objects, in Thomas' view the source of all our knowledge comes from God as well.

Goal of Human Life

In Thomas' thought, the goal of human existence is union and eternal fellowship with God. Specifically, this goal is achieved through the beatific vision, an event in which a person experiences perfect, unending happiness by seeing the very essence of God. This vision, which occurs after death, is a gift from God given to those who have experienced salvation and redemption through Christ while living on earth.

This ultimate goal carries implications for one's present life on earth. Thomas stated that an individual's will must be ordered toward right things, such as charity, peace, and holiness. He sees this as the way to happiness. Thomas orders his treatment of the moral life around the idea of happiness. The relationship between will and goal is antecedent in nature "because rectitude of the will consists in being duly ordered to the last end [that is, the beatific vision]." Those who truly seek to understand and see God will necessarily love what God loves. Such love requires morality and bears fruit in everyday human choices.

The After Life and Resurrection

A grasp of Aquinas' psychology is essential for understanding his beliefs around the afterlife and resurrection. Thomas, following Church doctrine, accepts that the soul continues to exist after the death of the body. Because he accepts that the soul is the form of the body, then he also must believe that the human being, like all material things, is form-matter composite.

Substantial form (the human soul) configures prime matter (the physical body) and is the form by which a material composite belongs to that species it does; in the case of human beings, that species is rational animal. So, a human being is a matter-form composite that is organized to be a rational animal. Matter cannot exist without being configured by form, but form can exist without matter—which allows for the separation of soul from body. Aquinas says that the soul shares in the material and spiritual worlds, and so have some features of matter and other, immaterial, features (such as access to universals). The human soul is different from other material and spiritual things; it is created by God, but also only comes into existence in the material body.

Human beings are material, but the human person can survive the death of the body through continued existence of the soul, which persists. The human soul straddles the spiritual and material worlds, and is both a configured subsistent form as well as a configure of matter into that of a living, bodily human. Because it is spiritual, the human soul does not depend on matter and may exist separately. Because the human being is a soul-matter composite, the body has a part in what it is to be human. Perfected human nature consists in the human dual nature, embodied and intellection.

Resurrection appears to require dualism, which Thomas rejects. Yet, Aquinas believes the soul persists after the death and corruption of the body, and is capable of existence, separated from the body between the time of death and the resurrection. Aquinas believes in a different sort of dualism, one guided by Christian scripture. Aquinas knows that human beings are essentially physical, but that that physicality has a spirit capable of returning to God after life. For Aquinas, the rewards and punishment of the afterlife are not only spiritual. Because, of this, resurrection is an important part of his philosophy on the soul. The human is fulfilled and complete in the body, so the hereafter must take place with souls enmattered in resurrected bodies. In addition to spiritual reward, humans can expect to enjoy material and physical blessings. Because, Aquinas' soul requires a body for its actions, during the afterlife, the soul will also be punished or rewarded in corporeal existence.

Aquinas states clearly his stance on resurrection, and uses it to back up his philosophy of justice; that is, the promise of resurrection compensates Christians who suffered in this world through a heavenly union with the divine. He says, "If there is no resurrection of the dead, it follows that there is no good for human beings other than in this life." Resurrection provides the impetus for people on earth to give up pleasures in this life. Thomas believes the human who has prepared for the afterlife both morally and intellectually will be rewarded more greatly; however, all reward is through the grace of God. Aquinas insists beatitude will be conferred according to merit, and will render the person better able to conceive the divine. Aquinas accordingly believes punishment is directly related to earthly, living preparation and activity as well. Aquinas' account of the soul focuses on epistemology and metaphysics, and because of this he believes it gives a clear account of the immaterial nature of the soul. Aquinas conservatively guards Christian doctrine, and thus maintains physical and spiritual reward and punishment after death. By accepting the essentiality of both body and soul, he allows for a heaven and hell described in scripture and church dogma.

Contribution of Aquinas to Political Thought

St. Thomas Aquinas is one of the most outstanding personalities of the middle ages. He was an intellectual and liberal thinker. He attempted to revive Aristotelian philosophy in so far as it did not come in conflict with the Church philosophy. He was the best scholastic and an influential writer and a systematic philosopher. It has rightly been said that he presented middle ages.

Thomas Aquinas was not an original writer but he possessed astonishing power of synthesis and blended book Divinity and Humanity into one compact whole and he was able to blend book Faith and Reason in simple manner. According to Dr. Jazi "In this new world the Roman Catholic Church urgently needed a comprehensive of Christianity in harmony with the world diplomacy of the Pope's power." The task was admirably accomplished by St. Thomas, not much by the originality of his ideas or the brilliancy of his analysis as by his extraordinary gift for combining and unifying different elements of thought in an apparently logical and convincing...his work was an attempt to graft the logical idea of the church, and the lightness of the Pope as a noble thing on the wild system of Aristotelian theory of state. He has contributed to the political philosophy in many ways, for example—

1. Idea of Welfare State

Aquinas, in his philosophy, has mooted the idea of a welfare state. By pleading that the state should unkeep the population, look after the poor, promote justice and make roads safe and living peaceful, he sowed the seeds of the welfare state which is being adhered to even today by all the advanced countries of the world.

2. Idea of Constitutional Government

Aquinas favoured the idea of limited monarchy as the ideal form of government. According to him, monarch should be bound by the laws of the state because their violation would make him a tyrant. By imposing limitations on the authority of monarchs he has put forth the idea of the constitutional government which is today considered as the ideal form of government.

3. Classification of Laws

His contribution is the method with which he has classified the laws based on reason. He has not made law as the command of the superior but only that of product of reasonable thinking. According to him, no law should be obeyed for being merely command of the superior but dictates of law should be honoured because of their being based on sound reasoning alone.

4. Idea of Democracy

He was the first political thinker in the Middle Ages who declared that the state was not the result of fall of man or due to his sins but that it was a moral institution and stood to promote the welfare of its subjects. It had no contractual origin but outcome of social instinct of man. The state was not only required to perform negative function of punishing the guilt but also positive functions of promoting virtue and good life.

5. Source of Authority

Before St. Aquinas, it was believed that the source of authority was impersonal but he said that is derived from some person. He did not believe in imperceptible forces as the source of either that of the law or that of the authority not even personal Christian God. This is what is being accepted by our modern jurists today.

6. Idea of Systematic Knowledge

Aquinas gave the idea to subsequent political thinkers that philosophy should best be studied in a systematic way and that diametrically opposite ideas could be studied by way of synthesis. His system was so perfect that Foster has described him as one of the greatest systematic philosophers of the world. He assimilated various fragments of knowledge and combined them together into a solid philosophy. He systematized reason with faith and tried to reconcile the two. He was compiler and systematizer of ideas and exponent of new philosophies.

7. Idea of Secular State

It was due to his efforts that the old idea that the religions acting through the machinery of the state should dominate science and philosophy gained ground. He substituted national sentiment for religious authority as the dominating force behind Government. In this way he contributed to the idea of nation state as against the Greek concept of the city state.

8. Concept of Natural Law

Aquinas gave the concept of natural law in a very systematic manner. He subordinated human law to natural law. His ideas about natural law influenced the thinkers of Glorious Revolution, including Locke.

9. Welfare of the People

Aquinas' another contribution is that he did not ignore the masses and cared for their welfare as well, e.g. he said that the ruler should look after the poor and the masses, should make roars secure for them and so on. He also believed that the masses should care to see that the laws of the state were not violated by the ruler and that he did not turn himself to be a tyrant in anyway.

10. Revival of Aristotle's Philosophy in the West

Aquinas borrowed heavily from Aristotle in many ways and is so much indebted to him that he had been called as 'Christianized Aristotle'. He was mainly responsible for the revival of Aristotle's philosophy in the West. He agreed with his philosophy so long as it did not clash with church ideals. He made an effort to merge doctrines of Aristotle with traditional doctrines.

Unit-III
Secular Political Thought

The Secularists

Secularism is the principle of separation between government institutions and the persons mandated to represent the State from religious institutions and religious dignitaries. In one sense, secularism may assert the right to be free from religious rule and teachings, and the right to freedom from governmental imposition of religion upon the people within a state that is neutral on matters of belief (*See* also separation of church and state and *Laïcité.*). In another sense, it refers to the view that human activities and decisions, especially political ones, should be unbiased by religious influence (*See* also public reason.). Some scholars are now arguing that the very idea of secularism will change.

Secularism draws its intellectual roots from Greek and Roman philosophers such as Marcus Aurelius and Epicurus; medieval Muslim polymaths such as Ibn Rushd; Enlightenment thinkers such as Denis Diderot, Voltaire, Baruch Spinoza, John Locke, James Madison, Thomas Jefferson, and Thomas Paine; and more recent freethinkers, agnostics, and atheists such as Robert Ingersoll and Bertrand Russell.

The purposes and arguments in support of secularism vary widely. In European laicism, it has been argued that secularism is a movement towards modernization, and away from traditional religious values (also known as secularization). This type of secularism, on a social or philosophical level, has often occurred while maintaining an official state church or other state support of religion. In the United States, some argue that state secularism has served to a greater extent to protect religion and the religious from governmental interference, while secularism on a social level is less prevalent. Within the countries as well, differing political movements support secularism for varying reasons.

In political terms, secularism is a movement towards the separation of religion and government (often termed the separation of church and state). This can refer to reducing ties between a government and a state religion, replacing laws based on scripture (such as the *Torah* and *Sharia* law) with civil laws, and eliminating discrimination on the basis of religion. This is said to add to democracy by protecting the rights of religious minorities.

Secularism is often associated with the Age of Enlightenment in Europe and plays a major role in Western society. The principles, but not necessarily practices, of separation of church and state in the United States and *Laïcité* in France draw heavily on secularism. Secular states also existed in the Islamic world during the Middle Ages (see Islam and secularism).

Due in part to the belief in the separation of church and state, secularists tend to prefer that politicians make decisions for secular rather than religious reasons. In this respect, policy decisions pertaining to topics like abortion, contraception, embryonic stem cell research, same-sex marriage, and sex education are prominently focused upon by American secularist organizations such as the Centre for Inquiry.

Most major religions accept the primacy of the rules of secular, democratic society but may still seek to influence political decisions or achieve specific privileges or influence through church-state agreements such as a concordat. Many Christians support a secular state, and may acknowledge that the conception has support in Biblical teachings, particularly the statement of Jesus in the Book of Luke: "Then give to Caesar what is Caesar's, and to God what is God's."However, some Christian fundamentalists (notably in the United States) oppose secularism, often claiming that there is a "radical secularist" ideology being adopted in current days and see secularism as a threat to "Christian rights" and national security. The most significant forces of religious fundamentalism in the contemporary world are Fundamentalist Christianity and Fundamentalist Islam. At the same time, one significant stream of secularism has come from religious minorities who see governmental and political secularism as integral to preserving equal rights.

Some of the well known states that are often considered "constitutionally secular" are USA, France, India, Mexico, South Korea, and Turkey although none of these nations have identical forms of governance.

The studies of religion, modern Western societies are generally recognized as secular. This is due to the near-complete freedom of religion (beliefs on religion generally are not subject to legal or social sanctions), and the lack of authority of religious leaders over political decisions. Nevertheless, religious beliefs are widely considered a relevant part of the political discourse in many of these countries. This contrasts with other Western countries where religious references are generally considered out-of-place in mainstream politics.

The nature of a secular society could characterize a secular society as one which:

1. Refuses to commit itself as a whole to anyone view of the nature of the universe and the role of man in it.
2. Is not homogenous, but is pluralistic.
3. Is tolerant. It widens the sphere of private decision-making.
4. While every society must have some common aims, which implies there must be agreed on methods of problem-solving, and a common framework of law; in a secular society these are as limited as possible.
5. Problem solving is approached rationally, through examination of the facts. While the secular society does not set any overall aim, it helps its members realize their aims.
6. Is a society without any official images? Nor is there a common ideal type of behavior with universal application.

Secularism as a Philosophy

Secularism is a code of duty pertaining to this life founded on considerations purely human, and intended mainly for those who find theology indefinite or inadequate, unreliable or unbelievable. Its essential principles are three:

- The improvement of this life by material means.
- That science is the available Providence of man.
- That it is good to do well. Whether there is other good or not, the good of the present life is good, and it is good to seek that good.

Secularism is the religion of humanity; it embraces the affairs of this world; it is interested in everything that touches the welfare of a sentient being; it advocates attention to the particular planet on which we happen to live; it means that each individual counts for something; it is a declaration of intellectual independence; it means the pew is superior to the pulpit, that those who bear the burdens shall have the profits and that they who fill the purse shall hold the strings.

It is a protest against ecclesiastical tyranny, against being a serf, subject or slave of any phantom, or of the priest of any phantom. It is a protest against wasting this life for the sake of one we know not of. It proposes to let the gods take care of themselves. It means living for us and each other; for the present instead of the past, for this world instead of another. It is striving to do away with violence and vice, with ignorance, poverty and disease.

Secularism is:...a variety of utilitarian social ethic which seeks human improvement without reference to religion and exclusively by means of human reason, science and social organization. It has developed into a positive and widely adopted outlook which aims to direct all activities and institutions by a non-religious concern for the goods of the present life and for social well-being.

According to these descriptions, secularism was a positive philosophy that is concerned entirely with the good of human beings in this life. The improvement of the human condition is treated as a material question, not spiritual, and is best achieved through human efforts rather than supplications before deities or other supernatural beings.

We should remember that at the time that Holyoake coined the term secularism, the material needs of the people were very important. Although "material" needs were contrasted with "spiritual" and thus also included things like education and personal development, it is nevertheless true that very material needs like adequate housing, food, and clothing loomed large in the minds of progressive reformers. None of these meanings for secularism as a positive philosophy are still in use today.

Today, the philosophy that was called secularism tends to be labelled humanism or secular humanism and the concept of secularism, at least in the social sciences, is much more restricted. The first and perhaps most common understanding of "secular" today stand in opposition to "religious." According to this usage something is secular when it can be categorized with the worldly, civil, non-religious sphere of human life. A secondary understanding of "secular" is contrasted with anything that is regarded as holy, sacred, and inviolable. According to this usage something is secular when it is not worshipped, when it is not venerated, and when it is open for critique, judgement, and replacement.

MARSIGLIO OF PADUA (1270-1342)

Marsiglio of Padua (Italian Marsilio or Marsiglio da Padova) (1270–1342) was an Italian medieval scholar, physician, philosopher, and political thinker. He collaborated with the Averroist philosopher Jean de Jandun on *Defensor pacis* (1324), one of the most extraordinary political and religious works of the fourteenth century. Crafted in response to the excommunication of Louis IV, Holy Roman Emperor elect, by Pope John XXII, *Defensor pacis* laid out an elaborate theory of government by popular sovereignty and challenged the authority of the Pope and clergy over secular affairs. Marsiglio supported the supremacy of the Empire as a government independent of the Holy See by declaring that all political power came from the people, and that the supreme coercive power in a community should be in the hands of a secular body chosen by popular consensus. He denied the anointing of a special leader of the church by St. Peter; said that all priests and bishops were equally invested with the authority to perform sacraments but did not have the right to judge their parishioners; and presented the position that scriptures should be interpreted by councils of the faithful rather than by authorities of the church. Marsiglio was one of the first to apply the methods of Aristotelian logic to Biblical scripture, theology and church doctrine.

Life

Marsiglio was born at Padua, Italy in 1270. He served for a time in the army of the emperor, and then began to study medicine at the University of Padua. Around 1311 he travelled to Paris to complete his medical studies, and in December of 1312 he became rector of the University of Paris. Soon after that, he went to Avignon and obtained letters from Pope John XXII appointing him as a canon of the Church of Padua. In Paris, Marsiglio made the acquaintance of Averroist philosopher Jean de Jandun, canon of Senlis, and together they composed "*Defensor pacis*" in 1324, to support Louis of Bavaria in his struggles with Pope John XXII.

At this time a conflict had arisen between Pope John XXII and Louis of Bavaria, the Roman emperor elect (elected 1314, died 1347). The Pope had denounced Louis for supporting heretics, excommunicated him and ordered him to step down within three months. At issue was whether or not the Roman emperor could rule without the confirmation of the Pope. In 1326, when it became known that they were the authors of *Defensor pacis*, Marsiglio and Jean de Jandun went to Nuremberg to seek the protection of the emperor Louis of Bavaria. Startled by the boldness of their political and religious theories, he was at first inclined to regard them as heretics. He soon changed his mind, however, and admitted them to the circle of his intimates. In the Papal Bull of April 3, 1327, John XXII reproached Louis of Bavaria for having welcomed Marsiglio and Jean de Jandun to his court. On the ninth of April the Pope summoned them and excommunicated them. On October 23rd, 1327, a commission appointed by the Pope condemned five of the propositions of Marsiglio and supported their claims with evidence from history and the scriptures. The propositions of Marsiglio and Jean de Jandun were declared to be erroneous, against the Holy Scriptures, heretical and dangerous to the Catholic church.

Marsiglio accompanied Louis to Italy, where he saw some of his revolutionary ideas being put into practice. On January 17, 1328, Louis had himself crowned by Colonna syndic of the Roman people. He removed John XXII as Pope and replaced him with a mendicant friar, Pietro de Corbara, raised by an imperial decree to the throne of St. Peter as Nicholas V after a supposed popular election on May 12, 1328. Marsilius was appointed Imperial Vicar and began to persecute the clergy who had remained faithful to John XXII. In recompense for his services, he seems to have been appointed archbishop of Milan, while his collaborator, John of Jandun, obtained from Louis the bishopric of Ferrara. Marsilius was apparently abandoned by the emperor in October of 1336 and died towards the end of 1342.

His Works

An addition to *Defensor pacis*, Mariglio of Padua also composed a treatise *De translatione imperii romani*, which is merely a rearrangement of a work of Landolfo Colonna, *De jurisdictione imperatoris in causa matrimoniali*. It was intended to prove the exclusive jurisdiction of the emperor in matrimonial affairs, in order to justify the actions of Louis of Bavaria, who had just annulled the marriage of the son of the king of Bohemia and the countess of Tirol. In the *Defensor minor*, an unpublished work preserved in the Bodleian Library at Oxford, Marsilius completed and elaborated certain points from the *Defensor pacis*. It further expounds his democratic theory and deals with ecclesiastical jurisdiction, penances, indulgences, crusades and pilgrimages, vows, excommunication, the pope and the council, marriage, and divorce.

Background

The conflict between Louis of Bavaria and Pope John XXII was one of many political disputes which arose between the powerful Roman Catholic Church and the European monarchs over issues such as marriage alliances, land ownership, taxation of church property, and territorial sovereignty. Marsiglio did not believe that the Roman Catholic Church should involve itself in secular politics and saw the church as a divisive force that was disrupting the peace of Europe. Cæsarian theologians like Guilaume Durand and the Dominican John of Paris had already begun to challenge the hegemony of the Roman church.

Within the religious community there was also disgust at the corruption and materialism which existed at the highest levels of the church hierarchy, and which seemed at odds with the teachings of Christ.

Political Theory

Marsiglio wrote *Defensor pacis* in 1324. This treatise was created in the context of a power struggle between Pope John XXII and Louis of Bavaria (or Ludwig of Bavaria), the elected candidate for Holy Roman Emperor. Louis' policies in the Italian peninsula, where the Empire had important territories, threatened papal territorial sovereignty. In 1323 Louis had sent an army to Italy to protect Milan against the powerful Kingdom of Naples. Naples, along with France, was a powerful ally of John XXII. John excommunicated Louis and demanded that he relinquish his claim to the imperial crown. Louis responded to John XXII with fresh provocations.

In Defensor pacis, Marsiglio sought to demonstrate, by arguments from reason (in Dictio I of the text) and by argument from authority (in Dictio II) the independence of the Holy Roman Empire from the Papacy and the emptiness of the prerogatives alleged to have been usurped by the sovereign pontiffs. This demonstration was regarded as heretical.

Marsiglio and John of Jandun, who has sometimes been credited as a co-author of *Defensor pacis*, left France for Louis' court in Bavaria. Louis admitted Marsiglio and John to his circle. Others were also under his protection, including Michael of Cesena and the philosopher William of Ockham, an advocate of an early form of church and state separation. In 1326, Marsiglio accompanied Louis to Italy, where he preached or circulated written attacks against the Pope. The Lord of Milan Galeazzo I Visconti, suspected of conspiring with John, was deposed and Louis was crowned King of Italy in Milan in 1327.

In January 1328 Louis entered Rome and had himself crowned emperor by the aged senator Sciarra Colonna, called captain of the Roman people. Three months later Louis published a decree declaring "Jacque de Cahors"–Pope John XXII—deposed on grounds of heresy. He then installed the Franciscan Pietro Rainalducci as Nicholas V. Nicholas was deposed upon Louis' departure from Rome in 1329.

In Bavaria, as imperial vicar, Marsiglio persecuted the clergy who had remained faithful to John XXII. In recompense for his services, he was appointed archbishop of Milan, and John of Jandun obtained from Louis IV the bishopric of Ferrara.

Marsiglio also composed a treatise *De translatione [Romani] imperii*, which some authorities consider is a rearrangement of a similar work by Landolfo Colonna called *De jurisdictione imperatoris in causa matrimoniali*. This work, and Marsiglio's variation, sought to justify the exclusive jurisdiction of the emperor in matrimonial affairs: Louis of Bavaria had recently annulled the marriage of the son of the King of Bohemia.

Impact of Aristotle

The thought of Marsiglio was greatly influenced by the views of Aristotle. In fact the impact of Aristotle on him was so deep that scholars have taken the view that his *Defensor pacis* completed the work left undone by Aristotle. In fact Marsiglio supplemented the rationalism with the spiritualism and others worldliness of Christian Faith.

Most legal words are derived from the Latin word lex, meaning "law" or "statute." Interestingly, the word lex itself seems to be related to the Latin 'legere' which means "to read." Etymologically, legal things are readable. This idea may be linked with Marsiglio of Padua's belief that law must be written because the spoken law of the monarch is not adequate for society. With writing and codification, law is distinguished from and raised above the mere customs or practices of a given society. Aristotle (whose works are quoted through the great extent of *Defensor Pacis*) provides a simple explanation of law in terms of two distinct categories: particular law and universal law. Universal law is "the law of nature" whereas particular law refers to a set of rules which is laid down by the members of a community.

Marsiglio of Padua had deeply imbibed Aristotle's Politics, and his own understanding of city-states was strengthened by his knowledge of the institutions of Lombard city-republics. He wrote about the "perfect" form of government intended by Nature through the gradual growth of human communities. Such communities would include various classes of men including the priesthood, Principans, the executive, and the legislator.

In *Defensor pacis*, Marsiglio explains that there can be several meanings of the word "law" but among its various implications the most significant meaning is "a natural inclination of the senses towards some action or passion." He explores the importance of the government of a perfect community by a set of laws or customs, and what such laws actually mean, and the application of laws by various agents.

"Law has coercive power, being speech for a certain prudence and understanding" (Nicomachean Ethics X, 1180a21–2). Marsiglio refers to this understanding of law in Aristotle when he describes law as a command or "coercive power" applied by someone who is guided by his sense of observation of what is right and just. The understanding of this "coercive power" which is relevant for maintaining peace in a community is what makes Marsiglio's understanding of law distinctive from others. Thomas Aquinas, for example, asks "Can anybody's reason make law?" (Summa theologiae IaIIae q. 90 a. 3) because he does not entirely believe that law is guided by reason. For him, the idea of coercive power is linked rather with the idea of giving penalties to a wrongdoer because reasoning with a criminal may not be enough for the larger community.

The primary necessity of law, according to Marsiglio, lies in civil justice and common advantage. Law also ensures the security of the position of the prince and their long principate. In order for a community to function properly laws are necessary and it is equally important for the law to be appropriated by someone who can judge rightly. When the laws are written down for a community, and thus made objective, it is not possible for even a corrupt prince to let his own intemperance affect judgment. The written law is universal and independent of external influence. Drawing upon Aristotle, Marsiglio asks "whether it is better for a polity to be ruled by the best man without law, or by the best law."

Aristotle had emphasized the importance of the politician as an able lawgiver (*nomothetês*), as one who frames the laws, customs and institutions of the city state. But Marsiglio recognizes that it is not always possible for a single lawgiver to be just and right at all times. In discussing this, he comes to the conclusion that the best judgement can be passed when the element of passion is absent. But this is not entirely possible because personal feelings often come into effect while giving a verdict. Moreover, ignorance can result in wrong judgement. Marsiglio provides a solution for the appropriation of law in the right way—it has to be written and made accessible to all so that it is easier to refer back to it whenever the need arises. For Marsiglio, the purpose of law is to "exclude malice and error from the civil judgements or sentences of judges." Important to Marsiglio discourse is the role of the legislator, the lawmaker.

Although he quotes extensively from Aristotle's work, Marsiglio also seems to be influenced by Plato's Nomoi or Laws. Plato emphasizes the importance of a legal order which is passed democratically by an assembly of people, and mentions that government should be subject to the rule of law. In this dialogue Plato also explores the important question of who lays down the laws. This very question is taken up by Marsiglio while trying to establish how a body of people is relevant for passing laws. For him, the human legislator is ideally a community of people, not a single person. When Marsiglio was writing about the human legislator he was aware of the tension between *populo grasso* and *populo minuto* in the Italian cities. Marsiglio carefully treads a middle path while exploring whether the whole multitude should rule or just some people. It is important to understand who can speak in legal matters of the community because women, children, and slaves are entirely excluded from this process. The 'collective' is important because according to Marsiglio the "whole" is more reliable than the "part". When a community or a collective passes a law it is more likely that everyone's interests will be taken into account. It is important to remember here that medieval canonists also maintained that acts need to be authorized by *major et saniors partes* ("greater and sounder parts") of the community.

Marsiglio also notes that people do not necessarily need to use their collective legislative powers, and instead can entrust it to a ruler who can act as a representative of the larger community. This is how the installation of the ruler is relevant, but again this can only be done by popular consent. Marsiglio was radical not only in his idea of state and law but even more so in his conception of the Church. He felt that in all types of appointments, and functions of the priesthood is responsible to the legislator and its deputy, the principan.

In the wake of Plato and Aristotle, Romans believed that all men had, by nature, an instinctive knowledge of what was right and what was wrong and they also believed that it was possible to frame laws in accordance with nature. To them, law was *Ius Gentium*—of all people. Propelled by this universalism they found it difficult to understand how Barbarians had different laws and how the Barbarians could claim that their own laws were peculiar to them. These laws were not founded on nature or reason but on the dictates of their own '*divine ancestors*'. The Barbarians, who subsequently felled the Roman Empire in 476 A.D., accepted Christianity as the state religion and brought about the 'Medieval Age' in Europe. This presented the first break with classical Graeco-Roman thought with regard to laws. Medieval Europe was encompassed by the Christian Church and theological laws overshadowed natural law, rational law, and even local customs. Marsiglio of Padua challenged the Church's authority to frame laws on behalf of civil society except in spiritual matters, and revived Aristotelian understandings of law. As a scholastic, Marsiglio tried to harmonize classical theories of law with the views of medieval theologians.

Marsiglio's idea that law is sovereign, and above the human legislators who instituted it, remains powerful today. Indeed, it may even be said to be the essence of our modern democracy.

Marsiglio on State

Following the footsteps of Aristotle, Marsiglio supposes the state as living organism, having its origin in the family. He agrees with Aristotle that the state is a self-sufficient and good community for life on the earth and also for eternal life. The efficiency of the state consists in ordinary working of its organs and if the parts collide, efficiency or peace of the state cannot be maintained. As such state should be independent of any control to promote general welfare and preserving peace and allowing free development of its members. All interests in the state should discharge its functions for the common welfare.

Following Aristotle, he enumerates the classes which co-operate to form a society. The artisans and the farmers supply the material wants and in strict sense, soldiers, officials and priest make up the state. He states that the function of priests is to know and teach these things which according to Scriptures, is necessary to believe, to do or to avoid in order to attain eternal salvation and escape. As such, he comes to conclusion that the secular questions are to be decided on their own rational merits without the help of faith or religion, secondly priest is only class of the society whose function is to preach salvation and the state possesses the right to control priests as the other classes such as farmers and traders etc. Finally, separation of faith and reason is scepticism.

He believes that the preservation of peace is the most important function of the state and duty of priest's to supplement the work of police and judge by the fear of hell. He holds that the work of the priest is to attain salvation for the next world and they have to do nothing about in this function of the world. Ideas of Marsiglio strike a deadly blow on the basic foundation of the church and at the theory of two swords and reduces the Church to the level of the department of the state.

Views on Law

Marsiglio's theory of Law constitutes the most important part of his thought. He gave a lucid exposition of the sources of law, kinds of law, and sanction behind the law. It may be observed that thought like Aquinas, Marsiglio also classified the laws into four categories, viz. Eternal, Natural, Divine and Human, his views in this regard completely differ from Aquinas. He does not accept the contention of Thomas Aquinas that the four categories of laws are manifestation of one and the same Cosmic reason and saw only a negative relation among the four laws. He said they are related only by equivocation as having the same but no common content of source. He also does not accept Aquinas view that justice was the sense of law and emphasised the coercive character of law. Marsiglio asserted that a law which cannot be enforced coercively is not law at all. Again Marsiglio does not consider law essentially as a dictate of reason duly constituted authority. In other words his concept of law is more political and less moral. In the next place he rejected Aquinas view that 'Law' makes the state and asserted that "far from the state being based upon a subsistent moral law, law will rather be based upon the state, and will derive its essential characteristics from the attributes which in that context had entailed for the state." Finally,

Marsiglio does not accept the contention of Thomas Aquinas that the Human Law in order to retain the force of law must be subservient to Divine Law and asserts that a Human Law may disagree with the Divine Law. He considered the Human Law superior in so far as it prevailed in case of conflict with the Divine law also possessed coercive power.

Though Marsiglio talks of four types of laws, he discussed only about the Divine Law. Out of these two he is primarily concerned with Human Laws and discusses about the Divine Law in very brief. Further, he subordinates the Divine Law to the Human Law and emerges as the extreme secularist among the medieval thinkers. Marsiglio's position is this regard has been summed up by Sabine thus "In so far as it is really a Divine Law, its penalties are other-worldly, in so far as it assesses earthly penalties it is part of human law and so within the power of the secular community."

Marsiglio defines Human Law as "command of the whole body of citizens or of its prevailing part, arising directly from the deliberation of those empowered to make law, about voluntary acts of human beings to be done or avoided in this world for the sake of attaining the best end, or some condition desirable for man, in this world. I mean a command the transgression of which is enforced in this world by a penalty or punishment imposed on the transgressor." A perusal of the above definition will highlight the following features of Law. Firstly, Marsiglio treats law as a coercive command of the legislator enforceable in the courts. Secondly, the source of the law is the will of the community rather than Divine Providence or Natural Reason. Thirdly, law emanates from Human Will as a kind of command to the subjects. Fourthly, coercion is the essential of law. Fifthly, it envisages a duly constituted authority with power to make, promulgate and enforce the laws. Sixthly, Marsiglio clearly accepts the concept of popular sovereignty and asserts that the source of all legal authority is always the people of its prevailing part. Seventhly, it shows preference for Rule of Law over rule of Men and asserts that the laws rightly laid down must be dominant. Finally, Marsiglio also emphasised the principle of positivism and asserted that all laws must be made by men. Even the unwritten law or custom must be laid down by men.

Thus, we find that Marsiglio in his theory of law combines the ideas of Aristotle with the medieval tradition and evolved a theory of law around which his whole philosophy revolves.

Views on Sovereignty

According to Marsiglio, the people should be sovereign in a state because it is in the collective interest of the community as a whole. He felt that combined wisdom was always better than the individual wisdom and that the people could collectively find defects in the laws. He also felt that the people were the best judge to enact a law and that the collective virtue could better be promoted by the community as a whole. He also felt that laws enacted by the community had no chances of being enacted in the interest of a single class and will also be readily obeyed. Accordingly he felt that elected monarchy was the best form of government. Monarch should be responsible to the community as a whole. A monarch should only perform administrative functions and should not go beyond these. These people have a right to remove a king from authority who abuses his powers or exceeds his legitimate rights. In order to make the rule of the people effective it is essential that the people should be educated. He also pleaded that the state should arrange for the education of the people and also see that there is not much of disparity in the wealth among different classes in a society. The state should also regulate economic life of the people. He had preference for limited monarchy and believed that a monarch should be elected by the people. Monarchy brings unity in executive because authority is vested in the hands of one person. Maxey has thus expressed his views on the subject, "The head of the Government should be elected or appointed by the people, and should be circumscribed in such a way that he cannot put himself above law."

The Organs of Government

He holds that executive and judiciary be set up or elected by the body of citizens. He agrees that there are various way of election but all other authority comes from the legislative act of whole body. It must be powerful and supreme to supervise the functions of the state. The executive organ is to carry out the laws in force made by the legislators. He prefers monarchy because its unity is safeguarded against internal disorders and peace is secured. He supports elective monarchy than hereditary monarchy. He puts emphasis on unity of the executive and opposes separate jurisdiction of the Church.

Representative Government

Intimately linked with his theory of popular sovereignty is Marsiglio's idea on representative government. Marsiglio asserts that the sanction behind the government is not knowledge of law, or practical wisdom or moral virtue but election by the whole body of citizens. The body of citizens has the right to correct the government and even to depose it if it becomes expedient for the common interest. He justified representative government through teleological argument. He argued that if the citizens are the material from which law emanates, the law-maker too must derive its authority from the same matter. "For whoever has the power to create a form has the power to determine its underlying substance as may be seen in all the productive acts...In all things, both artificial and natural, this is apparent by induction. There is a reason for this, for the forms and their operation are the ends, the material are the means. Since then it belong to the whole body of citizens to create the form according to which civil acts are to be regulated that is, the law—it belongs to the same body to determine the material or subject matter of this form...From this it seems possible to infer consistently that a ruler who is elected without hereditary succession is greatly to be preferred to rulers who are hereditary.

View on Church

The Church also, he extends principles of representative government which took shape of councillor movement. According to him, Church includes all the Christians and not only clergymen whose ultimate authority lies in the whole body which is superior to Pope. The Pope should be elected by the general council and should be responsible to it. In general council of the Church, there should be both ecclesiastical and secular delegates. He gives even power of disposing Pope to the General Assembly because the Pope derives his authority from the General Council. Which meant that the power of the Pope is not of divine origin. He regards the Church as a Christian common wealth and the Pope as its head. He holds that only duty of clergy is that of preaching for the salvation of the soul and nothing else even the judgement of excommunication is to enforced by secular authority if it things proper to enforce. As such he makes Church and Clergy as not entity.

He was an Erastian and wanted to subordinate the Clergy and the Church of the state. He even gives power to the state to make law for regulating the organization of the Church in the state on the ground that it will help the state in maintaining peace and order. He regarded the Pope as bishop of Rome, having no claim or superiority over other bishops. Thus he completely subordinated the Church under the state and for the state and to the state.

Relation between Church and the State

As regards the relationship between the Church and the State Marsiglio assigned a subordinate position to the Church. He refused to accept the divine origin and the past only in order to help the state keep the perverse and recalcitrant people under control by placing before them the terror of hell. Thus, the priests supplement the police and the judge in preventing people from committing crimes. He saw nothing sacrosanct about religion, clergy and the Church and considered religion merely as a social phenomenon. He thus reduced the Church to the position of the department of the state. He treated the clergy merely as a class "set apart to perform religious services, subject to regulation like any other class and like laymen which was amenable to the civil courts for violation of human law. He held that there was no such thing as spiritual offence and every offence as such was an offence against human law.

In the interest of unity and place of civil society he wanted the church to be subordinate to the secular government. He argued that unity, which was an essence of the state, suffered if the Church was given independent status and jurisdiction. He held that the presence of two equal and co-ordinate powers each trying to assert its supremacy over the other was a potent and persistent cause of discord and strife. The Priests which constituted one of the six classes of the state had to submit to the 'greater whole' for the preservation of peace, which constituted the life blood of the state.

Marsiglio asserted the superiority of the state over the Church by denying it coercive power. He argued that a Divine Law did exist but it could not be enforced in this world in so far as the rewards or punishment sanctioned by it were to be meted out by God alone in future life. There was no earthly punishment meant for its violation. Since Divine Law did not possess any power of coercion in this world, it could only be described as Divine Doctrine. On the other hand it could only be described as Divine Doctrine. On the other hand, coercion was one of the essential features of Human Law and this power emanated from human enactment. Hence if the Divine Law is to be enforced it is only the Human Legislator who can do so and not the priest or the Church.

Marsiglio described the Clergymen as physicians of the diseases of soul. Like physicians of the body they could act as healer of the souls and exhort them to follow rules of external health of soul. He argued that as no physician is competent to expel a leper and no one has authority to do so except the body of the citizens or their deputy, so on power of pronouncing coercive judgement based on the law of God belongs to any priest or to any body of priests' knowledge of that law. Marsiglio allowed the Church the power to issue decrees of excommunication and interdiction but asserted that these punishments could be given effective shape only by the civil authority.

Estimate or Contribution of Marsiglio to the Political Philosophy

Marsiglio is considered as one of the most important secularists of his age. His theory has been characterised as one of the most remarkable creations of medieval political thought. Unlike many other political thinkers of Middle Ages he had original thoughts. His important contribution was in the following fields:

(i) He brought to focus that the church had degenerated itself and accordingly it was not delivering spiritual goods. Thus, he was forerunner of renaissance movement.
(ii) He rightly felt that the sovereignty should have coercive authority without which sovereign cannot exercise his power. He thus, gave Austin the idea about absolute sovereignty, which the latter fully developed.
(iii) He separated ethics from politics and gave a definite and superior place to state and thus paved the way for the philosophy of Machiavelli.
(iv) He has given a definite and superior place to the people and thus has helped the cause of democracy. As already said he laid stress on the sovereignty of the people.
(v) He has put the state at par with the Church and has in fact given rather superior position to the latter. He has thus brought modernism in his ideas.
(vi) He has distinguished functions of all the three organs of government and is thus the forerunner of the theory of separation of powers as expounded by Montesquieu.
(vii) He was the first medieval thinker who gave the idea of limited or constitutional monarchy.

We may thus conclude by saying that Marsiglio has done full justice to the cause to which he had devoted himself. He clearly brought to the front the defects of church organisation—a cause for which he had set for himself. In mind a perfectly normal feature of monarchy, a preference for something like a modern limited monarch with another government organ independent of prince clothed with authority to judge him. He was original in many respects. His views about secularism, sovereignty of the people and limited monarchy were almost new and expounded and developed by him only.

NICCOLO MACHIAVELLI (1469-1527)

Niccolò di Bernardo dei Machiavelli (3 May, 1469–21 June, 1527) was an Italian historian, diplomat, philosopher, humanist and writer based in Florence during the Renaissance. A founder of modern political science, he was a diplomat, political philosopher, playwright, and a civil servant of the Florentine Republic. He also wrote comedies, carnival songs, and poetry. His personal correspondence is renowned in the Italian language. He was Secretary to the Second Chancery of the Republic of Florence from 1498 to 1512, when the Medici were out of power. He wrote his masterpiece, *The Prince after the Medici* had recovered power and he no longer held a position of responsibility in Florence.

Life

Machiavelli was born in Florence, Italy, the first son and third child of attorney, Bernardo di Niccolò Machiavelli, and his wife, Bartolomea di Stefano Nelli. The Machiavelli family is believed to be descended from the old Marquesses of Tuscany and to have produced thirteen Florentine Gonfalonieres of Justice, one of the offices of a group of nine citizens selected by drawing lots every two months, who formed the government, or Signoria. Machiavelli, like many people of Florence, was however not a full citizen of Florence, due to the nature of Florentine citizenship in that time, even under the republican regime.

Machiavelli was born in a tumultuous era—popes waged acquisitive wars against Italian city-states, and people and cities might fall from power at any time. Along with the pope and the major cities like Venice and Florence, foreign powers such as France, Spain, the Holy Roman Empire, and even Switzerland battled for regional influence and control. Political-military alliances continually changed, featuring condottieri (mercenary leaders) who changed sides without warning and short lived governments rising and falling.

Machiavelli was taught grammar, rhetoric, and Latin, and became a prolific writer. It is thought that he did not learn Greek, even though Florence was at the time one of the centres of Greek scholarship in Europe. In 1494, Florence restored the republic—expelling the Medici family, who had ruled Florence for some sixty years. In June 1498, shortly after the execution of Savonarola, Machiavelli, at the age of 29, was elected as head of the second chancery. In July 1498, he was also made the secretary to the Dieci di Libertà e Pace. He was in a diplomatic council responsible for negotiation and military affairs. Between 1499 and 1512 he carried out several diplomatic missions: to the court of Louis XII in France; to the court of Ferdinand II of Aragón, in Spain; in Germany; and to the Papacy in Rome, in the Italian states. Moreover, from 1502 to 1503 he witnessed the brutal reality of the state-building methods of Cesare Borgia (1475–1507) and his father Pope Alexander VI, who were then engaged in the process of trying to bring a large part of central Italy under their possession. The pretext of defending Church interests was used as a partial justification by the Borgias.

Between 1503 and 1506 Machiavelli was responsible for the Florentine militia, including the City's defence. He distrusted mercenaries (a distrust he explained in his official reports and then later in his theoretical works), preferring a politically invested citizen-militia—a philosophy that bore fruit. His command of Florentine citizen-soldiers defeated Pisa in 1509. However, in August 1512 the Medici, helped by Pope Julius II, used Spanish troops to defeat the Florentines at Prato. Piero Soderini resigned as Florentine head of state and left in exile. The Florentine city-state and the Republic were dissolved. Machiavelli was deprived of office in 1512 by the Medici. In 1513 he was accused of conspiracy, arrested, and imprisoned for a time. Despite torture ("with the rope", where the prisoner is hanged from his bound wrists, from the back, forcing the arms to bear the body's weight, thus dislocating the shoulders), he denied involvement and was released. Machiavelli then retired to his estate at Sant'Andrea in Percussina (near San Casciano in Val di Pesa), and devoted himself to study and to the writing of the political treatises that earned his intellectual place in the development of political philosophy and political conduct. Despairing of the opportunity to remain directly involved in political matters, after a time Machiavelli began to participate in intellectual groups in Florence and wrote several plays that (unlike his works on politics/political theory) were both popular and widely known in his lifetime. Still politics remained his main passion and to satisfy interest he maintained a well-known correspondence with better politically connected friends, attempting to become involved once again in political life.

Machiavelli's Cenotaph in the Santa Croce Church in Florence

In a letter to Francesco Vettori, he described his exile: When evening comes, I go back home, and go to my study. On the threshold, I take off my work clothes, covered in mud and filth, and I put on the clothes an ambassador would wear. Decently dressed, I enter the ancient courts of rulers who have long since died. There, I am warmly welcomed, and I feed on the only food I find nourishing and was born to savor. I am not ashamed to talk to them and ask them to explain their actions and they, out of kindness, answer me. Four hours go by without my feeling any anxiety. I forget every worry. I am no longer afraid of poverty or frightened of death. I live entirely through them. Machiavelli died in 1527 at the age of 58. He was buried at the Church of Santa Croce in Florence, Italy. An epitaph honouring him is inscribed on his monument. The Latin legend reads: TANTO NOMINI NULLUM PAR ELOGIUM ["so great a name (has) no adequate praise" or "no eulogy (would be appropriate to) such a great name"].

His Works

The Prince

Machiavelli's best-known book, "*The Prince*," contains a number of maxims concerning politics, but rather than the more traditional subject of a hereditary prince, it concentrates on the possibility of a "new prince." To retain power, the hereditary prince must carefully maintain the socio-political institutions to which the people are accustomed; whereas a new prince has the more difficult task in ruling, since he must first stabilize his new-found power in order to build an enduring political structure. He believed that social benefits of stability and security could be achieved in the face of moral corruption. Aside from that, Machiavelli believed that public and private morality had to be separate in order to rule. To do this required that the prince be concerned not only with reputation but that he is also willing to act immorally. As a political scientist, Machiavelli emphasizes the occasional need for the methodical exercise of brute force, deceit, and so on.

Scholars often note that Machiavelli glorifies instrumentality in state building—an approach embodied by the saying that "the ends justify the means." Violence may be necessary for the successful transfer of power and introduction of new legal institutions. Force may be used to eliminate political rivals, to coerce resistant populations, and to purge previous rulers who will inevitably attempt to regain their power. Machiavelli has become infamous for this political advice, ensuring that he would be remembered in history as an adjective, and "Machiavellian."

Notwithstanding some mitigating themes, the Catholic Church banned *The Prince*, registering it to the Index *Librorum Prohibitorum*, and humanists also viewed the book negatively—among them, Erasmus of Rotterdam. As a treatise, its primary intellectual contribution to the history of political thought is the fundamental break between political Realism and political Idealism—thus, *The Prince* is a manual to acquiring and keeping political power. In contrast with Plato and Aristotle, Machiavelli insisted that an imaginary ideal society is not the model for a prince to orient himself by.

Concerning the differences and similarities in Machiavelli's advice to ruthless and tyrannical princes in *The Prince* and his more republican exhortations in Discourses on Livy, many have concluded that *The Prince* although written in the form of advice for a monarchical prince, contains arguments for the superiority of republican regimes, similar to those found in the Discourses. In the 18th century the work was even called a satire, for example by Jean-Jacques Rousseau. More recently, commentators such as Leo Strauss and Harvey Mansfield have agreed that *The Prince* can be read as having a deliberate comical irony. Other commentators have not seen the irony as deliberate comedy, but most commentators agree that *The Prince* is in any case republican to some extent.

Discourses on Livy

The Discourses on the First Ten Books of Titus Livy (Discorsi) nominally discuss a classical history of early Ancient Rome. Machiavelli presents it as a series of lessons on how a republic should be started and structured. It is a larger work than *The Prince*, and it more openly explains the advantages of republics. It includes early versions of the concept of checks and balances, and asserts the superiority of a republic over a principality. It became one of the central texts of republicanism.

From The Discourses:

- "In fact, when there is combined under the same constitution a prince, a nobility, and the power of the people, then these three powers will watch and keep each other reciprocally in check." Book I, Chapter II.
- "Doubtless these means [of attaining power] are cruel and destructive of all civilized life, and neither Christian, nor even human, and should be avoided by everyone. In fact, the life of a private citizen would be preferable to that of a king at the expense of the ruin of so many human beings." Bk I, Ch XXVI.
- "Now, in a well-ordered republic, it should never be necessary to resort to extra-constitutional measures." Bk I, Ch XXXIV.
- "...The governments of the people are better than those of princes." Book I, Chapter LVIII.
- "If we compare the faults of a people with those of princes, as well as their respective good qualities, we shall find the people vastly superior in all that is good and glorious." Book I, Chapter LVIII.
- "For government consists mainly in so keeping your subjects that

they shall be neither able, nor disposed to injure you." Bk II, Ch XXIII.

- "...no prince is ever benefited by making himself hated." Book III, Chapter XIX.
- "Let not princes complain of the faults committed by the people subjected to their authority, for they result entirely from their own negligence or bad example." Bk III, Ch XXIX.

Other Political and Historical Works

— *Discorso sopra le cose di Pisa* (1499)

— *Del modo di trattare i popoli della Valdichiana ribellati* (1502)

— *Del modo tenuto dal duca Valentino nell' ammazzare Vitellozzo Vitelli Oliverotto da Fermo, etc.* (1502)—A Description of the Methods Adopted by the Duke Valentino when Murdering Vitellozzo Vitelli, Oliverotto da Fermo, the Signor Pagolo, and the Duke di Gravina Orsini.

— *Discorso sopra la provisione del danaro* (1502)—A discourse about the provision of money.

— *Ritracto delle cose della Magna* (1508–1512)—Portrait of the affairs of Germany.

— *Dell'Arte della Guerra* (1519–1520)—*The Art of War*, high military science.

— *Discorso sopra il riformare lo stato di Firenze* (1520)--A discourse about the reforming of Florence.

— *Sommario delle cose della citta di Lucca* (1520)—A summary of the affairs of the city of Lucca.

— *The Life of Castruccio Castracani of Lucca* (1520)—*Vita di Castruccio Castracani da Lucca*, a short biography.

— *Istorie Florentine* (1520–1525)—*Florentine Histories*, an eight-volume history book of the city-state, Florence, commissioned by Giulio di Giuliano de' Medici, *later Pope Clement VII.*

Fictional Works

Besides being a statesman and political scientist, Machiavelli also translated classical works, and was a dramaturge (*Clizia*, *Mandragola*), a poet (*Sonetti*, *Canzoni*, *Ottave*, *Canti carnascialeschi*), and a novelist (*Belfagor arcidiavolo*).

Some of his Other Works

- *Decennale primo* (1506), a poem in terza rima.

- *Decennale secondo* (1509), a poem.
- *Ritratti delle cose di Francia* (1510)–Portrait of the affairs of France.
- *Andria* or *The Woman of Andros* (1517), a Classical comedy, translated from Terence.
- *Mandragola* (1518)–*The Mandrake*, a five-act prose comedy, with a verse prologue.
- *Clizia* (1525), a prose comedy.
- *Belfagor arcidiavolo* (1515), a novel.
- *Asino d'oro* (1517)—*The Golden Ass* is a terza rima poem, a new version of the *Classic work by Apuleius*.
- *Frammenti storici* (1525)—Fragments of stories.

Other Works

Della lingua (1514), a dialogue about the language is also normally considered to be by Machiavelli.

Machiavelli's literary executor, Giuliano de'Ricci, also reported having seen that Machiavelli, his grandfather, made a comedy in the style of *Aristophanes* which included living Florentines as characters, and to be titled *Le Maschere.* It has been suggested that due to such things as this and his style of writing to his superiors generally, there was very likely some animosity to Machiavelli even before the return of the Medici.

Machiavelli as a Modern Thinker

Machiavelli was a modern thinker only in the sense that he ceased to be a medieval thinker and ushered in certain new ideas which are symbolic of the modern age. Some of the important ideas of Machiavelli which can be cited for this purpose are as follows:

1. Divorce of Religion and Politics

Credit goes to Machiavelli for boldly and clearly divorcing religion from politics. He strongly stood for the doctrine that the religion should have no place in state activities and that the Prince should not act according to the wishes of the Pop.

2. Distinction in Public and Private Morality

Machiavelli's another contribution to the political thought was that for the first time he distinguished between public and private morality which he felt must be separated from each other.

3. Refutation of Natural and Eternal Law

Machiavelli was the first political thinkers of his time who abandoned the idea of natural law and in its place gave the idea that the law was positive rule created by the sovereign in the state. He did not believe that there were certain eternal laws. Thus he refuted the idea of natural and eternal law.

4. Rejection of Divine Law

He also did not contribute to the idea of Divine Law. According to him, man has no super natural ends and as such it is wrong to believe that Divine Law has any purpose to perform.

5. State as an End

As a modern thinker Machiavelli made a valuable contribution by saying that the state was an end in itself. He did not care for the morality of means but believed that end always justified the means. No doubt a little later Hobbcs also stood for the elevation of state, but the lead was given by Machiavelli. For the first time he put forth the idea that individual conscience should be sacrificed over the state. Like a realist he believed that history was an illustration of the strength and nothing else and, therefore, he worshipped strength was the only deity to be worshipped. Without strength there was nothing which a Prince could rely upon.

6. Nationalism

Machiavelli was a symbol of nationalism and pleaded that there was nothing above or beside it and that it was an end in itself. It may not sound us of much importance today, but it was his greatest contribution to the age in which he was living.

7. Secularism

He was again the 1st political thinker who believed in secularism. Living in the days of theocracy he stood for secularism which can in no way be underestimated.

8. Naturalistic Theory of State

Another contribution of Machiavelli to the modern political thought is that for the 1st time he pleaded that man had no supernatural ends and was not governed by the Divine Law. He, thus method the conception of naturalistic theory of state as a logical one.

9. Fare-well to the Medieval Philosophy

Another contribution of Machiavelli is that he bade fare-well to the philosophy of middle ages. His conception of autonomous authorities, with which he replaced central authority, is both original and novel in so far as his age was concerned. In an age of Feudalism he shook its vary basis and thus invited the wrath of the feudalist and faced that.

10. Elected Authority

Machiavelli also gave food to modern thinkers by suggesting that the Republican form of Govt. was the best one and stood for the elected rather than a hereditary head of state. His conception of elected head of state though quite new yet that fully materialised in the theory of General Will as expounded by Rousseau.

11. Logical Concept of Sovereignty

Credit again goes to Machiavelli for attempting to give logical conception of sovereignty by defining it as independent and supreme authority both internally as well as externally; a definition which even today is considered as the most logical one. It was put on scientific basis by Austin.

12. Theory of State Craft

Machiavelli also contributed to the theory of state craft when he shook the foundations of the age long Greek philosophy of 'city state' had outlived its utility. The world needed another conception which Machiavelli rightly pleaded. His conception of national state is being followed even today.

13. Use of Historical Methods and Events

In contrast to the medieval thinkers, Machiavelli made use of inductive method along with historical method. He based his conclusions on the observation of the contemporary situation and wherever possible fortified his findings with the help of past historical events.

14. Separation of Ethics from Politics

The most important factor which separates Machiavelli from the medieval thinkers is that he separated ethics from politics. He asserted that there were two different codes of conduct—one for individual and the other for the state. He justified the use of unfair means by the ruler for the security and safety of the state.

15. Separation of Morality from Politics

Unlike other medieval thinkers, Machiavelli denied the place of morality in political affairs. He pleaded that the main force behind the government was utility. However, he limits this utility to the protection of life and property and ignores concepts like freedom, equality etc.

Machiavelli's Methods

Machiavelli was a man of practical affairs and as keen observer of men and situations. Machiavelli followed the following method in his study:

1. Method of Observation

Machiavelli had a keen power of observing men and situations. He went abroad on diplomatic missions many times and observed the condition in the countries which he visited. He was a realist and practical psychologist.

2. Inductive Method

He followed inductive and not the deductive method. In inductive method, we start with facts or particulars and arrives universal principles or generalizations.

3. Empire Method

He followed empirical method. His two books, *The Prince* and *The Discourse* are based on his own experience.

4. Scientific Method

He was the first great political thinker of modern times to free politics from religion. He made politics a real science. His method was scientific.

5. Comparative Method

He used comparative method to understand and explain the political problems. His aim was to build a strong and unified Italy under a strong ruler.

6. Historical Method

Machiavelli studied the past. He believed that the study of the past would enable us to better understand the present and to predict the future. He used the historical method in his discourse. He studied particularly the history of Rome. Machiavelli was concerned with the things as they are and not things as they ought to be. In other words, he was concerned with the facts and not with ideals.

Machiavelli's View on Human Motives

Machiavelli's view of human nature is found in his masterpiece "*The Prince.*" Machiavelli gives a long list of human motives which determines human conduct. A brief description of some of these motives are given below:

1. Love of Novelty

Machiavelli is of the opinion that human beings love novelty. All people they are well off are not desire novelty. The rise of new leaders is the result of the people's desire for novelty.

2. Love and Fear

Machiavelli believes that some people acquire influence by arousing love in the minds of others. He said, some people become popular and influential by creating love or fear in the minds of others. Machiavelli is of opinion that fear is more powerful than love. People will follow more readily the men whom they fear than the men whom they love.

3. Love of Wealth

Another powerful motive which determines human conduct is the love of wealth. Men are greedy after wealth and this greed becomes the cause of strife.

4. Ambition

Machiavelli says ambition is very forceful motive to determine human conduct. Men are not satisfied with their achievements. The more they achieve, the more they desire to achieve.

5. The Desire for Liberty

There is a strong desire in the hearts of all men to be free from the control of others. Men want to lead an independent life in their own way. They do not want to be restricted or controlled by others. In order to become independent, they make others dependent. The unavoidable result is the strife among the individuals and the state.

Views on Human Nature

Machiavelli's view of human nature is found in his masterpiece "*The Prince*." Machiavelli gives a long list of human character which determines human conduct. A brief description of some of these characters is given below:

1. Men are Selfish

Men is essentially selfish and self-centric by nature. He is greedy. According to Machiavelli, man always cares for himself and are selfish and self-centred and always run after their own interests. They do not care the interests and the welfare of others. Their behaviour is anti-social.

2. No Limit or End to Human Desires

Men have endless desires. There is no limit to the desires of men. According to him, human desires are insatiable. If one desire is satisfied, another arises in mind. Sometimes desires arise in our minds in clusters. If many desires are satisfied, many more are dissatisfied. This is satiable nature of desire creates discontent in the human mind and the struggle, competition, strife and war are the results.

3. Men are Wicked

Men are wicked. They work against the collective interests. Men are wicked and are always ready to deceive others for their selfish motives. Men are fickle in their love and friendship. They are ungrateful, fickle, deceitful, cowardly and avaricious. Thus they are ungrateful and greedy. They show love and friendship so long as their own selfish interests are satisfied. As soon as their own purpose is served, they break the bond of love and friendship.

4. Men are Jealous and Envious

According to Machiavelli, envy and jealousy also determine human contact. Men are jealous and envious of those who make more progress and try to harm them. Envy and jealousy are the cause of quarrels and disputes.

5. Men are Aggressive

Human beings are always aggressive and everyone is interested in acquiring more and more and not interested in leaving what has been once acquired. They are aggressive because they always want to promote their own selfish interests. Men want to acquire more and more and do not want to lose what they possess. They result is strife and war.

6. Men are Timid

Men are always timid and creature of his own habits. Being timid, he follows the line of least resistance. They want to follows only well establishes customs so that he is not opposed by the society. Men are simple minded and they judge the things altogether by appearances. Men are weak ignorant and vicious. Most of the men by nature are stupid and irrational. Men always want maximum liberty and want to be independent of others.

7. Men Loves Private Property

Machiavelli was of the views that by nature men love private property more than their kiths and kins. He can forget and forgive murder than patrimony.

Machiavelli's View on State

Machiavelli had seen that the state which do not try to expand, soon see their ends. He, therefore, believed that the state must expand and try to become self-sufficient. His views about state may briefly be discussed as under.

In so far as state is concerned, Machiavelli was clear that the state was the highest form of human association. The state came into being because the human beings were selfish, weak and fickle minded. The state came into being to check the selfish interests of human beings. Since the people have endless desires, the state is to check them and also to satisfy them and to the extent possible. He also said that the state was not natural to the human beings and thus, not in keeping with his social instincts. On the other hand it was an artificial creation. He disliked Aristocracy as a form of Government and favoured monarchy. He also said that the state was nothing unearthly but came into being to satisfy material interest of the people. He said that the Church had no big role to play in state affairs and expected that a good ruler in a state should take full advantage of such religious feelings of the people as humanity and submission. He very strongly believed that in order to become strong it was essential that the state must have a strong and powerful army. Such an army should consist of its own citizens and be most prepared not only to defend its national order but also to expand. The citizens must be trained for army service and there should be compulsory military training for all able bodied persons. According to his view point it was very difficult for a state to survive without a national army.

Normal and Perverted State

Machiavelli also distinguished between a normal and perverted state. According to him, in a normal state, the citizens were always faithful and law abiding. They were patriots and most prepare to defend their mother land. In a perverted state, these qualities are not to be found. He also said that a normal state always would have a tendency to expand and grow. But he also said that in a perverted state such a tendency was unavoidable. He pleaded that expansion of state was nothing new because in the past the states had expanded to become empires. In his own words, "All free Governments have two principal ends—one of which is enlarge their dominions and the other to preserve their liberties." A good, healthy and normal state must try to be self-sufficient and if it fails to expand, then it must be understood that it has some unhealthy tendencies in the body politics. According to Machiavelli in a state law givers have a big role to play. According to him, good laws and legislators could change the very foundations of the state.

Machiavelli on Forms of Government

Machiavelli, like Aristotle, has classified the governments into normal and perverted forms. In its normal form the government was monarchy, aristocracy and limited democracy or constitutional democracy while correspondingly perverted forms being tyranny, oligarchy and democracy. He, however, agreed with Polybius and Cicero that only a mixed form of government was the best or ideal attainable one. As a realist he felt that in a state there should be close relationship between economic development and political stability. According to him, the stability of a government depended on the economic development of its subjects. He liked rule of many on elected basis rather than rule of one on hereditary basis. He had definite preference for elected elements over hereditary system. He argued that the people no doubt were unable to understand intricate and complicated policy matters but their sharing of government in ordinary affairs was bound to bring stability to the state. He believed in this suppression and extirpation of nobility as their interests were against the monarchy and middle classes. He also believed that training and equipping of a citizen army was the primary need of a nation and as such for a successful ruler it was most essential to know the art of war. He pleaded for compulsory military training for all able bodied persons.

Machiavelli's View on Morality

Machiavelli is the first famous philosopher who completely separates ethics, morality from politics. He is perturbed by political corruption and moral degeneration in Italy of his times. Therefore, he suggests that only a strong ruler can control the people who are by nature wicked, stupid, irrational, selfish, aggressive and anti-social.

Machiavelli suggests that ethics and politics are two different sciences. Ethics is concerned with what is right and wrong, good and bad, moral and immoral, rational and irrational, just and unjust in the conduct of the individual. Politics is the science of the state. Machiavelli does not expect the 'prince' to follow the principles and standards of morality. The prince should strengthen his position internally and externally and to expand his territories. To achieve the end of building a strong and powerful state, the prince is free to break the rules of morality.

Machiavelli suggests doubt standard of morality—one for the individuals and the other is for the ruler. It goes to the credit of Machiavelli that he completely divorced religion and morality from politics and separated them completely from each other. In fact, he tried to subordinate religion to the state but at the same time agreed that morality had its own limited place in society which must be preserved and exploited. He also differentiated between public and private morality and assigned the former a preferential place and position over the latter.

According to Machiavelli, the ruler creates law. It also creates morality, because all moral obligations must in the long run have the sanction of law. The ruler is, therefore, above law and morality. The ruler has to face the problems of internal and external security of the state. We should not judge the ruler's actions on the basis of individual standards of morality. It will bring ruin and destruction to the state if we apply strict standards of individual morality to the ruler. It is always wrong for the individual to break the moral law. It is essential and good for the prince to tell lies and break the promises in the interest of the state.

Machiavelli says that the prince has to deal with human beings who are selfish, wicked, aggressive and anti-social. Therefore, he should not be bound by any strict moral law. The prince should break treaties and promises and use force and evidence whenever it is useful for the strength of the state and welfare of the people. The prince must appear all sincerity, all uprightness, all humanity, all religion, but must have his mind. So disciplined that when it is necessary to save the state, he can act regardless of them.

Machiavelli subordinates moral judgements to political considerations. He suggests that the ruler should violate all moral principles when circumstances require. The highest consideration is the state, not morality. Machiavelli does not deny morality. He only gives it a secondary place to political considerations. The prime consideration is the state. The prime consideration is the welfare of the people. Morality is only a secondary consideration.

According to Machiavelli a prince who is a violator of the principles of morality and is cruel for the purpose of keeping his subjects united and faithful is better than one who follows moral principles and is tender and creates disorders by his tenderness.

Machiavelli's View on Religion

Machiavelli is famous for separating religion from politics. He subordinated the Church to the state and freed politics from the doctrines of the divine law. According to him, the Church was one of the major causes of degeneration and downfall of Italy. The state was detached by him from the Church. He made the state as an organization of force. The state according to him existed only for earthly ends.

Machiavelli does not believe in the supernatural end for man. Human am is earthly, not heavenly. Earthly end is not only material well being. It is something higher than this. Machiavelli recognises the values of greatness, power and fame. According to Machiavelli, the individual is capable of winning fame which will bring immorality to him.

The central point in Machiavelli's philosophy of separating religion from politics is that the primary consideration is the safety of the state. The wise statesmen should use religious sentiments of the people to achieve reforms which otherwise would be beyond their power.

Machiavelli is by temperament a hero worshipper. He has every word of praise for a strong and powerful man Machiavelli was pessimistic in one sense regarding the ordinary man, but optimistic regarding the exceptional man. He said the religious teachings and principles must be subordinated to the end of attaining power. There is nothing higher than power. Religion is subordinate to power. According to Machiavelli the divine law has no function to perform is human life because there is no supernatural end for men. Machiavelli does not believed like St. Thomas Aquinas that men are government by two laws, the human law and the Divine law. According to St. Thomas Acquinas, the ruler is the custodian of human law and the church is the custodian of Divine law. St. Thomas Aquinas also believes that the Church is superior to the state. According to Machiavelli, the Church is not superior to the state. It is not even independent. It is definitely subordinate to the state.

Machiavelli is a realist. He believes in practical politics. His political philosophy is guided by realities, facts, and actual and not by ideas. He is concerned with the actual working of and not by ideas. He is concerned with the actual working of the government, and not with the ideal state. Machiavelli thinks that religion can prove useful if it is subordinate to the state and the ruler wins the co-operation and obedience of the people by appealing to their religious sentiments. Religion according to Machiavelli cannot be given a superior position to that of the state. It must function within the state position to that of the state. It must function within the state and must serve the end of the ruler. He is against the Christian virtues of mercy, tenderness, gentleness etc. and glorifies virtues like bravery and courage.

Machiavelli's Suggestion to the Prince Regarding Retention of Power

As has already been pointed out, Machiavelli was no political philosopher and was concerned mainly with the art of government. He, therefore, only made casual references to the theory of state and dealt at length with the principles which the prince should observe to maintain himself in power. Some of the suggestions offered by Machiavelli to the Prince are as follows:

1. The prince should crush all opposition to his authority with an iron hand and should not hesitate to make use of ruthless force. He should enforce his will without bothering about the privations of his subjects.
2. As force is an expensive and inefficient method of attaining the objective, Machiavelli says that a shrewd ruler should also use the methods of propaganda and religion to lull the people into submission. He holds that a tactful use of these devices can obviate the need of force. He wants the rulers to be both fox and a lion.
3. The prince should try to take quick firm decisions, because hesitation can prove very harmful. He would like the prince to act promptly and make mistakes rather than lose initiative through delay and uncertainty.
4. A good prince should try to maintain peace and plenty in the country so that the people can lead a comfortable and contended life.
5. The prince should maintain a well-trained regular national army of his own citizens and should not depend on mercenary soldiers, because the national army alone can defend the state and make it powerful.

6. The prince should be a good soldier and commander. He should possess thorough knowledge of the war strategy and maintain best possible arms and equipments. He must also keep the morale of his forces high.
7. The prince must try to maintain his popularity with the people and earn their love and affection.
8. The prince should try to cultivate public spirit and patriotism among his citizens through education, religion and propaganda.
9. The prince must maintain utmost secrecy in the conduct of the state's affairs.
10. It was not essential for the prince to be always honest. If the interests of the state so demand he should not mind resort to fraud and other dishonest means. The prince should not mind even violating his promises for the good of the state.
11. The prince should not under any circumstances touch the property and women of his subjects, because people are very touchy about these things.
12. The prince should be a good showman and project himself as the embodiment of qualities like generosity, kind-heartedness chivalry, mercy, sincerity, humanity, bravery, and religiousness.
13. The prince must avoid the company of flatters because it has a debasing effect on his sense of judgement.
14. The prince should not have permanent friends or enemies.
15. The prince should not listen to every known or unknown person because this could undermine his respect with his subjects. He should mix up only with a handful of counsellors, who have proved their sincerity and collect all necessary information from them.

In addition to the above suggestions, Machiavelli made numerous other suggestions to his prince, but it is not possible to reproduce all of these here. We get a fairy good idea about the shrewd insight of Machiavelli from these tips to the prince. In fact some of the principles laid down by Machiavelli for his prince hold good even today.

Evaluation

Machiavelli was not systematic philosopher and he mainly deals with the preservation of the state in face of disruptive forces and tendencies but to say that Machiavelli was not a philosopher at all as Sabine says is to go a long way. Machiavelli was realist thinker, who dealt with actual problems and enunciated a modern doctrine of state. To sum up we can say he was the first, if not the noblest of the great pragmatist though he was more clearly sighted than a far-sighted thinker. In spite of all this according to Dunning, "He was the first modern Political Philosopher." He based his ideas on realistic outlook.

Machiavelli is the first political thinker who separated politics from morality. He pleaded for strong, united national state based on patriotism. He supported that aim of gaining and preserving power ought to be achieved by hook or crook or by fair and foul means as end justified he means. As such he has been considered as a great realist and shrewd thinkers, who gave pragmatic ideas without caring for morals.

Unit-IV
Contractual Political Thought

THE CONTRACTUALISTS

THOMAS HOBBES (1588-1679)

Thomas Hobbes of Malmesbury (5 April, 1588–4 December, 1679), in some older texts Thomas Hobbes of Malmsbury, was an English philosopher, best known today for his work on political philosophy. His 1651 book *Leviathan* established the foundation for most of the Western political philosophy from the perspective of social contract theory.

Hobbes was a champion of absolutism for the sovereign but he also developed some of the fundamentals of European liberal thought: the right of the individual; the natural equality of all men; the artificial character of the political order (which led to the later distinction between civil society and the state); the view that all legitimate political power must be "representative" and based on the consent of the people; and a liberal interpretation of law which leaves people free to do whatever the law does not explicitly forbid.

He was one of the founders of modern political philosophy. His understanding of humans as being matter and motion, obeying the same physical laws as other matter and motion, remains influential; and his account of human nature as self-interested cooperation, and of political communities as being based upon a "social contract" remains one of the major topics of political philosophy.

In addition to political philosophy, Hobbes also contributed to a diverse array of other fields, including history, geometry, the physics of gases, theology, ethics, and general philosophy.

Early Life and Education

Thomas Hobbes was born at Westport, now part of Malmesbury in Wiltshire, England, on 5 April, 1588. Born prematurely when his mother heard of the coming invasion of the Spanish Armada, Hobbes later reported that "my mother gave birth to twins: myself and fear." His childhood is almost a complete blank, and his mother's name is unknown. His father, also named Thomas, was the vicar of Charlton and Westport. Thomas Sr. abandoned his three children to the care of an older brother, Thomas junior's uncle Francis, when he was forced to flee to London after being involved in a fight with a clergyman outside his own church. Hobbes was educated at Westport church from the age of four, passed to the Malmesbury school and then to a private school kept by a young man named Robert Latimer, a graduate of the University of Oxford. Hobbes was a good pupil, and around 1603 he went up to Magdalen Hall, which is most closely related to Hertford College, Oxford. The principal John Wilkinson was a Puritan, and he had some influence on Hobbes.

At university, Hobbes appears to have followed his own curriculum; he was "little attracted by the scholastic learning." He did not complete his B.A. degree until 1608, but he was recommended by Sir James Hussey, his master at Magdalen, as tutor to William, the son of William Cavendish, Baron of Hardwick (and later Earl of Devonshire), and began a lifelong connection with that family.

Hobbes became a companion to the younger William and they both took part in a grand tour in 1610. Hobbes was exposed to European scientific and critical methods during the tour in contrast to the scholastic philosophy which he had learned in Oxford. His scholarly efforts at the time were aimed at a careful study of classic Greek and Latin authors, the outcome of which was, in 1628, his great translation of Thucydides' History of the Peloponnesian War, the first translation of that work into English from a Greek manuscript. It has been argued that three of the discourses in the 1620 publication known as *Horea Subsecivae: Observations and Discourses*, also represent the work of Hobbes from this period.

Although, he associated with literary figures like Ben Jonson and thinkers such as Francis Bacon, he did not extend his efforts into philosophy until after 1629. His employer Cavendish, then the Earl of Devonshire, died of the plague in June 1628. The widowed countess dismissed Hobbes but he soon found work, again as a tutor, this time to Gervase Clifton, the son of Sir Gervase Clifton, 1st Baronet. This task, chiefly spent in Paris, ended in 1631 when he again found work with the Cavendish family, tutoring the son of his previous pupil. Over the next seven years as well as tutoring he expanded his own knowledge of philosophy, awakening in him curiosity over key philosophic debates. He visited Florence in 1636 and later was a regular debater in philosophic groups in Paris, held together by Marin Mersenne. From 1637 he considered himself a philosopher and scholar.

Leviathan

In *Leviathan,* Hobbes set out his doctrine of the foundation of states and legitimate governments—originating social contract theory. Leviathan was written during the English Civil War; much of the book is occupied with demonstrating the necessity of a strong central authority to avoid the evil of discord and civil war.

Beginning from a mechanistic understanding of human beings and the passions, Hobbes postulates what life would be like without government, a condition which he calls the state of nature. In that state, each person would have a right, or licence, to everything in the world. This, Hobbes argues, would lead to a "war of all against all" (*bellum omnium contra omnes*). The description contains what has been called one of the best known passages in English philosophy, which describes the natural state mankind would be in, were it not for political community: and such a state, people fear death, and lack both the things necessary to commodious living, and the hope of being able to toil to obtain them. So in order to avoid it people accede to a social contract and establish a civil society. According to Hobbes, society is a population beneath a sovereign authority, to whom all individuals in that society cede some rights for the sake of protection. Any abuses of power by this authority are to be accepted as the price of peace. There is no doctrine of separation of powers in Hobbes' discussion. According to Hobbes, the sovereign must control civil, military, judicial, and ecclesiastical powers.

Later Life

Hobbes published, in 1658, the final section of his philosophical system, completing the scheme he had planned more than twenty years before. De Homine consisted for the most part of an elaborate theory of vision. The remainder of the treatise dealt cursorily with some of the topics more fully treated in the Human Nature and the Leviathan. In addition to publishing some controversial writings on mathematics and physics, Hobbes also continued to produce philosophical works. From the time of the Restoration he acquired a new prominence; "Hobbism" became a byword for all that respectable society ought to denounce. The young king, Hobbes's former pupil, now Charles II, remembered Hobbes and called him to the court to grant him a pension of £100.

The king was important in protecting Hobbes when, in 1666, the House of Commons introduced a Bill against atheism and profaneness. That same year, on 17 October, 1666, it was ordered that the committee to which the Bill was referred "should be empowered to receive information touching such books as tend to atheism, blasphemy and profaneness, in particular the book of Mr. Hobbes called the *Leviathan*." Hobbes was terrified at the prospect of being labelled a heretic, and proceeded to burn some of his compromising papers. At the same time, he examined the actual state of the law of heresy. The results of his investigation were first announced in three short Dialogues added as an Appendix to his Latin translation of Leviathan, published at Amsterdam in 1668. In this appendix, Hobbes aimed to show that, since the High Court of Commission had been put down, there remained no court of heresy at all to which he was amenable, and that nothing could be heresy except opposing the Nicene Creed, which, he maintained, Leviathan did not do.

The only consequence that came of the bill was that Hobbes could never thereafter publish anything in England on subjects relating to human conduct. The 1668 edition of his works was printed in Amsterdam because he could not obtain the censor's licence for its publication in England. Other writings were not made public until after his death, including *Behemoth*: the History of the Causes of the Civil Wars of England and of the Counsels and Artifices by which they were carried on from the year 1640 to the year 1662. For some time, Hobbes was not even allowed to respond, whatever his enemies tried. Despite this, his reputation abroad was formidable and noble or learned foreigners who came to England never forgot to pay their respects to the old philosopher.

His final works were a curious mixture: an autobiography in Latin verse in 1672, and a translation of four books of the Odyssey into "rugged" English rhymes that in 1673 led to a complete translation of both *Iliad* and *Odyssey* in 1675.

In October 1679, Hobbes suffered a bladder disorder, which was followed by a paralytic stroke from which he died on 4 December, 1679. He is said to have uttered the last words "A great leap in the dark" in his final moments of life. He was interred within St. John the Baptist Church in Ault Hucknall in Derbyshire, England.

Hobbes' Writings

Hobbes was great writer and great political philosopher. He spent many years of his life in France. He had a chance of coming in content with great writers and philosopher of his times. He came in contact, with Francis Bacon. He also met the great philosopher Descartes.

Thomas Hobbes wrote the following books:

1. The Leviathan
2. De Cive
3. De-Corpore

4. De Homine
5. Two Essays: Human Nature and DE Corpore Politics
6. Thucydides
7. Elements of Law

The Leviathan is Hobbes' greatest book. It has made him immortal. This famous book was written when Hobbes was in exile in France. The *Leviathan* has 4 parts—1 of men, 2 of commonwealth, 3 of Christian Commonwealth, and 4 of the kingdom of darkness.

Hobbes View about Human Nature

Hobbes, like Machiavelli was concerned with the secure origins of human conduct, for he did not theorise about proper behaviour from an understanding of the idea of God, or from a revelation of Devine commands, contrary to Aristotle and the medieval thinkers, who saw human nature as innately social. Hobbes viewed human beings as isolated, egoistic, self-interested and seeking society as a means to their ends. Individuals were creatures of desire, seeking pleasure and avoiding pain.

Hobbes maintained that men by birth were equal and intelligent. It was the desire for having one and the same thing which made them quarrel with each other. Competition, glory and difference make people brute and quarrelsome. It was an uncontrolled society. Hobbes' conception of human nature was essentially based on two basic factors.

(a) Men are Equal

In his '*Laviathan*' Hobbes said nature has made men so equal with the faculties of body and mind, as that though there be found one man sometimes manifestly stronger in body, or of the quicker mind than the other; yet when all is reckoned together, the difference between man and man is not so considerable, as that one man thereupon can claim o himself any benefit to which another may not pretend.

(b) Man Fight with Each Other

Unlike Machiavelli, Hobbes believed that men were not an idle spectator in political drama. He was always ready to struggle and achieve something novel, gentle and higher.

This desire makes men fight with each other. It makes man nasty and brutish while in the state of nature. It makes him stand against the valid desires of others to satisfy his own desires. Out of this view of man and man's relation with each other Hobbes construct his political philosophy.

By equality, Hobbes meant equal ability and the equal hope of attaining the ends individuals desired for. The physically weak may achieve by cunning what the strong could accomplish through force Hobbes accepted differences in physical and natural endowments.

Hobbes also saw human beings as active creatures with a 'will'. Since they were creatures endowed with both reasons and passions (reason being passive while passion active). So difference in passions created differences in wits with a desire to excel others. Since individuals were equal and active, those who succeed would have more enemies and competitors and face maximum danger. A permanent rivalry existed between human beings for honour, riches and authority, with life as, nothing but potential warfare, a war of everyone against the other.

Hobbes View about State of Nature

Hobbes views on the state of nature, a period of human history preceding the establishment of the civil state, are an extension of his view of human nature. The pre-society of pre-state is thus, a state of conflict and of war of all against all not merely actual fight, but the anticipation of war, its fears and apprehension, for war s the absence of assurance of peace. There is no peace in the state of nature. There is positive law to govern them. This state is called a negative state. Men are constantly troubled by continuous fear and danger of violent death. It was a state of every man against every other man. There was no property, no justice, no mine and no light and no wrong. Hobbes gives a negative, gloomy and desperate description of state of nature.

There is no peace, no industry and no culture in the state of nature. There is no industry. Hobbes says there were no laws in the state of nature. Men cannot know what is right and what is wrong. Hence, there was no law; there was no question of justice and injustice, right or wrong. In such a state of war, nothing was unjust. The ideas of right and wrong, justice and injustice have no place in the state of nature. Men distrusts not only his fellow-citizens, but even his servants, wife and children. Hobbes, therefore, says that the validity of the argument of the state of nature is not affected by the lack of historical argument or evidence. The state of nature as depicted by Hobbes has no existence in history. Hobbes gives only an imaginary and hypothetical picture of the kind of life which men lead if there is no state. History does not give any example of the type of life which Hobbes describes.

Each man has the fear of the other. Men live in constant fear of others. Hobbes asserts that in the state of nature men live in a condition of perpetual war. Each man is the enemy of every other man. The hand of each is against all. Each man lives in the condition of cut-throat competition. There is endless war in the state of nature. According to Hobbes, there is no security of life in the state of nature because all men are equal in physical and mental strength and there is no common power to control them. There is always a danger of violent death. Life of man in the state of nature is the life of man is "solidary, poor, brutish, nasty and short." There is no progress in Arts, Literature and Science. Hobbes says, men live without security. All signs of trade, industry, culture and civilization are totally non-existent in the state of nature.

Men in the state of nature can be controlled only by the use of force. Hobbes comes to the conclusion that selfish, brutish, aggressive and competitive men living in the state of nature are actuated by instincts and passions. The instinct of self-preservation is the main instinct in them. The men are not guided by reason. Men in the state of nature can be controlled only by the use of force.

Hobbes' View on Natural Laws and Natural Rights

Hobbes has given his idea about most of the important political problems like the liberty of the individuals and their rights etc. In all walks of life he has tried to tighten the grip of the sovereign over his subjects. He strongly pleaded that the church was a department of state.

Hobbes was of the view that in the state of nature and even prior to that there were certain rights which were very dear and precious to man. He struggled and fought for their preservance and had a strong desire to retain the. By liberty Hobbes means the absence of external impediments. Natural law on the other hand implies primarily restriction rather than liberty. It prescribes a rule based on reason. Hobbes said that natural rights were at a stake when people thought of joining the civil state and subjected himself to the authority of sovereign in order to retain those very rights. For their sake he gave up all his rights accept those of life and property. He could give up everything but not these rights. He also reserved with himself the right to disobey the sovereign if its rights were being snatched. Such rights which he kept with himself even after joining the state of nature are called natural rights.

Hobbes, however, clearly distinguished between natural rights and natural laws. He was of the view that the natural rights of men were based on their selfish views and if strictly and closely followed, these were the basis of war. On the other hand natural laws would positively lead to peace and avoid war. With natural rights men could struggle to preserve what they had with them; whereas on the basis of natural laws men gave up some of their rights in order to have sure realisation of rights of all. The natural laws according to Hobbes are 'immutable and eternal.'

In addition to these laws, other laws are based on the similar ideas of cultivating the spirit of freedom and avoiding of any and every spirit of revenge. He has based his laws not on the basis of morality but on the basis of utility. But, he did not believe that utility was the only consideration for arriving at conclusions. On the other hand, he felt that if left alone that would give an opportunity to a clever person to use these laws for their personal ends. He thus pleaded for a common coercive power to use these laws for their common ends.

He believed that the laws of nature by their very character were eternal and necessary for the fullest desire and satisfaction of mankind. He also distinguished between the 'law proper' and the 'natural law'. To him the former was the will expressed by a person or assembly of persons who had command over others and had a right to get them obeyed but the later were those laws by which the individuals mutually agreed to act in a manner which was conducive to peace and goodwill of the society as a whole.

Hobbes' View on Social Contract

After having deduced the principles of human nature, natural law and natural rights, Hobbes proceeds to develop the theory of social contract. Hobbes, theory of social contract is fundamentally different from the earlier contracts. The earlier contracts were governmental contracts. They were agreements between the ruler and the people. Hobbes contract is a social contract, a contract between the people themselves. It is a contract by which the state is established.

Hobbes tells that there are two ways by which a common wealth may come into existence. First, by institution. Main of their own impulse unites. Second, by acquisition. When some superior threatens them with destruction, the fear of being destroyed induces natural men to unite and seek peace. Thus, it is not the desire for power and glory that induces man to enter into a contract. It is the desire for securing the minimum life, if possible the means of commodious existence. Hobbes is a rationalist and believes that reason is an integral part of man. Once man realises that fear of death is primary due to brutal competition, resulting n perpetual war of all against all, reasons shows the way out to accept the principle of not doing that to anther which is unreasonable. So man enters into a contract not to do one another what he would not wish to have done to himself. So, social impulse was not the 1st cause of the state. On the other hand, self-preservation brought the state into existence.

Hobbes writes a common wealth is said to be constituted when a multitude of men agreed and covenanted everyone with everyone, that this man or the assembly of men would be the sovereign. Each individual would say in effect, "I authorise and give up my right of governing myself to this man or to this assembly of man on this condition that thou give up thy right to him and authorise all his actions in like manner." So, men enter into a contract, not to do to one another what they would not wish to have done to themselves. This contract is not thought of as a definite historical event. It is an explanatory myth use to explain why men should submit to the authority of the state. The purpose of submission is self-preservation from the universal war resulting from our love of liberty.

The parties to the contract are the individual natural men and not the people nor groups of individuals. The sovereign is not a party to the contract but its creation. The subject is the creator of the sovereign. The state thus conceived is a real unity, a single personality, taking the place of many. The individual has resigned his natural rights. The state has assumed them. Such is the origin and nature of that great Leviathan or that Mortal God to which we owe our peace and defence.

Thus, we find that Hobbes' Social Contract is characterised by the following features:

First, the parties to the contract are individuals (the natural men), not groups of any sort. The Sovereign is not a party to the contract but rather the product of the contract.

Secondly, the Commonwealth or State is based on reason and not on fear. People render obedience to the authority of the state because of the rational apprehension that the end of self-preservation is better served within the state.

Thirdly, the Sovereign is not a party to the contract and hence cannot be guilty of violating the contract. Justice lies in adherence to the contract and sovereign cannot be unjust. Though the sovereign is the creature of the contract, he is above it.

Fourthly, the contract once concluded by the individuals cannot be revoked because once the individuals submit their wills to will of the sovereign they have no right to withdraw their consent without the permission of the sovereign.

Fifthly, the minority has no right to object to the choice of the majority in the selection of the sovereignty. The minority by becoming a part of the commonwealth tacitly accepts the will of the majority does not accept the authority of the Commonwealth, it remains outside it and can be justly destroyed by it.

Sixthly, as the contract was concluded primarily for the protection of individual's life, it implies that the individual surrendered all his rights, except the right to live, to the sovereign. Thus, the sovereign can encroach on all the rights of the individual, except the right to live.

Seventhly, the people are bound to submit to the will of the state or the ruler and enjoy no right against the sovereign. This is why it has been said that instead of being the charter of liberty, it is a bond of slavery for the people. However, Hobbes does concede to the people to withhold obedience to the sovereign under some special circumstances.

Thus, he permits the individual to disobey the sovereign if the latter commands him "to kill, wound or maim him", or not to resist those that assault him or to abstain from the use of food, air, medicine or any other thing without which he cannot live. In short, Hobbes permits disobedience to a command which frustrates the end of self-preservation for which the sovereign authority was created.

Different Stages of Social Contract

We can explain the different stages in Hobbes' argument about the social contract by means of the following chart:

1. Selfish, self-seeking, brutish, anti-social, aggressive and competitive men living in the state of nature which is a state of ceaseless war. There is the ganger of violent death. Each individual has the right of nature to do what he likes to preserve his life.
2. Laws of nature or dictates of reason tell men to strive for peace and surrender their rights for the protection of their life.
3. Reason is too weak to control passions. Control of reason is not dependable.
4. Need of a strong sovereign authority with absolute power to enforce laws of nature will force.
5. Sovereign is the result of the social contract among the people themselves.

Criticisms

Hobbes' theory of social contract occupies a very important place in the history of political philosophy. His theory of social contract, however, is full of defects and shortcomings and has been subjected to a very severe criticism.

We may note the following points of criticism against Hobbes' theory of social contract:

1. Hobbes takes a very poor view of human nature.
2. His description of the state of nature is incredible and unhistorical.
3. Hobbes' argument is consistent. It is impossible to believe that selfish and brutish men become so civilised and rational that they create a civil society.
4. Hobbes bases his theory on fear and attaches too much importance to force.
5. Hobbes does not explain why and how the contract can be binding on the coming generations.
6. Hobbes makes his sovereign unlimited and absolute.
7. One party contract is impossible.

Hobbes View on Sovereignty

Hobbes has not only expounded his political philosophy about the social contracts but has also given his ideas about many other important political problems like he liberty of the individuals and their rights etc. In all walks of life he has tried to tighten the grip of sovereign over his subjects. He strongly pleaded that church was a department of the state. He was, however, more individualist than Plato who absolutely subjected his citizens to the sovereign.

Rights of nature allow men to do what they like to preserve their life. Laws of nature or dictates of reason restrict them from doing what may take away their life. Laws of nature tell them to put an end to insecure state of nature and to choose a sovereign by a contract among themselves. Reason is, however, too weak to make men follow the laws of nature. Men's passions can be controlled by force alone. Therefore, by contract, men surrender all their rights to the sovereign for the protection of their lives. The contract is only among the people and the sovereign is not a party to it. The people submit to the sovereign unconditionally. They can neither place limitations upon his authority, nor can they remove him.

As noted above the sovereign was created as a result of the contract and enjoys all the powers which were surrendered by the people at the time of concluding the contract. As Hobbes puts it "By this authority, given to him by every particular man in the commonwealth, he has the use of so much power and strength conferred on him, that any error thereof, he is enabled to form wills of them all, to peace at home and mutual aid against their enemies abroad. And in him consists the essence of commonwealth and he shall think expedient, for the peace and common defence." In simple language it means that the sovereign enjoys the power to determine on behalf of the entire community as to what should be done to maintain peace and order and promote their welfare. He had right to make laws which are binding on all the subjects.

Characteristics of Sovereign

According to Hobbes, the person to whom rights were surrendered was the sovereign: a great Leviathan before whom all were to bow. He was the preserver of peace, hope for prosperity, development and security. The sovereign of Hobbes has the following salient features:

1. Above Law

Sovereign shall not be party to the contract and remain above all laws.

2. Custodian of Rights

He shall accordingly retain all the rights which he used to enjoy in the state of nature. Since all have surrendered their rights willingly to the sovereign, the sovereign was the custodian of their rights. None should challenge sovereign on the ground of infringing his rights.

3. Beyond Constitutional Check

The sovereign according to Hobbes had no constitutional checks.

4. Soul Interpreter of Law

He was the soul interpreter of law and his actions could not be pre-judicial to social interest.

5. Beyond Break of Truth

He could not be charged with the break of contract because he was not a party to the contract.

6. Symbol of National Unity

He was the symbol of national unity and as such any challenge to his authority is irrational.

7. Final Authority to the Contracts

No contract can be quoted against the sovereign. He was the final authority to approve all contracts. There could be no contract against him. Hobbes maintained that the obedient to authority was universal. The minority should not disobey the commands of a sovereign on the grounds that it was not party to the contract.

8. Sovereignty

Hobbes could not reconcile himself to the idea of limited sovereignty. Sovereignty must be indivisible and inalienable. The right of choosing his own ministers and magistrates was valid in the hands of the absolute and inalienable sovereign. He was, however, in the way bound by the advice of his ministers or magistrates.

9. Ultimate Authority

The sovereign was the ultimate authority for making war and peace with other nations and commonwealth. That is to say of judging when it is for the public good and how great forces are to be assembled; armed and paid for that end; and to levy money upon the subjects, to defray the expenses thereof.

10. Absolute Dictator

Hobbes has thus created his absolute indivisible and inalienable sovereign. His sovereign was the dictator. He was one of the most undemocratic persons. After having been elected in a most democratic way he tried to stress that his subjects, ministers and magistrates might shine ir his absence but they cannot find a place in his presence.

Rights and Duties of the Sovereign

Hobbes gives a description of the rights and duties of the sovereign. A brief account of some of the rights and duties of the sovereign as mentioned by Hobbes is given below:

1. The Sovereign is the Sole Law-making Authority

According to Hobbes, the sovereign is the sole law-making authority. He is the source of all positive law. The subjects cannot disobey the law of sovereign. Law is the command of the sovereign. The sovereignty alone has the power to enforce law. It is the duty of the sovereign that he should make equitable and necessary laws. The sovereign has a right and duty to interpret law.

2. The Sovereign is not Bound by his Own Laws

According to Hobbes, the sovereign is not bound by the laws of his own making. There is no law which the sovereign cannot make. There is no law which the sovereign cannot repeal.

3. The Sovereign is not Bound by Laws of Nature or Laws of God

According to Hobbes, the sovereign is not found by Laws of Nature or Laws of God. Hobbes says clearly that the people have no right to disobey the sovereign even in the name of the Law of God.

4. The Sovereign is the Judge of the Means of Peace and Defence

It is the right and duty of the sovereign to protect the society from civil dissolution and to follow a policy suited for the protection of peace and security. He has the right to judge what opinion and doctrines are averse to peace. He has also the right to judge what opinions and doctrines are conducive to peace.

5. The Sovereign has the Right to Declare War and Make Peace

According to Hobbes, the sovereign has the right to declare war and make peace, with other nations and commonwealths. He can judge when it is in the interest of public good to declare war.

6. Right to Judicature

According to Hobbes, the sovereign has the right to judicature. He is the highest judicial officer to decide disputes among the individuals. This right is essential for protection of the individuals against injuries by one another.

7. Right to choose Counsellors, Ministers, Magistrates and Officers

According to Hobbes, the sovereign has the right to choose Counsellors, Ministers Magistrates, and Officers. It is, therefore, his right to choose his Counsellors, Magistrates, Ministers and Officers in peace and war.

8. The Sovereign has Right to Make Rules about Property

According to Hobbes, the sovereign has right, to make rules about property. The sovereign makes rules to determine what goods belong to the different individuals. Before the sovereign was chosen as a result of the contract, all men had right to all things.

Hobbes View on Liberty

In *Leviathan*, Hobbes creates a conception of liberty that is persuasive and holds true so far as it concerns both rational and irrational beings existing in the state of nature. However, once Hobbes condemns the state of nature to being a state of undesirable existence and moves his argument towards establishing peace under an absolute sovereign, he loses the persuasiveness of his argument for liberty. I find myself in disagreement with the concept that liberty must be surrendered to an absolute sovereign, and he will choose which liberties to return. Man is, as John Locke argues in the Second Treatise of Government, in a "state of perfect freedom without asking leave or depending upon the will of any other man."

In Hobbes' view of the state of nature, mankind exists in a state of uninhibited liberty, dictated only by the law of nature. It is in this state that Hobbes makes his most persuasive argument for his conception of liberty, likening it to the total absence of opposition other than "the necessity of doing that which God will." Liberty takes on a philosophical sense of being free will within the state of nature, due to its consistency with fear and necessity, which are some of the driving factors of Hobbes' theory. Hobbes states "when a man throweth his goods into the sea for fear the ship should sink, he doth it nevertheless very willingly, and may refuse to do it if he will," demonstrating that although fear motivates the man to a certain action, it still allows him the liberty of deciding whether he will act in the manner dictated or go against it.

The argument put forth by Hobbes for the liberty existing in the state of nature is very persuasive because it fits with the views of even his critics, such as John Locke. Locke, however, continues his same conceptions of liberty throughout the establishment of a sovereign, or government, while Hobbes believes that liberties must be surrendered to a sovereign in order to escape the state of nature. In the transition from the state of nature to the creation of a sovereign, the people must "consider what rights we pass away, when we make a commonwealth, what liberty we deny ourselves by owning all the actions of the man or assembly we make our sovereign." While Locke agrees that "the liberty of man is to be under no other legislative power, but that established, by consent, in the commonwealth," he differs in the idea that we must give up our liberties to the legislative power, because people cannot surrender what they do not own in the first place.

Hobbes derives his argument for the surrendering of our liberties from the idea that mankind must find an escape from the state of nature and the only possible way of accomplishing this is through the establishment of a sovereign. Hobbes conceives this sovereign in relation to liberty as "an artificial man," made "for the attaining of peace and the conservation of themselves" by people wishing to leave the state of nature. Because the people have entered into a contract with the sovereign, and have either established him as a representative by appointment or by being conquered, the sovereign, therefore, fully represents the will of the people.

Because the sovereign's will is seen to be the will of the people, "every subject is author of every act the sovereign doth." This means that, in essence, although a person has surrendered their liberties to the sovereign, all of their liberties remain intact. Since Hobbes defines liberty as "the absence of external impediments of motion", a person's liberty is not truly impeded by the establishment of a sovereign. Firstly, because said person had the liberty in the first place to establish the sovereign and enter into a contract with him/her, and secondly, because with the will of the sovereign being the will of the people, the people are not "hindered to do what [they have] a will to do." This second point is due to the fact that the people are the authors of the sovereign's actions, so the liberties granted to the people by the sovereign are the liberties that they have authored themselves to desire, and there is no necessity for any greater degree of liberty than that which is in the will of themselves and their sovereign.

While this argument follows a logical path in its construction, it has a clear flaw in assuming that the will of the sovereign is the will of the people in any form of government. While Hobbes believes that "whether a commonwealth be monarchical or popular, the freedom is still the same," (Hobbes, XXI 8) the reality of the matter is that in Hobbes' system, the liberties of the individual are ignored because the individual has become a part of the commonwealth which acts on the part of all individuals combined. The consequence of this fact is that people within the commonwealth may desire to exercise their liberties to different ends, but because they have surrendered them to the sovereign, they are all seen as only wanting the liberty to meet the end that the sovereign, and therefore, the body of the commonwealth, desires to meet.

In ignoring individual liberties, Hobbes grants the power to the sovereign to take the lives of his subjects. Although, like Locke, Hobbes believes that men are entitled to the preservation of their own lives, Hobbes does not exclude the sovereign the right to "demand or take anything by pretence of his power" because "there Leith in that case no action of law, for all that is done by him in virtue of his power, is done by the authority of every subject." While in Hobbes' theory the people have the right to defend their lives whether they are guilty or innocent of what they are being accused of, if the sovereign kills them, there has been no injustice committed because "nothing the sovereign representative can do to a subject, on what pretence so ever, can properly be called injustice."

This flaw in Hobbes' argument creates a clear distinction between the liberties held while existing in the state of nature and those held while under the rule of an absolute sovereign. One of the greatest critics of this shift, John Locke, found no truth in Hobbes' conception of liberty because of the idea that liberties must be surrendered in order to escape the state of nature. Locke argues that "no man can, by agreement, pass over to another which he hath not in himself, a power over his own life." This directly conflicts with Hobbes' views, because, although Hobbes believes that we do not have power over our own lives as well, he does believe that the power over our lives can be, in a sense, surrendered to the sovereign. Locke's argument hinges on the idea that we cannot make a contract which passes over to another party something that we have no authority over in the first place.

By Locke's very conception of liberty, the purpose of a government, or sovereign, is only to "have a standing rule to live by .and not to be subject to the inconstant, uncertain, unknown, arbitrary will of another man." This is because Locke realizes that "absolute monarchs are but men" and, as such, can never be truly representative of the will of the people. Thus, there can be no liberty found in surrendering individual liberties to a sovereign. An absolute sovereign simply strips the people of their liberties, and imposes his will on the people, making them accept the sovereign's will as their own, and the liberties he grants them as the only ones they need. Locke questions,

> "How much better is it than the state of nature, where one man, commanding a multitude, has the liberty to be judge in his own case, and may do to all his subjects whatever he pleases, without the least liberty to anyone to question or control those who execute his pleasure?"

This exemplifies the contradiction in Hobbes' theory, noting that there can be no liberty existing under a sovereign if the sovereign himself cannot be held accountable by the liberties of the people.

Although Hobbes initially establishes a persuasive argument for the conception of liberty while existing in the state of nature, he falters in his transference to the liberties held while under the rule of an absolute sovereign. Hobbes attempts to make a claim that although liberties must surrendered, they still exist for the sovereign to reinstate, and those reinstated are the only ones necessary for the people. While this claim follows a logical development process, the ideas that it is based upon are not accurate enough for the claim to be persuasive. That is why Locke successfully countered that there can be no existence of liberties under the rule of an absolute monarchy. Therefore, Hobbes' conception of liberty is accurate only while man exists in the state of nature, and once the state of nature is left behind, Hobbes' argument must be abandoned for a more accurate assessment of the liberties that mankind is entitled to, which is that of John Locke.

Contribution of Hobbes as the Father of Modern Political Philosophy

Thomas Hobbes was one of those political philosophers who, by their writings and preaching, played a great role in a social and political life of the people of their times. He created a sense of great dissatisfaction in many of the then existing institutions. He stood for secularism. The church could not reconcile itself to the philosophy of Hobbes, which so elevated the state and sovereign that the church became merely a department of the state. The unqualified low position assigned to the church was a source of constant criticism by church fathers. Similarly, the believers of Divine Rights of kings could not support Hobbes in the theory of social contract. On the same lines the followers of Parliamentary system of Government could not adjust themselves to the ideas of Hobbes which virtually left very little ground for the parliament and much within the preview of the monarch. His philosophy was not followed till the times of Bentham and Austin. But, today the significance of his philosophy has been fully realised. The following points show the importance of Hobbes in the history of political thought.

1. Subordination of Church to the State

He was the 1st political philosopher of the middle ages who ventured to subordinate church and religion to the state.

2. Secularism

Machiavelli separated religion and morals from politics but Hobbes subordinated both to politics. He thus stood for secularism which even today is considered as the best basis for the stability of the Government.

3. Theory of Sovereignty

He was the first political thinker who declares sovereignty as the indivisible and inalienable personality. In this respect he even surpassed Machiavelli who could not dare to say that the Natural law and Divine law would find their expression through a sovereign. His theory of sovereignty is the basis of all definitions given by the political thinkers today. He was the 1st political philosopher who stood for unlimited sovereignty.

4. Synthesis of Absolute Sovereignty and Individualism

His contribution to the political philosophy was the beauty with which he synthesise absolute sovereignty and individualism. Both were combined together and made dependent upon each other.

5. Equality of Man

It was in his philosophy for the first time that the masses were taken into consideration for the formation of the state and the human equality was brought to the front. In his political philosophy all men were considered equal in talent and development.

6. Synthesis of Elected and Absolute Authority

Hobbes skilfully combined the elected element with the unlimited and absolute authority of the sovereign. He very efficiently made community and agency for the creation of *Leviathan.* He pleaded absolutism when in the form of "Theory of Divine Rights of King" that theory had lost ground throughout the world.

7. Rejection of Divine Origin and Divine Right Theory

God has nothing to do with the origin of the state. Hobbes did not believe that there was any mystery in the creation of the state. The state was a contrivance of man. Hobbes gave a serious setback to the theory of Divine Rights of kings and the theory of Divine Origin of the state.

8. State as Conciliator of Interests

Credit goes to Hobbes for giving the idea that the state was the conciliator of interests. This was otherwise difficult to solve. In this regard Bentham borrowed from him.

9. Realism and Utility

Realism and utility are the contribution of Hobbes. He was clear in his mind that the people left the state of nature and joined civil society, only because they wanted to gain something out of that. Unless the state proved useful and was capable of discharging its obligations it had no right to demand obedience from the citizens. He thus gave the concept of utility and portrayed utilitarian approach to the people.

10. Materialism

It was for the first time that Hobbes gave the idea that matter alone was everything and he based his philosophy on this basic conception. This idea was further developed theory about Materialistic Interpretation of History.

11. Scientific Legislation

Hobbes proved a guiding generous for the scientific legislation. He clearly said that in all matters of legislation relating to human affairs man made law and not the natural law mattered. Thus, Hobbes gave the concept of positive law.

12. Theory of Social Contract

Hobbes says that the sovereign is the creature of a contract signed between the individuals. On the one hand, he introduced the idea that the individuals were competent and capable of signing a contract. On the other hand, he made it amply clear that the sovereign was a creature or product of the contract which of course was a novel idea in those days. As A. Hacker said, "But it is Hobbes who has created a theory which embraces a psychology, a sociology, and a Political Science, which integrates this into a coherent theoretical framework."

To sum up, we can say that Thomas Hobbes, the most famous English philosopher of the Stuart period, the writer of one of the greatest books on political thought—the *Leviathan* has made a remarkable contribution to political thought. His theory of social contract about the origin of the state, his secularism, his individualism, his utilitarianism and above all, his theory of absolute sovereignty and his theory of law have made him immortal.

JOHN LOCKE (1632-1704)

John Locke was born on August 29, 1632, in Warrington, a village in Somerset, England. In 1646 he went to Westminster school and in 1652 to Christ Church in Oxford. In 1659 he was elected to a senior studentship, and tutored at the college for a number of years. Still, contrary to the curriculum, he complained that he would rather be studying Descartes than Aristotle. In 1666 he declined an offer of preferment, although he thought at one time of taking up clerical work. In 1668 he was elected a fellow of the Royal Society, and in 1674 he finally graduated as a bachelor of medicine. In 1675 he was appointed to a medical studentship at the college. He owned a home in Oxford until 1684, until his studentship was taken from him by royal mandate.

Locke's mentor was Robert Boyle, the leader of the Oxford scientific group. Boyle's mechanical philosophy saw the world as reducible to matter in motion. Locke learned about atomism and took the terms "primary and secondary qualities" from Boyle. Both Boyle and Locke, along with Newton, were members of the English Royal Society. Locke became friends with Newton in 1688 after he had studied Newton's *Principia Mathematical Philosophise Naturalis*. It was Locke's work with the Oxford scientists that gave him a critical perspective when reading Descartes.

Locke admired Descartes as an alternative to the Aristotelians dominant at Oxford. Descartes' "way of ideas" was a major influence on Locke's An Essay Concerning Human Understanding.

Locke studied medicine with Sydenham, one of the most notable English physicians of the 17th century. His skills in medicine led to an accidental encounter with Lord Ashley (later to become the Earl of Shaftesbury) in 1666, which would mark a profound change in his career. Locke became a member of Shaftesbury's household and assisted him in business, political and domestic matters. Locke remained at Shaftesbury's side when the Earl was made Lord Chancellor in 1672, making presentations to benefices, and eventually becoming his secretary to the board of trade until 1675, when Shaftesbury lost his title.

Locke's ideas on freedom of religion and the rights of citizens were considered a challenge to the King's authority by the English government and in 1682 Locke went into exile in Holland. It was here that he completed An Essay Concerning Human Understanding, and published *Epistola de Tolerantia in Latin.* The English government tried to have Locke, along with a group of English revolutionaries with whom he was associated, extradited to England. Locke's position at Oxford was taken from him in 1684. In 1685, while Locke was still in Holland, Charles II died and was succeeded by James II who was eventually overthrown by rebels (after more than one attempt). William of Orange was invited to bring a Dutch force to England, while James II went into exile in France. Known as the Glorious Revolution of 1688, this event marks the change in the dominant power in English government from King to Parliament. In 1688 Locke took the opportunity to return to England on the same ship that carried Princess Mary to join her husband William.

Locke had written Two Treatises of Civil Government in the early 1680s while Whig revolutionary plots against Charles II were still in the works, and in 1690 he was finally able to publish them. This work is a theory of natural law and rights in which he makes a distinction between legitimate and illegitimate civil governments and argues for the legitimacy of revolution against tyrannical governments. He saw that the reason government is established is to protect the life, liberty and property of a people, and if these goals are not respected, then rebellion is entirely permissible by the population who originally consented to the government's power. The first treatise is an attack on Sir Robert Filmer and his text Patriarcha (1680), which he wrote in defense of divine monarchy. Locke uses this critique to launch his criticism of the work of Thomas Hobbes. In the Second Treaties Locke states his theory of natural law and natural right, revealing a rational purpose to government. Locke felt that the public welfare made government necessary and was the test of good government, and he always defended the government as an institution.

In 1690 Locke was also able to publish An Essay Concerning Human Understanding, which he had been working on since 1671. In this book he establishes the principles of modern Empiricism, and attacks the rationalist concept of innate ideas. Drawing on earlier writings by Chilling worth in which human understanding is said to be limited, Locke sets out to determine these limits. He writes that we can be certain that God exists, and be as certain of mortality as we are of mathematics, because we create moral and political ideas. He states that we cannot, however, know the underlying realities of natural substances, as we can only know their appearance. He imagined that the human mind begins as a "*tabula rasa*," and that we learn by our experience.

The new government of England offered Locke the post of ambassador to Berlin or Vienna in recognition of his part in the revolution; however, Locke declined the honourable position. In 1689 he became commissioner of appeals, and from 1696 to 1700 acted as commissioner of trade and plantations. In 1691 Locke responded to financial difficulties in the government by publishing Some Considerations of the Consequences of Lowering of Interest, and Raising the Value of Money, and in 1695 Further Considerations on the topic of money. In 1693 he published Some Thoughts Concerning Education, and in 1695 The Reasonableness of Christianity. He was later inspired to write two Vindications of this last work in response to some criticism. Locke invested a great deal of energy in theology in his later years, and among his work published post mortem are commentaries on the Pauline epistles, a Discourse on Miracles, a fragment of the Fourth Letter for Toleration, and An Examination of Father Malebranche's Opinion of Seeing all things in God, Remarks on Some of Mr. Norris' Books. After his death another chapter of "An Essay Concerning Human Understanding" was published under the title "The Conduct of the Understanding."

In his final years he lived in the country at Oates in Essex at the home of Sir Francis and Lady Masham (Damaris Cudworth). Locke had met Cudworth in 1682, a philosopher and daughter of the Cambridge Platonist Ralph Cudworth. They had an intellectual and amorous relationship, which was cut-short by Locke's exile in Holland. Cudworth had married Sir Francis Masham in Locke's absence, yet she and Locke remained close friends. Before his death, Locke saw four more editions of *An Essay Concerning Human Understanding* and entertained controversy and critiques regarding the work, engaging in a series of letters with Edward Stilling Fleet, Bishop of Worcester, which have since been published. He died at Oates in Essex on October 28, 1704.

Writings of Locke

List of Major Works

- (1689) A Letter Concerning Toleration
- (1690) A Second Letter Concerning Toleration
- (1692) A Third Letter for Toleration
- (1689) Two Treatises of Government
- (1690) An Essay Concerning Human Understanding
- (1693) Some Thoughts Concerning Education
- (1695) The Reasonableness of Christianity, as Delivered in the Scriptures
- (1695) A Vindication of the Reasonableness of Christianity

Major Unpublished Manuscripts

- (1660) First Tract of Government (or the English Tract)
- (c.1662) Second Tract of Government (or the Latin Tract)
- (1664) Questions Concerning the Law of Nature (definitive Latin text, with facing accurate English trans. in Robert Horwitz *et al.*, eds., John Locke, Questions Concerning the Law of Nature, Ithaca: Cornell University Press, 1990)
- (1667) Essay Concerning Toleration
- (1706) Of the Conduct of the Understanding
- (1707) A paraphrase and notes on the Epistles of St. Paul to the Galatians, 1 and 2 Corinthians, Romans, Ephesians

Influences

Locke exercised a profound influence on political philosophy, in particular on modern liberalism. Michael Zuckert has argued that Locke launched liberalism by tempering Hobbesian absolutism and clearly separating the realms of Church and State. He had a strong influence on Voltaire who called him "*le sage Locke.*" His arguments concerning liberty and the social contract later influenced the written works of Alexander Hamilton, James Madison, Thomas Jefferson, and other Founding Fathers of the United States. In fact, one passage from the Second Treatise is reproduced verbatim in the Declaration of Independence, the reference to a "long train of abuses." Such was Locke's influence that Thomas Jefferson wrote: "Bacon, Locke and Newton. I consider them as the three greatest men that have ever lived, without any exception, and as having laid the foundation of those superstructures which have been raised in the Physical and Moral sciences." Today, most contemporary libertarians claim Locke as an influence.

But Locke's influence may have been even more profound in the realm of epistemology. Locke redefined subjectivity, or self and intellectual historians such as Charles Taylor and Jerrold Seigel argue that Locke's An Essay Concerning Human Understanding (1690) marks the beginning of the modern Western conception of the self.

Theories of Religious Tolerance

Locke, writing his Letters Concerning Toleration (1689–92) in the aftermath of the European wars of religion, formulated a classic reasoning for religious tolerance. Three arguments are central: (1) Earthly judges, the state in particular, and human beings generally, cannot dependably evaluate the truth-claims of competing religious standpoints; (2) Even if they could, enforcing a single "true religion" would not have the desired effect, because belief cannot be compelled by violence; (3) Coercing religious uniformity would lead to more social disorder than allowing diversity.

Constitution of Carolina

Appraisals of Locke have often been tied to appraisals of liberalism in general, and also to appraisals of the United States. Detractors note that (in 1671) he was a major investor in the English slave-trade through the Royal African Company, as well as through his participation in drafting the Fundamental Constitution of the Carolinas while Shaftesbury's secretary, which established a feudal aristocracy and gave a master absolute power over his slaves. For example, Martin Cohen notes that as a secretary to the Council of Trade and Plantations (1673–4) and a member of the Board of Trade (1696–1700) Locke was, in fact, "one of just half a dozen men who created and supervised both the colonies and their iniquitous systems of servitude." Some see his statements on unenclosed property as having been intended to justify the displacement of the Native Americans. Because of his opposition to aristocracy and slavery in his major writings, he is accused of hypocrisy and racism, or of caring only for the liberty of English capitalists.

Theory of Value and Property

Locke uses the word property in both broad and narrow senses. In a broad sense, it covers a wide range of human interests and aspirations; more narrowly, it refers to material goods. He argues that property is a natural right and it is derived from labour.

In Chapter V of his Second Treatise, Locke argues that the individual ownership of goods and property is justified by the labour exerted to produce those goods or utilise property to produce goods beneficial to human society.

Locke stated his belief, in his Second Treatise, that nature on its own provides little of value to society; he provides the implication that the labour expended in the creation of goods gives them their value. This is used as supporting evidence for the interpretation of Locke's labour theory of property as a labour theory of value, in his implication that goods produced by nature are of little value, unless combined with labour in their production and that labour is what gives goods their value.

Locke believed that ownership of property is created by the application of labour. In addition, he believed property precedes government and government cannot "dispose of the estates of the subjects arbitrarily." Karl Marx later critiqued Locke's theory of property in his own social theory.

Political Theory

Locke's political theory was founded on social contract theory. Unlike Thomas Hobbes, Locke believed that human nature is characterised by reason and tolerance. Like Hobbes, Locke believed that human nature allowed men to be selfish. This is apparent with the introduction of currency. In a natural state all people were equal and independent, and everyone had a natural right to defend his "Life, Health, Liberty, or Possessions." Most scholars trace the phrase, "life, liberty, and the pursuit of happiness," in the American Declaration of Independence to Locke's theory of rights, though other origins have been suggested.

Like Hobbes, Locke assumed that the sole right to defend in the state of nature was not enough, so people established a civil society to resolve conflicts in a civil way with help from government in a state of society. However, Locke never refers to Hobbes by name and may instead have been responding to other writers of the day. Locke also advocated governmental separation of powers and believed that revolution is not only a right but an obligation in some circumstances. These ideas would come to have profound influence on the Declaration of Independence and the Constitution of the United States.

Limits to Accumulation

Labour creates property, but it also does contain limits to its accumulation: man's capacity to produce and man's capacity to consume. According to Locke, unused property is waste and an offence against nature. However, with the introduction of "durable" goods, men could exchange their excessive perishable goods for goods that would last longer and thus not offend the natural law. The introduction of money marks the culmination of this process. Money makes possible the unlimited accumulation of property without causing waste through spoilage. He also includes gold or silver as money because they may be "hoarded up without injury to anyone," since they do not spoil or decay in the hands of the possessor. The introduction of money eliminates the limits of accumulation. Locke stresses that inequality has come about by tacit agreement on the use of money, not by the social contract establishing civil society or the law of land regulating property. Locke is aware of a problem posed by unlimited accumulation but does not consider it his task. He just implies that government would function to moderate the conflict between the unlimited accumulation of property and a more nearly equal distribution of wealth and does not say which principles that government should apply to solve this problem. However, not all elements of his thought form a consistent whole. For example, labour theory of value of the Two Treatises of Government stands side by side with the demand-and-supply theory developed in a letter he wrote titled Some Considerations on the Consequences of the Lowering of Interest and the Raising of the Value of Money. Moreover, Locke anchors property in labour but in the end upholds the unlimited accumulation of wealth.

On Price Theory

Locke's general theory of value and price is a supply and demand theory, which was set out in a letter to a Member of Parliament in 1691, titled Some Considerations on the Consequences of the Lowering of Interest and the Raising of the Value of Money. Supply is quantity and demand is rent. "The price of any commodity rises or falls by the proportion of the number of buyer and sellers." and "that which regulates the price...[of goods] is nothing else but their quantity in proportion to their rent." The quantity theory of money forms a special case of this general theory. His idea is based on "money answers all things" (Ecclesiastes) or "rent of money is always sufficient, or more than enough," and "varies very little." Regardless of whether the demand for money is unlimited or constant, Locke concludes that as far as money is concerned, the demand is exclusively regulated by its quantity. He also investigates the determinants of demand and supply. For supply, goods in general are considered valuable because they can be exchanged, consumed and they must be scarce. For demand, goods are in demand because they yield a flow of income. Locke develops an early theory of capitalisation, such as land, which has value because "by its constant production of saleable commodities it brings in a certain yearly income." Demand for money is almost the same as demand for goods or land; it depends on whether money is wanted as medium of exchange or as loanable funds. For medium of exchange "money is capable by exchange to procure us the necessaries or conveniences of life." For loanable funds, "it comes to be of the same nature with land by yielding a certain yearly income or interest."

Monetary Thoughts

Locke distinguishes two functions of money, as a "counter" to measure value, and as a "pledge" to lay claim to goods. He believes that silver and gold, as opposed to paper money, are the appropriate currency for international transactions. Silver and gold, he says, are treated to have equal value by all of humanity and can thus be treated as a pledge by anyone, while the value of paper money is only valid under the government which issues it.

Locke argues that a country should seek a favourable balance of trade, lest it fall behind other countries and suffer a loss in its trade. Since the world money stock grows constantly, a country must constantly seek to enlarge its own stock. Locke develops his theory of foreign exchanges, in addition to commodity movements, there are also movements in country stock of money, and movements of capital determine exchange rates. The latter is less significant and less volatile than commodity movements. As for a country's money stock, if it is large relative to that of other countries, it will cause the country's exchange to rise above par, as an export balance would do.

He also prepares estimates of the cash requirements for different economic groups (landholders, labourers and brokers). In each group the cash requirements are closely related to the length of the pay period. He argues the brokers—middlemen—whose activities enlarge the monetary circuit and whose profits eat into the earnings of labourers and landholders had a negative influence on both one's personal and the public economy that they supposedly contributed to.

The Self

Locke defines the self as "that conscious thinking thing, (whatever substance, made up of whether spiritual, or material, simple, or compounded, it matters not) which is sensible, or conscious of pleasure and pain, capable of happiness or misery, and so is concerned for itself, as far as that consciousness extends." He does not, however, ignore "substance", writing that "the body too goes to the making the man." The Lockean self is, therefore, a self-aware and self-reflective consciousness that is fixed in a body.

In his Essay, Locke explains the gradual unfolding of this conscious mind. Arguing against both the Augustinian view of man as originally sinful and the Cartesian position, which holds that man innately knows basic logical propositions, Locke posits an "empty" mind, a *tabula rasa*, which is shaped by experience; sensations and reflections being the two sources of all our ideas.

John Locke's formulation of *tabula rasa* in An Essay Concerning Human Understanding was influenced by a 17th century Latin translation *Philosophus Autodidactus* (published by Edward Pococke) of the Arabic philosophical novel *Hayy Ibn Yaqzan* by the 12th century Andalusian-Islamic philosopher and novelist Ibn Tufail (known as "Abubacer" or "Ebn Tophail" in the West). Ibn Tufail demonstrated the theory of *tabula rasa* as a thought experiment through his Arabic philosophical novel *Hayy ibn Yaqzan* in which he depicted the development of the mind of a feral child "from a tabula rasa to that of an adult, in complete isolation from society" on a desert island, through experience alone.

Locke's Some Thoughts Concerning Education is an outline on how to educate this mind: he expresses the belief that education maketh the man, or, more fundamentally, that the mind is an "empty cabinet", with the statement, "I think I may say that of all the men we meet with nine parts of ten are what they are, good or evil, useful or not, by their education."

Locke also wrote that "the little and almost insensible impressions on our tender infancies have very important and lasting consequences." He argued that the "associations of ideas" that one makes when young are more important than those made later because they are the foundation of the self: they are, put differently, what first mark the *tabula rasa*. In his Essay, in which is introduced both of these concepts, Locke warns against, for example, letting "a foolish maid" convince a child that "goblins and sprites" are associated with the night for "darkness shall ever afterwards bring with it those frightful ideas, and they shall be so joined, that he can no more bear the one than the other."

"Associationism", as this theory would come to be called, exerted a powerful influence over eighteenth-century thought, particularly educational theory, as nearly every educational writer warned parents not to allow their children to develop negative associations. It also led to the development of psychology and other new disciplines with David Hartley's attempt to discover a biological mechanism for associationism in his Observations on Man (1749).

Locke on Human Nature

Like other political thinkers we start the study of his philosophy with his views on human nature. However, unlike Hobbes, Locke did not express his views about human nature in a systematic manner and one had to collect his views from the scattered ideas in the Essays Concerning Human Understanding and the Second Treatise. Locke believed that if everyone is given proper opportunities, he is bound to have equal mental development. According to Locke, it was mental and not physical development which always counted. He agreed with Hobbes that men had desire and wants to substitute their pains for pleasure. He, however, did not agree with Hobbes that for the sake of pleasures men become cruel some, savage and brutish. On the other hand, he felt that the people always want to achieve ends by peaceful and rational methods. He also believed that nature itself had blessed mankind. With the sparks of reason with motivate his actions in the darkness. In pre-state civil society it was goodwill, mutual understanding and sense of co-operation which prevailed and governed their social relations. Locke considered all human beings as equal, in the moral sense and asserts that every individual enjoys certain natural rights, viz. the right of life, liberty and property. Man enjoys these rights not because of any position, strength, wealth etc., but, because he is a human being and possesses reason. Thus, Locke's views about human nature are just the opposite of Hobbes. However, unlike Hobbes, he failed to provide any scientific basis for his views about human nature.

Locke on State of Nature

Locke believed with Hobbes that before man came in the civil state, he was living in the state of nature. But according to Locke, the state of nature was not as bad as that of Hobbes. Men living in the state of nature where there was law, order, peace and prosperity. It was a state of goodwill. His state was state of pre-political rather than pre-social condition. People lived a free and happy life. They also enjoyed rights and freedoms. Men were not quarrelsome. They were sympathetic towards one another. The state of nature was a state of equality and reason. There was a state of peace, good will and mutual assistance. Locke believed with *Grotius* that law of nature was not only legal in character but it represented moral and rational reasoning of the society. He stood for the idea that it was personal liberty that mattered in the state of nature rather than physical liberty. He further believed that in the state of nature though there was no common authority, the result was not anarchic. He himself said that "Men living together, according to reason without a common superior on earth with authority to judge between them are properly the state of nature."

We may note the following main points about Locke's state of nature—

1. The State of Nature is a Pre-political Rather than a Pre-social Condition

According to Locke, the state of nature is a pre-political condition. It is not a pre-social condition. There is no political authority. In other words, there is no state. The state of nature is a pre-state period. It is not a pre-society period. Men in the state of nature live in an organised society, though there is no political authority.

2. Men in the State of Nature have Obligations

Locke points out that, men in the state of nature have obligations like men in the state living under a political authority, though these obligations differ to a certain extent.

3. Perfect Peace of Harmony in the State of Nature

According to Hobbes, the state of nature is a state of endless war. The hand of each is against all and everybody is the enemy of everybody else. According to Locke, men in the state of nature live in perfect peace, co-operation and harmony. They are guided by reason which is the spark of divine nature.

4. Men are Social and Sociable in the State of Nature

Men in the state of nature are social and sociable. They are governed by sympathy and fellow feeling. They are united by the bond of sociability. Their life is peaceful and happy. Men in the state of nature are innocent. Men in the state of nature are equal and free. Locke's description of the state of nature is quite in contrast with that of Hobbes description. Whereas for Hobbes, life in the state of nature is the life of a creature solitary, poor, brutish, nasty and short. Locke's state of nature is peaceful and social in character.

5. Law of Nature—Liberty and Equality

In the state of nature, men are governed by the law of nature. Reason interprets the law of nature. The basic principle of law of nature is equality among men. By law of nature, Locke means rules for human behaviour. Law of nature does not tell us how human beings behave but how they ought to behave.

6. Men's Natural Rights

From the basic principle of equality arise men's natural rights. These natural rights are: (i) Right to Life (ii) Right to Liberty (iii) Right to Property.

According to Locke, everyone has the right to punish the violator of the law of nature. Every injured person is the judge in his own case to punish the culprit.

7. Law of Nature not only Gives Rights but also Imposes Duties

According to Locke, law of nature not only gives men rights to life, liberty and property, but also imposes duties on them. Law of nature commands men to try to preserve others, if their preservation does not come in competition. All men are commanded to restrain themselves from invading the rights of others and from doing hurt to one another. All men are commanded to observe the law of nature.

8. Law of Nature Provides Moral Standards

According to Locke, the law of nature provides moral standards and is applicable to the ruler and the ruled alike. According to Locke, the law of nature is based on reason. It provides moral standards for social actions. It tells men to keep faith. It tells them to observe contract. It is for the preservation of all mankind. It represents a moral standard. It is applicable to the ruler and the ruled alike. Since law of nature is identical with reason, if regulates human conduct not only in the state of nature, but also in civil society.

9. Rights of Nature Cannot be Taken Away by any Person

Locke says that the law of nature gives men rights of nature. These rights cannot be taken away by any person. The individual cannot be deprived of his rights of life, liberty and property by any person. No one can take away his right of equality. The right to enforce the law of nature is in the hands of the individual. Each individual has a right to protect his rights. He has also a right to protect the rights of his neighbours.

10. Punishment to the Violator of the Law of Nature should be in Proportion to the Crime and should not be Arbitrary

Locke says that the violator of the law of nature should be punished. Every man has the right to punish the violator of the law of nature. But, according to Locke, punishment should be in proportion to the crime and should not be arbitrary.

Locke on Social Contract Theory

Locke believed that in the state of nature the people were neither nasty, nor uncivilised nor brutish but they lived happily and peacefully with each other. They enjoyed certain natural rights and there was no perpetual state of war. They enjoyed certain natural rights and there was no perpetual state of war. But even then they decided to leave the state of nature and join civil state.

According to Locke, the people joined civil state because it was their internal desire to establish contracts with each other. Uncertainty about common decisions and common interpreter to enforce those decisions and acceptability of commonly approved social laws in right spirit were other consideration with the people to join civil state and leave the state of nature. Locke realised that there were inconveniences in the state of nature. Laws were not definite and determinant. There was no competent authority to enforce law and there was no arbitrator to settle disputes. In order to escape from this situation people entered into an agreement with one another to form a civil society. Locke believed that men were capable, considerate and efficient beings. Locke's concept of social contract revolves round the idea that the individual is a dependable and rational being.

In the state of nature people enjoyed peace and prosperity and there was no fear of war, then why did they leave the state of nature. According to Locke, it was the internal desire to establish social contract which motivated the people in this direction. The uncertainty of common decision and common interpreter of acceptable social laws as we have discussed above was another factor which made men think of leaving the state of nature. Yet, as a political theorist, Locke has some reservations about man's ability to act and as an objective to judge.

People abandoned the state of nature and joined the civil state in order to avoid inconvenience and confusion which arouse because of everyone becoming a soul interpreter of law. Locke believed that these rational beings could not be driven like dumb cattle of Hobbes. They preserved their natural rights with them. They had the legislative powers with them. They created contract that there should be authority to interpret laws and that the interpreter could himself be subject to this own interpretation. Locke's contract unlike Hobbes was double sided. His sovereign was a party to the contract. He was neither above his fellow being nor did he remain in the state of nature and thus uncivilised. He also left the state of nature and became cultured, responsible and civilised. The idea of absolute monarch was foolish because monarchs were also human beings and suffered from 'love and hatred' feelings.

We may note the following main points about Locke's Social Contract Theory—

1. To get out of the State of Nature, Locke points out: men make contract to enter into a civil society. This is a contract of all with all. This is a social, or more truly a political contract, since it establishes political society. It is not a contract made with the government which is to be set up later on. The end for which the contract is made is the protection and preservation of life, liberty and property—the three natural rights which people enjoyed in the State of Nature—against danger both from within and without the community.

2. It is a contract to which all must consent. A society thus becomes by the acts of individuals who formed it, vested with it the functions of determining what is offence against the law of nature and punishing violation of that law—and these functions constitute in Locke's view, the whole scope of political authority. The community becomes the sole interpreter and executor of the laws it makes for the protection of these rights.

3. Though the original contract itself is unanimous, all parties, to it agree, henceforth "to submit to the determination of the majority." Since unless men agree to majority rule, decisions cannot be taken and the State cannot survive.

4. The social contract once made cannot be revoked. He who has signed it "can never again be in the liberty of the State of Nature."

5. This contract does not, as with Hobbes, put an end to the Law of Nature as it does to the State of Nature. Man in the State continues to be under that law, as he was before.

6. According to Wayper, this contract is the first step to the drawing up of a trust. People, having formed a society, must then institute a government. They do not do this by making a contract with the government—that, as Rousseau was so clearly to point out, would be to invest government with too much dignity and authority.

7. It is a contract to which each generation must have consent. This is in contrast to Hobbes who had conceived of a contrast in which once the agreement was made it was binding on all future generations.

8. Locke here lacks clarity. He neither talks of any contract between people and government, nor does he deny it. But the use of the word trust shows that there was no second contract. So, power of the government is always derivative and hence limited by the covenant of the trust and thus the community is both the creator and beneficiary of the truth.

Criticism

The theory of social contract put forth by Locke has been subjected to severe criticism.

1. Protection of Propertied Class

That natural man had some property and authority. He wanted that a good government should protect those rights. Thus, Locke stood for the protection of propertied class. This philosophy cannot be justified on the basis of quality and common principles of justice.

2. Misunderstanding of Human Nature

Like Hobbes, Locke miss-understood the nature of man. Man was not nasty, brutish and uncivilised as Hobbes conceived him. Man was also never gentle, self-realising and responsible to the extent to which Locke thought. At no stage of human history, man has acted as restrained person in the absence of any authority. Locke is thus a victim of miscalculation of man's nature and his basic instinct.

3. Society or Government

It is doubtful whether Locke created a society or a government. Government is an agent which has executive, legislative and judicial powers. In case of Locke, it has only limited legislative functions which were assigned to supreme authority and that is only of interpreting the laws. It is doubtful whether Locke created a sovereign or only a judge and thus whether state came into being at all.

4. Social Contract not a Fact

As expounded by Locke the theory of social contract postulates the individual who was given indefeasible rights and also the legislature which was the only organ of the government. This is not correct.

5. Sacrifice of Legal Sovereign

Locke's main task was to bring a man from pre-civil state to a civil state and thus to create a legal sovereign. In his defence of revolution he has felt in this main task as well. He rather sacrificed his legal sovereign at the altar of popular sovereign.

Locke's View on Property

Private property is an age old institution and a subject matter of many controversial theories both in political as well as economic fields. Perhaps no serious political philosopher could afford to ignore discussion of this subject.

Locke is famous for his theory of property. He believes that every individual has the right to property. According to Locke, all land and all things of the world were given by God in common to all men, in the beginning. Originally nobody had an exclusive right to anything. All things were common. Man had a right of property to his own person. The labour of his body and fruit of his labour were his property. The labour of his body and the work of his hands, are properly his.

Locke, however, firmly believed that institution of private property was essential for the development of mankind. He believed that man was an entrepreneurial animal. He has right to own private property. In fact commonwealth came into being to protect his natural rights of life, liberty and property. Of them all the right to property was the most sacred and valuable one. Locke neither agreed with Aristotle about the notion of private property nor did he agree with Rousseau when he said "that property ownership has become concentrated in too few hands and hence can no longer enter a claim to legitimacy." He believed that private property must be preserved if state desired that citizens should live happily. Thus he believed that private property was always source of joy.

Locke believed that ownership of private property was justified on the following grounds:

1. Religious Ground

Firstly that God did not commit himself on public or private ownership of earth resources. He himself said that "The appropriate means for making use of the resources which God has given to men is for individuals to develop them so that they can actually sustain life."

2. Property a Result of Labour

Another justification for the retention of private property was that men had mixed labour in that. Men put in their labour by way of tilling and sowing the land. It is his labour which makes the land worthy of possession and converts lands into private property.

3. Socially Sanctioned

Still another reason given for the justification of private property was that its possession had social approval and sanction from times past. It has social sanction and recognition.

4. Social Product

Locke also justified the retention of private property on the grounds that it emerged in the society and continues to exist even today whether we like that or not. According to him, the very fact that it has got social approval throughout these ages is sufficient to indicate that it was an unobjectionable institution.

5. Historical Grounds

Locke's another justification of private property was based on historical grounds. According to him, history is a witness that only those have suffered under tyrannies who did not own property. Similarly, liberty of those people was only snatched who were without private property. He was of the view that possession of private property was essential particularly for middle classes. He, however, suggested a degree of social control over private property.

We may mention the following points in Locke's theory of property—

1. All land and Things Common in the Beginning

Locke says that in the beginning there was no private property in the form of land and things. All land and all things were held in common by all men. God had created different gifts of nature to be the common possession of all mankind.

2. Man's Person was his Own

According to Cocke, man had full possession of his person, everybody had the exclusive right to his own person. Nobody had any claim on his personality.

3. By Mixing his Labour Man Makes Common Things his Private Property

According to Locke, man creates private property by mixing his labour with it. The labour of his body and the fruit of his labour are his property. By mixing his labour with a thing, man makes that thing his own. He extends his personality and energy of thing and makes it his own property.

4. Labour Theory of Value

According to Locke, the greater the labour spent by man in making a thing, the greater is the value of a thing. The value of a thing goes on increasing in proportion to the labour spent on it.

5. No Equality in Private Property

Locke points out that some men are more industrious than others. Some are clever than others. There cannot be equality in the matter of private property. Some men may possess more property than others because of their industrious habit and clever nature. Locke who is an upholder of equality with regard to natural rights in general does not apply the principle of equality to private property.

6. No Man has Right to Unlimited Property

We may interpret Locke's theory of property men that no man has a right to unlimited property. Man must make proper use of things which he possesses. Man should take only as much as he needs. He should not encroach upon the right of his neighbour. Things can be spoiled, but not money.

7. Men Enter into a Contract to Safeguard Right to Property

Locke says that men enter into a contract to safeguard the right to property. The preservation of property is the chief end of the state.

Criticism of Locke's Theory of Property

Locke's theory of property, however, has many shortcomings. We may note the following points of criticism against Locke's theory:

1. Locke does not Explain the Need of Property

Locke says that the men are decent, good, social and co-operative. God has made land and all things in common in the beginning. Locke does not explain why a decent, social and co-operative individual feels the need of private property when land and other things are in common.

2. Locke does not give any Psychological and Scientific Explanation for the Desire for Property

Psychologists have explained that each man has an instinct of acquisitiveness. That is the basic reason why each man wants to acquire property. Locke does not mention this psychological factor.

3. There is a Contradiction in the Concept of Equality and Inequality

It is strange that Locke who is a great champion of equality in the state of nature says that the principle of equality cannot be observed in the matter of property. There is a contradiction in Locke's notion. If men have a right to equality, they should possess equal property.

4. Locke's Theory of Property is not Clear

Locke's theory of property is not clear. It is not definite and precise. It is vague and indefinite. He leaves many points in his theory unexplained. On account of this vagueness, there are different interpretations of his theory.

5. Locke's Labour Theory of Value not Applicable in Modern Times

Locke's labour theory of value is not applicable in modern times. In a complex age of science, machines and technology the quality and value of a thing do not depend upon the labour of man alone, but upon the quality of raw material and excellence of the machines. Raw materials and machines are in the hands of the capitalists. Locke's theory can be used to justify capitalism or socialism.

Locke's View on Revolution

Locke was in favour of Glorious Revolution of 1688 which he felt was morally just. He believed that the individual has every right to rise against tyranny and revolt against it if the government failed to protect their rights. In his view government holds power in trust only for the welfare of the community. If the government fails to perform the functions or purposes of the truth, the people have every right to revolt. They can take to arms and set-up new government.

The use of the authorised force should be checked with force and in such cases resistance becomes natural right of every citizen. The government loses its legitimacy as soon as it becomes arbitrary and exceeds its authority. He has, however, made it clear that right to revolution is a reserve right and need not be misunderstood as encouragement to rebellion. The people revolt to revolution when they have lost patience and all other methods have failed. He, however, has said this right should be treated valid if it has majority support.

It is his love for individualism which has moulded his ideas about the rights of the people to revolt against their sovereign. Like an individualist, he was of the opinion that the people had certain basic minimum rights and that no authority in the state had any right to snatch these rights from him. A state should bestow and not snatch rights.

Locke's love for individualism is also clearly reflected when he assumes that individual is everything and that the state is only means to achieve certain ends. It is the supreme duty of the state to preserve natural rights of the people and that revolution is justified when such rights are flouted, disregarded or disrespected.

We may note the following points in Locke's Theory of Revolution :

1. Government Holds Power as a Trust From the Community

Locke believes that the government holds power as trust from the community. There are certain ends for which the government has been created. These ends are peace and security, protection of the natural rights of the people, promotion of their interests and welfare. If the government does not perform its duties to achieve these ends, the people have a right to rise in revolt and to change the government. If the government overuses its authority, the people have a right to revolt.

2. The Right to Decide Whether or not the Government is Performing its Duties with the People

Locke believes that the people have a right to determine whether or not the government is performing its duties. If the people are convinced that the government is inefficient, they have a right to revolt and remove that inefficient government. If the people feel that the government is following the policy of oppression, they have a right to rise in rebellion against the oppressive government and get rid of it.

3. People can Revolt if the Ruler Rules Arbitrarily and does not Summon the Legislature

If the ruler rules in an arbitrary manner and ignores law, people have a right to revolt against such a ruler. If the ruler does not summon the law-making body or the legislature or the parliament, people are justified in revolting against such a ruler.

4. If the People Feel that the Legislature is not Performing its Duty of Law-making Honestly and Properly, they can Revolt.

According to Locke, "even the legislative power is held only on good behaviour and the final judge of this behaviour is the people itself." Locke says that in case the people feel that the legislature is not performing its duty of law-making honestly and properly, people can revolt and can change the legislature. The legislature has been given the power of law-making as a trust by the people. If the legislature violates this trust, people are fully justified in changing such a legislature.

5. Ultimately Sovereignty is with the People

Locke is convinced that ultimately sovereignty is in the hands of the people. The government exists to safeguard and protect the natural rights of the people and to promote their interests and welfare. As soon as the people feel that the ruler is not protecting their rights and is indifferent to their interests and welfare, they can revolt and remove such a ruler.

6. The Glorious Revolution of 1688

Locke wrote at a time when in 1688 James II and last Stuart King of England, was compelled by the people by means of a bloodless or glorious revolution to leave the throne and the country and people offered the throne to William III and Mary. The result of this revolution was victory of the Parliament. It resulted in limited monarchy. The arbitrary rule of the Stuart dynasty was over. We can understand Locke's philosophy of revolution very clearly if we study the causes and effects of the glorious revolution of 1688. Locke's theory of revolution becomes intelligible if we study it in the background of the glorious revolution of 1688 (Kafue).

Locke on Government

Locke basically believed that body politics and common wealth came into being for the welfare of the individuals and the community. Locke said in his social contract theory that there were inconveniences in the state of nature. Laws were not definite and determinate. There was no competent authority to enforce laws and there was no arbitrator to settle disputes. In order to escape from this situation, people entered into an agreement with one another to form a civil society. Locke's theory consists of two contracts. The first contract helped the people to form the state while the second one the Government. The first one was the 'social contract' and the second one was called the 'Government contract'. To Locke, people surrendered some of their rights to the society. The people as a whole authorised a particular person to make laws for the welfare of the people and to settle their disputes. The power of the government was defined and limited. The people had the right to overthrow the government if it made laws against their common good. The society was superior to the government. Locke, therefore, assigned following functions to the government:

1. To Fix Standards of Ethics

The Government should attempt to create standards by which the individual should be in a position to decide as to what was right or wrong. The law of nature which all followed in the state of nature was clear and rational yet selfish interests make men blind of proper understanding. These also influence his judgement of deciding as to what was right or wrong.

2. Impartial Authority to Settle Disputes

The Government should provide it subject with an impartial authority to decide the disputes arising out of social misunderstandings in the community. This was essential because men were usually partial towards themselves.

3. To Safeguard Peoples Interest

Locke believed that it was the duty of the state to safeguard the interest of its individuals and subjects against undue intervention from outside agencies. He went to the extent of saying that the state had a right to declare the war if it found that the life and property of its subjects was at stake. Thus the state should not hesitate to sacrifice anything when it felt that the rights of the individuals were being challenged.

As regards his concept of constitutional government it is worthwhile to note that he was perhaps the first thinker who realised that unless the rule of man against man was based on consent. It had no legal justification. He stressed for constitutional government was physically more in the days when he was expounding his philosophy.

Limitations on the Authority of Government

Locke did not agree with Hobbes that Government had absolute powers and authority. He was of the opinion that it was bounded by certain limitations.

1. The Government could have a right to destroy, enslave or impoverish the subjects.
2. The Government should govern not by unknown laws but by the laws which have been promulgated and are not to judiciary.
3. The Government had no authority to snatch rightly earned property of any of any subjects without its consent because it does not stand for snatching the property but for preserving that.
4. The legislation was trust for the nation and hence that could not be transferred to any other authority.
5. The Government could not abrogate the natural rights of the individuals.
6. The state should not act autocratically but on the other hand it should function for promoting utility.
7. The legislature must act according to the laws of nature.

Locke on Forms of Government

Locke believed with Aristotle that Government could be divided into three forms, viz. monarchy, aristocracy and democracy. But he was of the view that limited democracy was the best form of Government. From limited democracy, he understood that form of democracy in which the powers had been delegated to the representatives who were guided by the electorates.

Locke on Separation of Power

In Locke's philosophy legislature had a supreme authority and place. The other two organs, viz. the executive and the judiciary were subordinated to that. He believed that the legislature and the executive must be separated from each other. Both in functions of personnel. He, however, permitted the executive to issue ordinance when legislature was not in session. He, however, did not develop this idea further. In this connection it can be said that it was from Locke that Montesquieu picked up the idea and made that the basis of his theory of separation of power.

Shortcomings of Locke's Political Philosophy

With which the name of Locke is associated is full of certain anomalies/criticisms which have entered in his philosophy for having certain preconceived notions about certain basic principles of life. Anomalies and difficulties mainly have emerged because he has failed to make-up his mind as to the direction in which he was to move. This uncertainty resulted in a practical difficulty and he could not decide as to what the principles were and what then derivatives were. The difficulties of Locke are as follows—

1. Wrong Idea about State

He takes a mechanistic view of state and society which is not correct. The state and the society are not so simple institutions which can be created or destroyed by the individual at will. There were certainly more complicated motives which were involved in the formation of the community than Locke wanted us to believe.

2. Private Property

Locke laid so much stress on the institution of private property that he pleaded that it ought to be preserved at all costs. He felt that the society stood to preserve and not to snatch private property. But, in fact, one finds that primitive man is on his lips, but the portrait he paints is that of civil man.

3. Concept of Sovereignty and Individuals

Locke's conception of sovereignty if pressed to its logical conclusions makes state a corporate body. He believed that individual was ultimate sovereign and that the sovereignty was thus aggregate of individuals and not the supreme power which was the characteristics of sovereignty. He has intact, made sovereignty a limited inability company. It is very strange that he placed individual even before the state. The individuals have no doubt, a place in the state and in democracies play an important role but to believe that they were above the state was something which was undesirable.

4. Need to Create Civil Society

In his philosophy Locke has taken many things for granted, e.g. the moral and intellectual values of mankind without the coercive power of the state. But if in actual practice moral tone of the people of pre-civil society was so high as Locke assumed then there was very little need and necessary for the creation of political organisation and civil societies.

5. Minorities have no Right to Revolt

He allowed the people the right to revolt. This is unwanted because history is the evidence that revolutions are carried out by minorities and not by the majorities. A minority has no right to upset social order and thus harm the progress of the majority.

6. His Theories Stood against the Reality of Revolution

Locke based his theory on pleasure and pain principle. These are closely associated with the idea of preservation, welfare and well-being of the people. This is against the reality of revolution.

7. Logical Inconsistencies of his Philosophy

Locke's philosophy suffers from logical inconsistencies and he does not stick to any particular opinion. For example, at various times he asserts that the sovereignty resides with the individual, the community, the government and the legislature. At the very initial state of his theory of social contract he gives us the impression that the individual and his rights are absolute.

8. Conflict of Tolerance and Intolerance

Locke proposed the theory of tolerance for religious purpose and also of intolerance. The curious result in his social philosophy was a theory markedly tolerant and critical in defending religious freedom and capable of being highly dogmatic in defending rights of property.

9. Wrong Notion of Social Contract

It is very clear that Locke's social contract has become little better than efforts. If consent then be the hallmark of democracy, Mussolini's Italy and Nazi's Germany and Bolshevik Russia must be regarded as being much more democratic than those countries in which governments have perforce to reconcile themselves to persistent, vigorous and often widespread opposition.

10. Corporate Community vs. *Individualism*

Locke failed to reconcile his ideas about corporate character of the community on the one hand and his ideas about individualism on the other.

11. Mechanical Theories of State and Society

Locke has been criticised for his mechanistic views about state and society. His idea that the individual could destroy and create the state at all was not sound to reason and needed careful consideration.

12. No Source and Code of Law of Nature

Though according to Locke's philosophy law of nature is perfect yet he has not given its source and has not tried to modify that.

13. No Ground for Civil Society

Locke has been criticised for not providing any solid grounds which forced the people to leave the state of nature and instead join political or civil society.

Contribution of Locke in Political Philosophy

Despite the above noted deficiencies in the thought of Locke, it cannot be denied that he was one of the most influential thinkers in the realm of modern political thought. His chief contribution to the development of political thought can be numerated as follows—

Firstly, he was the first to draw a distinction between society, state and government, and to put them in proper chronological order.

Secondly, he contributed to the political theory the doctrine of natural rights, which according to Prof. Dunning is the most distinctive contribution of Locke.

Thirdly, Locke emphasised the doctrine of supremacy of the community on which later on Rousseau based his theory of General Will.

Fourthly, his views on right to revolt exercised profound influence on the people of America and France and they tried to put these views into actual practice.

Fifthly, Locke is the father of Liberalism in the sense that he for the first time emphasised that the people are the source of all authority and the state must formulate its policies in accordance with the wishes and interest of the people.

Sixthly, Locke worked on the concept of separation of powers and his ideas provided the basis for Montesquieu to present his classical theory of separation of powers.

Seventhly, Locke's thought contains seeds of utilitarianism. He greatly emphasised the principle of general happiness of people which was later on adopted by Bentham.

Eighthly, Locke provided the basis for the development of the idea of a democratic state based on popular institutions and constitutional government. He also emphasised the principles of consent of the governed and majority rule which form the basis of the modern democratic institutions.

Ninthly, Locke laid great emphasis on the principles of toleration and secularism. He for the first time reduced Church to a voluntary society which can exert no powers save over its members.

Tenthly, Locke laid the foundation of the labour theory which not only influenced the classical economists but also greatly influenced Marx's labour theory of value.

Lastly, Locke gave a death blow to the prevailing notions of Divine rights and asserted that the state is human institution. He did not favour interference of God or religious leaders in the affairs of the state. Prof. Maxey, "Laying hold of obstruse and important concepts that had been floating around in the back eddies of European political thought for many generations, he wove them into coercive kinetic body of doctrine that has gripped the political consciousness of Europe and America for two tremendous centuries. He further says "if, as critics are want to opine, there is little that is absolutely original in the political philosophy of John Locke—few ideas and doctrines that had not been previously conceived and declared to the world—it is none the less a fact that this frail and bookish physician of seventeenth century England must be ranked as one of the few political thinkers whose work will never die." It does not matter that he was a mediocre, it does not matter that his political ideas originated in the minds of other thinkers. What matters is that he became one of the "foremost combiners of ideas and compounder of systematic thought that the world has ever known."

Unit-V
Enlightenment Political Thought

The Age of Enlightenment (or simply the Enlightenment or Age of Reason) was a cultural movement of intellectuals in eighteenth century Europe and the United States, whose purpose was to reform society and advance knowledge. It promoted science and intellectual interchange and opposed superstition, intolerance and abuses by church and state. Originating about 1650 to 1700, it was sparked by philosophers Baruch Spinoza (1632–1677), John Locke (1632–1704), Pierre Bayle (1647–1706), physicist Isaac Newton (1643–1727), and philosopher Voltaire (1694–1778). The wide distribution of the printing press, invented in Europe in 1450, made possible the rapid dispersion of knowledge and ideas which precipitated the Enlightenment. Ruling princes often endorsed and fostered figures and even attempted to apply their ideas of government in what was known as Enlightened Despotism. The Enlightenment flourished until about 1790–1800, after which the emphasis on reason gave way to Romanticism's emphasis on emotion and a Counter-Enlightenment gained force.

In France, Enlightenment was based in the salons and culminated in the great Encyclopaedia (1751–72) edited by Denis Diderot (1713–1784) with contributions by hundreds of leading philosophers (intellectuals) such as Voltaire (1694–1778), Rousseau (1712–1778) and Montesquieu (1689–1755). Some 25,000 copies of the 35 volume set were sold, half of them outside France. The new intellectual forces spread to urban centres across Europe, notably England, Scotland, the German states, the Netherlands, Russia, Italy, Austria, and Spain, then jumped the Atlantic into the European colonies, where it influenced Benjamin Franklin and Thomas Jefferson, among many others, and played a major role in the American Revolution. The political ideals of the Enlightenment influenced the American Declaration of Independence, the United States Bill of Rights, the French Declaration of the Rights of Man and of the Citizen, and the Polish-Lithuanian Constitution of May 3, 1791.

Use of the Term

The term 'Enlightenment' did not come into use in English until the mid-eighteenth century, with particular reference to French philosophy, as the equivalent of the French term 'Lumières' (used first by Dubos 1733 and already well established by 1751). From Immanuel Kant's 1784 essay "Beantwortung der Frage: Was ist Aufklärung?" ("Answering the Question: What Is Enlightenment?") the German term became 'Aufklärung'.

"For Kant, Enlightenment was mankind's final coming of age, the emancipation of the human consciousness from an immature state of ignorance and error." According to historian Roy Porter, the thesis of the liberation of the human mind from the dogmatic state of ignorance that he argues was prevalent at the time is the epitome of what the age of enlightenment was trying to capture. According to Bertrand Russell, however, the enlightenment was a phase in a progressive development, which began in antiquity, and that reason and challenges to the established order were constant ideals throughout that time. Russell argues that the enlightenment was ultimately born out of the Protestant reaction against the Catholic counter-reformation, when the philosophical views of the past two centuries crystallized into a coherent world view. He argues that many of the philosophical views, such as affinity for democracy against monarchy, originated among Protestants in the early sixteenth century to justify their desire to break away from the pope and the Catholic Church. Though many of these philosophical ideals were picked up by Catholics, Russell argues, by the eighteenth century the Enlightenment was the principal manifestation of the schism that began with Martin Luther.

Chartier (1991) argues that the Enlightenment was only invented after the fact for a political goal. He claims the leaders of the French Revolution created an Enlightenment canon of basic text, by selecting certain authors and identifying them with The Enlightenment in order to legitimize their republican political agenda.

Historian Jonathan Israel dismisses the post-modern interpretation of the Enlightenment and the attempts of modern historians to link social and economical reasons for the revolutionary aspect of the period. He instead focuses on the history of ideas in the period from 1650 to the end of the eighteenth century, and claims that it was the ideas themselves that caused the change that eventually led to the revolutions of the later half of the eighteenth century and the early nineteenth century. Israel argues that until the 1650s Western civilization "was based on a largely shared core of faith, tradition and authority." Up until this date most intellectual debates revolved around "confessional"—that is Catholic, Lutheran, Reformed

(Calvinist), or Anglican issues", and the main aim of these debates was to establish which bloc of faith ought to have the "monopoly of truth and a God-given title to authority." After this date everything thus previously rooted in tradition was questioned and often replaced by new concepts in the light of philosophical reason. After the second half of the seventeenth century and during the eighteenth century a "general process of rationalization and secularization set in which rapidly overthrew theology's age-old hegemony in the world of study", and thus confessional disputes were reduced to a secondary status in favour of the "escalating contest between faith and incredulity." This period saw the shaping of two distinct lines of enlightenment thought. Firstly, the radical enlightenment, largely inspired by the one-substance philosophy of Spinoza, which in its political form adhered to: "democracy; racial and sexual equality; individual liberty of lifestyle; full freedom of thought, expression, and the press; eradication of religious authority from the legislative process and education; and full separation of church and state." Secondly, the moderate enlightenment, which in a number of different philosophical systems, like those in the writings of Descartes, John Locke, Isaac Newton or Christian Wolff, expressed some support for critical review and renewal of the old modes of thought, but in other parts sought reform and accommodation with the old systems of power and faith. These two lines of thought were again met by the conservative Counter-Enlightenment, encompassing those thinkers who held on to the traditional belief-based systems of thought.

JEAN JACQUES ROUSSEAU (1712-1778)

Early Life

Jean-Jacques Rousseau was born to Suzanne Bernard and Isaac Rousseau on June 28, 1712, in Geneva, Switzerland. Nine days later his mother died. At the age of three, he was reading French novels with his father, and Jean-Jacques acquired his passion for music from his aunt. His father fled Geneva to avoid imprisonment when Jean-Jacques was ten. By the time he was thirteen, his formal education had ended and he was sent to work for a notary public (someone legally empowered to certify documents), but he was soon dismissed as fit only for watch making. Afterwards Rousseau spent three miserable years serving as a watchmaker, which he abandoned when he found himself unexpectedly locked out of the city by its closed gates. He faced the world with no money or belongings and no obvious talents.

Rousseau found himself on Palm Sunday, 1728, in Annecy, France, at the house of Louise Eleonore, Baronne de Warens. Rousseau lived under her roof off and on for thirteen years and was dominated by her influence. Charming and clever, a natural businesswoman, Madame de Warens was a woman who lived by her wits. She supported him and found him jobs, most of which he disliked. A friend, after examining the lad, informed her that he might aspire to become a village curé (priest) but nothing more. Still Rousseau read, studied, and thought. He pursued music and gave lessons, and for a time he worked as a tutor.

First Publication and Operas

Rousseau's scheme for musical notation, published in 1743 as Dissertation *surla musique moderne*, brought him neither fame nor fortune—only a fond letter from the *Académie des Sciences*. But his interest in music spurred him to write two operas—*Les Muses galantes* (1742) and *Le Devin du village* (1752)—and permitted him to write articles on music for Denis Diderot's (1713–1784) *Encyclopédie*; *the Lettre sur la musique française* (1753) and *the Dictionnaire de musique*, published in 1767.

From September 1743 until August 1744, Rousseau served as secretary to the French ambassador to Venice, Italy. He experienced at firsthand the stupidity and corruption (dishonesty and deception) involved in these offices. Rousseau spent the remaining years before his success with his first Discours in Paris, where he lived the poor lifestyle of a struggling intellectual.

In March 1745 Rousseau began an affair with Thérèse Le Vasseur. She was twenty-four years old, a maid at Rousseau's lodgings. She remained with him for the rest of his life—as mistress, housekeeper, mother of his children, and finally, in 1768, as his wife. They had five children—though some biographers have questioned whether any of them were Rousseau's. Apparently he regarded them as his own even though he assigned them to a hospital for abandoned children. Rousseau had no means to educate them, and he reasoned that they would be better raised as workers and peasants by the state.

By 1749 Rousseau had befriended the French philosopher Diderot. The publication of Diderot's Lettre sur les aveugles had resulted in his imprisonment at Vincennes, France. While walking to Vincennes to visit Diderot, Rousseau read an announcement of a prize being offered by the Dijon Academy for the best essay on the question, "Has progress of the arts and sciences contributed more to the corruption or to the purification of morals?" Rousseau won the prize of the Dijon Academy with his *Discours sur les sciences et les arts*. His famous "attack" on civilization called for sixty-eight articles defending the arts and sciences. Though he himself regarded this essay as "the weakest in argument and the poorest in harmony and proportion" of all his works, he nonetheless believed that it sounded one of his essential themes: the arts and sciences, instead of freeing men and increasing their happiness, had for the most part imprisoned men further.

Major Works

Rousseau's novel *La Nouvelle Héloïse* (1761) attempted to portray in fiction the sufferings and tragedy that foolish education and restrictive social customs had among sensitive creatures. Rousseau's two other major writings—*L'émile ou de l'éducation* (1762) and *Du contrat social* (1762)—undertook the more difficult task of constructing an education and a social order that would enable men to be natural and free; that is, to enable men to recognize no bondage except the bondage of natural necessity. To be free in this sense, said Rousseau, was to be happy.

La Nouvelle Héloïse appeared in Paris in January 1761. Originally entitled *Lettres de deux amants, habitants d'une petite ville au pied des Alpes*, the work was structurally a novel in letters, after the fashion of the English author Samuel Richardson (1689–1761). The originality of the novel won it harsh reviews, but its sexual nature made it immensely popular with the public. It remained a best seller until the French Revolution in 1789, a massive uprising calling for political and social change throughout France.

The reputation of *La Nouvelle Héloïse* was nothing compared to the storm produced by *L'émile* and *Du contrat social.* Even today the ideas set forth in these works are revolutionary. Their expression, especially in *L'émile*, in a style both readable and alluring made them dangerous. *L'émile* was condemned (officially dissaproved of) by the Paris Parliament (the governing body) and heavily criticized by the archbishop of Paris. Both of the books were burned by the authorities in Geneva, Switzerland.

Exile and Death

Forced to flee from France, Rousseau sought refuge at Yverdon in the territory of Bern. There he was kicked out by the Bernese authorities and would spend the next few years seeking a safe place to live. Finally, British philosopher David Hume (1711–1776) helped Rousseau settle in Wotton, Derbyshire, England, in 1766. Hume managed to obtain from George III (1738–1820) a yearly pension (sum of money) for Rousseau. But Rousseau, falsely believing Hume to be in league with his Parisian and Genevan enemies, not only refused the pension but also openly broke with the philosopher.

Rousseau returned to France in June 1767 under the protection of the Prince de Conti. Wandering from place to place, he at last settled in 1770 in Paris. There he made a living, as he often had in the past, by copying music. By December 1770 *the Confessions*, upon which he had been working since 1766, was completed, and he gave readings from this work at various private homes. His last work, *Les Rêveries du promeneur solitaire*, begun in 1776 and unfinished at his death, records how Rousseau, an outcast from society, recaptured "serenity, tranquility, peace, even happiness."

In May 1778 Rousseau accepted Marquis de Giradin's hospitality at Ermenonville near Paris. There, with Thérèse at his bedside, he died on July 2, 1778, probably from uremia, a severe kidney disease. Rousseau was buried on the Île des Peupliers at Ermenonville. In October 1794 his remains were transferred to the Panthéon in Paris. Thérèse, surviving him by twenty-two years, died in 1801 at the age of eighty.

Influences on Rousseau

Quarrels

Rousseau's emphasis on emotion over reason placed him at loggerheads with the general outlook of his day. His exploration of how man came to sublimate individual interests to the needs of society finds parallels with the speculation of the British philosophers, Hobbes and Locke. But his understanding of both "natural man" and of society differs significantly.

Rousseau's quarrels with his contemporaries were often more than philosophical. They were bitter and personal. He was at one time, a close friend of Diderot and contributed an article to his "Encyclopedia", but they fell out, each accusing the other of breaches of confidence. His visit with the philosopher Hume, who offered him a home in England, also ended in bitter argument.

Revolution

His concept of the State as an entity higher than the citizens that live in it greatly influenced a generation of thinkers, and had much appeal to advocates of the French Revolution. Many see Rousseau's political philosophy as the inspiration for the intellectual movement that instigated the revolution (although, as Marx stressed, the revolution was as much related to economic pressures as to demands for political freedom). Still, echoes of Rousseau's philosophy are clear in the revolutionary slogan "Liberty, Equality, Fraternity" and in Robespierre's concept of a Supreme Being, a republican deity that embodied civic virtue and opposition to tyranny, to whom choirs of citizens would sing hymns of praise.

Romanticism

Rousseau's glorification of "man in nature" initiated a Romantic movement that would dominate much of art and literature for generations. The Romantics spurned the mechanistic view of a nature whose laws could be understood through scientific investigation. They sought a more direct and emotional relationship with nature. Less than twenty years after Rousseau's idealised picture of "natural man" was formulated, Tahiti and other Pacific islands were discovered. Early navigators like Bouganville, an admirer of Rousseau, saw here idyllic societies unsullied by science and technology, living examples of the harmony envisaged by Rousseau. The inhabitants were not dismissed as primitives to be pitied for their lack of civilised ways, but were idealised as "noble savages." Their life was to be envied not despised.

Concept of Human Nature

According to Rousseau, man was basically good and it is only the wrong actions which make him wicked. He holds that man is government by the two instincts-self love and mutual aid or sympathy. According to Rousseau, man by birth had no evil tendencies but it was the result of wrong social action which made him evil.

Self-love

Rousseau believed that man by nature has only two instinct, of them one is 'self-love'. His first preference always is to attend to his own presentation, his first cares are those which he owes himself.

Sympathy

Man's second instinct is that of sympathy or instinct of mutual aid. These instincts, Rousseau believed, always make our struggle for existence easier and do us better than harm.

Conscience

There was very possibility of clashing of both these instincts at one time and the other and as a result of clash another instinct called 'conscience' emerges. It is this conscience which is something above education and reason and soles conflict between the first two instincts. Arguing father he says that reasoning comes only when the complexities of problems come to the front and the sentiments attached with those instincts do not successfully motivate the actions of men in the proper direction.

Pride

A problem which is bound to crop up is that if mankind was good by nature and gifted with the sentiments of love and sympathy. His simple answer was that because self-love went astray to become pride and the latter made men begin to feel ashamed or honoured over being deprived or getting something in competitions. He believed that this pride was the root cause of many evils.

Freedom to Choose

Rousseau also believed in addition to above instincts nature has also gifted mankind with another instinct, viz. the freedom to choose his own path which distinguished a man from an animal. This freedom according to him was essential for the perfection of mankind.

Rousseau on State of Nature

Rousseau starts with the conception of natural man and natural right. Hobbes had argued that the State of Nature was a state of war; that the life of man in it was solitary, poor, nasty, brutish and short. Locke held the view that the State of Nature was normally peaceful and pleasant but he argued that life in State of Nature was vexatious and inconvenient. Therefore, he entered into a contract and exchanged it for a civil state. Rousseau accepted with few qualifications of Locke's view of the state of nature but emphasised even more strongly the peaceful, pleasant, idyllic condition of these natural state. It was not a State of war. The liberty that natural man possessed was boundless and absolute. The State of Nature of Rousseau was completely stands for anarchic individualist freedom. Its essential characteristic is that in it man lives in isolation from his fellows. Though he was unsocial and immoral, he possessed an underdeveloped capacity for morality and reason. In this state, inequality, oppression and poverty which are the lot of the bulk of the inhabitants of the most modern political states were absent.

Rousseau believed that in the State of Nature people lived an isolated life and had neither ties of obligation nor duties. He did not know how to deliver a speech and had no cares for dress. He was free, self-contented and unknown to social good, evil or fear. He was not even afraid of death and had no fear of loss of property or family because he had neither proprty nor family. To him in this state man was in peaceful ignorance.

Rousseau believed that for man could not lead a solitary life. His social instinct compelled him to live in groups. Social institutions began to gradually develop. His instinct of self-love began to shape itself into pride and man began to think in terms of private property.

Rousseau believed that this institution of private property which entered in the society disturbed the whole atmosphere of pre-civil state. According to Rousseau, with the passage of time many other complicated problems also came to the front. The private property created a problem and the society was divided between the rich and the poor. It also resulted in the division of labour and thus whole social set up was disturbed.

In the State of Nature, man was guided by two sentiments—self-interest and pity. Having no normal obligations with others he could not be good or bad or virtuous or vicious. So, a natural man was an animal. He wholly lacked language. Without language any idea of general good is impossible. So, a natural man was neither moral nor vicious. He was not unhappy. Neither was he happy. He had no property. Property comes into existence as a result of ideas, wants, foreseen knowledge and industry. Selfishness, hate, regard for the opinion of others, arts, slavery, vice, conjugal and paternal affection, all exist in men only as social beings living together in larger or smaller groups. They do not exist in a natural man.

Rousseau's Social Contract Theory

The social contract of Rousseau opens with the famous sentence "Man is born free, however, he is everywhere in chains." The sentence as it stands may mean that man ought to be free independent and solitary. But conventions, customs of society, the various regulations and restrictions which political and economic institutions involve enslave him and cause his fall from his original and blessed state of freedom. Rousseau actually meant was man ought to be free not in the sense of being able to do just whatever he wants but in the sense of being able to do just whatever ought to do. Thus, freedom of which Rousseau is talking about is no longer licence. It is no longer the unrestricted conduct of a separate and independent individual. On the contrary, the term means participation by all individuals in a large life in such a manner so that the good of the community may be promoted. Then only the individual is free.

This is an unusual notion of freedom. It is not at all that physical freedom to do whatever we can as Hobbes would have understood this assertion. It is not even the moral autonomy of the individual man to judge and decide for himself which Locke would have meant. Rousseau's freedom implies certain amount of restraint. That is, free will is that which is subject to moral laws.

However, according to Rousseau, soon after the serpent, in the form of private property, entered into the society, the whole peaceful atmosphere and the order was disturbed and the men began to fill the necessity of bringing about the old order of calmness and happy life. The problem was solved by the creation of a social and political association to which all the members of the society agreed. Reconciliation between the individual on the one hand and the society on the other was to be arrived at by the way of contract. He agreed with Locke that individuals consent was necessary for binding him in the contract.

Like Plato and Hobbes, Rousseau also tried to completely merge individual in the state. He maintained that the system of equality made all to surrender their rights. But another serious problem was that the individuals who had by now become selfish and self-centred were not willing to subordinate themselves to any individual. Rousseau solved this problem by saying that the contract was concluded between the individuals and the society or the community. He made his contract a double sided one. His individual as a part of sovereignty was bound to other individuals and as a part of the state he was bound to the sovereign. Rousseau's individual thus executed a contract in his individual capacity as well as in his corporate capacity.

To sum up the discussion, salient features of Rousseau's contract were—

1. **Surrender to society**—Individual surrendered his everything to the society and yet as a member of the society he retained everything with himself.
2. **Gain to everyone**—In his contract everyone seem to be a gainer and none appear to be a loser.
3. **Surrender to the state**—The rights were surrendered not to an individual but to a body to whom everyone understood.
4. **Organic concept**—The contract had organic in nature. It was moral, collective and had a public person.
5. **Transformation**–under this contract an individual got material and moral transformation.

But there is an explicit difference between the contracts stipulated by Locke and Rousseau. According to A. Hacker, "This conception makes a departure from Hobbes and Locke's definition of freedom." Not only this but whereas Locke's contract was only for a specific object in view, Rousseau's contract was a continuous process because he believed that the community could grow rich and become fertile only with the constant participation of individuals in the welfare of the society.

Criticism

Rousseau's theory of social contract has been criticised on the following grounds:

(1) The contract of Rousseau is social like that of Hobbes. It is not governmental like that of Locke. It is a mutual agreement between the individuals. It is bound the individual with one another and also the sovereign state. Thus the ideas of Hobbes and Locke are combined together by Rousseau in his theory of social contract. It is not an original idea of Rousseau.

(2) According to Sabine, Rousseau in view of his criticism of the natural man ought to have avoided the notion of contract altogether as both meaningless and misleading.

(3) The imaginary act by which a society is produced is not even remotely like a contract, because the rights and liberties of individuals have no existence at all except as they are already members of groups.

(4) Rousseau's whole argument depended upon the fact that a community of citizens is unique and coeval with its members; they, neither make it nor have rights against it. It is an 'association' not an 'aggregation" a moral and collective personality. The word contract was about as misleading as any that Rousseau could have chosen.

(5) Lastly, Rousseau's theory of social contract is not compatible with his theory General Will. If General Will is supreme then social contract is unnecessary and meaningless and if social contract is necessary then General Will is not supreme.

Rousseau's General Will

Rousseau regarded consent as the basis of society but emphasised the importance of the community along with the need to protect individual freedom. A community was created for the benefit of the individual, and Rousseau attempted to reconcile the two claims: that of the community with that of the individual the claims of authority with those of liberty. A community that was constituted by all consenting individuals voluntarily submitting to the General Will was the solution to his paradox that though persons were born free, yet they were in chains. There was a moral transformation in the individuals once a community was created. This was because, having voluntarily created it, the community was seen as furthering the individuals moral autonomy. Since it was through society that individuals realised their full potential, it could be recognised to ensure the freedom that individuals enjoyed when they were in a state of nature. This was possible once the right society was created, for that would maximise individual liberty.

Rousseau described the community vested with a 'General Will', a will of all individuals thinking of general and public interests. It was the 'Common Me', meaning that the best spirit of the individual was represented in it. The selfish nature of the individual was transformed bringing forth co-operative instincts and essential goodness.

Rousseau was of the opinion that man having grown sick of the anarchy which the serpent of private property brought in the society thought of creating a sovereign. The contract was concluded by a pact between the individuals and the community consisting of individuals who formed the society. The individuals surrendered all their powers and rights to the community as a whole bowed before the General Will, which in the ultimate analysis was the sovereign.

The General Will would be the source of all laws. The human beings would be truly free if he followed the dictates of the law. Civil liberty, for Rousseau meant freedom from the assault of others, from the following arbitrary will of another person and obedience to one's notions of liberty. Of course, if one had to be free then one had to obey one's own will which meant that one's will and the law. Of the state and the laws of the state would have to be in harmony. Each individual would have to be a law maker, consenting to obey a law if it maximised freedom. It was for this reasons that he desired that the free state would be a consensual and participatory democracy. He was categorical that the General Will could emerge only in an assembly of equal law makers. It could not be alienated. The "Executive Will" could not be the General Will. Only the legislative will which was sovereign, could be the General Will. The individual participated in the articulation of the General Will, for citizenship was the highest that one could aspire for. The General Will could not be the will of the majority. In fact it did not represent the will of all. It was the difference between the sum of judgements about the common good and mere aggregate of personal fancies and individual desires. It would always aim and promote the general interest and the will of all its members.

In order to properly understand the theory of General Will, it is proper to understand the terms 'Actual Will' and 'Real Will'. From Actual Will, Rousseau understood the will which was selfish, irrational and thought of the good of the individual alone. It conceives of the individual alone and has no concern with the welfare of the society. On the other hand, he believed that the Real Will was something higher, nobler and supreme. It thought more about the well being of all than that of one individual. It was more social than anti-social, collective than individualistic. In other words, his Real Will was channel for promoting the well-being of the individuals and the society because when he thought of the society it also thought about the well fare of the individuals. This Real Will was permanent and not transitory. It did not take into consideration only the monetary aspects of life but also its permanent aspects. This will was based on reason and criticism.

According to Rousseau, General Will was the sum total of all the 'Real Wills' of the individuals which were based on reason farsightedness of the individuals.

It was the will of all the individuals for collective welfare. It was common consciousness. Rousseau has defined General Will as the public person, so formed by the Union of all other persons is called by its member state when passive, sovereign when active.

According to Rousseau, General Will was not the sum total of good and bad wills of the individuals by a method of plus and minus but was something nobler which was the product of deliberations, discussions and consciousness. General Will is concerned with general good but it might not be willed by the majority of the members of the society.

Rousseau believed that in General Will none was slave or under subordination to anyone else. Everbody was free.

Rousseau tried to distinguish between the General Will and the Will of all. General Will considered about the good of the community as a whole whereas will of all was all majority will and considered about the majority of a few only. But the will of all could become General Will of peculiar interests, which have selfish ends and are taken away from it.

Salient Feature of General Will

Thus, according to Rousseau, General Will has the following particular features:

(1) Unity

General Will was rational and not self-contradictory. It thus, gave us the unity in the sense that it was indivisible because once divided it will not be called 'General Will' but only 'Sectional Will'.

(2) Permanent Will

Since General Will was based on reason, wisdom and experience and thought about the good of all, it was not to sway with the time but was permanent. It cannot be altered or changed. Even though it may be dominated by other wills for some time yet in the ultimate analysis this will dominates others.

(3) Right Will

It was the will which takes into consideration not only the political and social but also moral conditions. As such it was right will based on right reasoning and presumptions.

(4) Inalienable

Rousseau's sovereign is General Will and not any human being. Rousseau's sovereign in fact cannot give up the sovereignty and also cannot pass that on to any other individual because sovereignty was vested in the community as a whole. Community could not pass on the sovereign authority to any other Individual Will. Thus, sovereignty and General Will were inseparable. For him, alienating General Will was killing that.

(5) Not representable

According to Rousseau's conception, people had no right to delegate their authority of representing themselves by anybody else. He believed in the theory of direct democracy through General Will.

(6) Rational

Rousseau based his theory of General Will on Rationalism and thus for him will was not force but the very basis of sustaining state.

(7) It is uninterested

According to Rousseau, General Will was uninterested firstly because it was not concerned with the individual but with the community as a whole and secondly, it promoted public spiritedness. Thus, General Will was not interested in any section of society but took into consideration will of society as a whole.

(8) It cannot be Executive

Another characteristics of General Will was that it was not executive. In his opinion since General Will was impersonal it could not be loaded with the responsibility of enforcing law. It was sovereign in nature and character and as such Government was only an agency of General Will. He has also suggested that General Will could not be executive as well as legislative body.

Criticism of General Will

(1) It boils down to striking the balances of Real Will and Actual Will and has thus tried to it an arithmetical touch. Even if Rousseau's notion is accepted General Will is a dynamic process and not arithmetical one. So, his theory of General Will is not very clear.

(2) Rousseau has tried to distinguish between General Will and will of all which in practice is impossible to differentiate.

(3) Rousseau's conception of General Will is more or less a unanimous will and decisions are possible only in the animal and not in human society.

(4) Rousseau has tried to divide the will of an individual into two integral parts, viz. essential and non-essential wills. According to him, essential will was rational and represented sum totals of essential wills. But who can deny that individuals and their wills are corporate and that it is impossible to distinguish and divide the wills.

(5) Rousseau himself has reduced his theory of 'General Will' to nothingness when he says that General Will was not majority will. He has in fact created such confusion that it is difficult to adjust his view.

(6) The notion of General Will was expounded by Rousseau might to some extent be possible in case where the community is small and the individuals have personal contacts with each other but it is impossible to follow this conception and put it into actual practice of nation states of today.

(7) Rousseau believed that in General Will there should only be direct and not indirect representation. This again is not practical in modern nation state. The system of direct representation can only be possible in small states.

(8) The conception of General Will is not practicable on human grounds as well. Who can deny that in normal time men are selfish and considered their own interest above everything else. It is only in the national crisis grave emergencies that they think of common good. To think of men giving up their selfish ends for collective ends is something extraordinary against human nature.

(9) Rousseau has failed to guide the community as to how it can be applied in actual practice and also how to achieve that.

(10) Rousseau has also been criticised because his theory of General Will is against his social contract theory. Not only this but his theory is against his ideas of individualism. Wayper has expressed

this opinion when he said that "For if the General Will is supreme, the social contract is unnecessary and meaningless, and if the social contract is necessary and significant, the General Will cannot be supreme."

Rousseau on Sovereignty and Government

Rousseau's concept of sovereignty was congruent with that of Hobbes regarding power as the basis of the sovereignty. Nevertheless, concerning the mere existence of the sovereign power as the sufficient basis for obedience to the sovereign, he strongly disagreed with him. Rousseau's theory belongs to the Classical theory of sovereignty because it meets at least two conditions of this theory. First, the sovereign power is unlimited. Second, sovereign power is the origin of all the rights in the state. Rousseau's theory of sovereignty fulfils both conditions. He defines sovereignty as unlimited. Rousseau excluded any possibility that the state of nature with its main element, freedom, could limit sovereign power. Rousseau holds that sovereignty was the only source of all the rights and the creator of the complete legal order in the state. The freedom along with all other rights, is a concession of the sovereign. It does not recognize them; it creates them.

Popular sovereignty, which is an important idea presented in Rousseau's political philosophy, also should be taken into account since, by its nature, it has the capacity to affect and modify the classical idea of unlimited sovereignty which Rousseau is advocate of.

The idea of popular sovereignty, in general, does not pay much attention to the organization of the state. The conception of popular sovereignty is not the conception of the state, but that of the community. Bodin and Hobbes had in mind the state organization when writing their works. Rousseau, on the other hand, was dissatisfied with the state in general. His First and Second Discourse, on the whole, offered a negative picture of the state and society. Hence, he believed that people could be happy and felicitous only after having established a very community of people. Rousseau assumed that sovereignty is the notion pertaining to the political community. He did not make any attempt to differentiate community from the state: they were the same thing. In this sense, people, as, the, community, are beyond the reach of the legal-state organization not only in the state of nature, but also after the creation of the state. And even if the state is once erected, established and organized, people are free to disobey to the state authority, and even to reorganize or to destroy the state organization itself. This is the final consequence of popular sovereignty taken in its most extreme form.

With no regard to the fact that the mere existence of sovereignty does not present the element of the Classical Theory of sovereignty, it is interesting to notice this distinction between Hobbes and Rousseau, since it points at the fact that Rousseau had an ethical understanding of the role of sovereignty, which was quite irrelevant for the Classical theory. This feature will be of significance later in the analysis of the relationship between Sovereignty and the General Will. Since in practice of erecting the state, it was impossible to establish the state on the basis of popular sovereignty, the latter concept itself was to be changed, if the state was to be erected. Therefore, in practice, Rousseau's principles of sovereignty have been constantly weakened "by accommodation to the facts of political organization; and this adjustment has constantly taken the form of compromise with the doctrine of Hobbes or the doctrine of Hobbes' constitutionalist and pre-Rousseau critics."

Strictly defined, a sovereign is the voice of the law and the absolute authority within a given state. In Rousseau's time, the sovereign was usually an absolute monarch. In The Social Contract, however, this word is given a new meaning. In a healthy republic, Rousseau defines the sovereign as all the citizens acting collectively. Together, they voice the general will and the laws of the state. The sovereign cannot be represented, divided, or broken up in any way: only all the people speaking collectively can be sovereign.

This is the executive power of a state, which takes care of particular matters and day-to-day business. There are as many different kinds of government as there are states, though they can be roughly divided into democracy (the rule of the many), aristocracy (the rule of the few), and monarchy (the rule of a single individual). The government represents the people: it is not sovereign, and it cannot speak for the general will. It has its own corporate will that is often at odds with the general will. For this reason, there is often friction between the government and the sovereign that can bring about the downfall of the state.

Rousseau on Individualism and Absolutism

In contrast to Locke, Rousseau did not emphasize individualism. Rousseau's political philosophy was encapsulated in the idea of the "General Will." Wolin correctly explains that Rousseau believed that the precondition for dependence upon the whole as opposed to nature, individuals, or classes, required "the voluntary and total surrender by each individual of all his rights and powers."As Rousseau himself stated, "each of us puts his person and all his power in common under the supreme direction of the general will." Rousseau claims that there is a great difference between the "general will," which considers "only the common interest," and the "will of all," which considers the "sum of private wills." At the same time Rousseau argues that the "general will is always right and always tends towards the public utility."

It is his straying from the groundbreaking thinking of Lockean individualism that makes Rousseau's philosophy dangerous. Rousseau naively assumes that there is one "general will" which benefits everyone. In my estimation, the common good is an aggregate of private interests. A truly free society must protect competing interests. Rousseau also makes no distinctions between "will" and "utility" saying the "general will" is always in the best interest. What makes this thinking perilous is that, despite the fact that Rousseau attempts to differentiate between "general will" and "will of all," he leaves unexplained the mechanism to determine whether something is "general will" or not. This only leads to the worst forms of tyranny as totalitarian regimes can exploit this concept and force the people to act against their true will. Furthermore, an inevitable result on reliance on the "general will" is tyranny of the majority. Rousseau famously said that if someone does not abide by "the general will" then he must be "forced to be free," a paradox to the very concept of freedom from a classical liberal perspective.

Locke is the greatest modern thinker because of his emphasis on freedom and equality. He provides the framework for a government that is meant to protect the rights of its citizens. He importantly argues that property is the result of hard labour, recognizing that not only are individual rights important, but the advancement of individual interests as well. Rousseau thought he could increase freedom through the "general will" because "private interest tends always to preferences, the public interest to equality." Rousseau was paving a dangerous path that would be taken up by succeeding writers stressing "subordination of the individual to the group," a concept that I do not value. In my opinion, it is important to value individual rights and preferences. It is essential to encourage hard work with incentive and property. It is imperative to have a government that protects the people's rights.

Rousseau had no purpose to serve like Hobbes and Locke. His was only a philosophical attempt to explain the origin of civil society. He tried to combine Hobbes absolutism with Locke's idea of popular sovereignty. He was an original genius. Lason says that "he is to be found at the entrance to all paths leading to the present." But Rousseau and contradiction go together. He is an idealist and at times, confused. For him property is both an evil and a sacred institution. He preaches toleration for all but banishes atheists from his state. He is the extreme absolutist and the extreme individualist.

Inconsistencies and Shortcomings of Rousseau

Rousseau's political philosophy suffers from serious contradictions. In his Discourses on the Origin of Inequality as well as Emile he condemns private property but subsequently he makes it one of the duties of the state to defend private property. Similarly, he makes a strong plea of democracy and maximum rights for the people, but actually creates an absolute sovereign with dictatorial powers. The main shortcomings of Rousseau's philosophy are mentioned below—

1. Rousseau's theory is as much unhistorical as that of Hobbes or Locke. Never was there any 'State of Nature' when man lived without society.
2. While the description of State of Nature by Hobbes was on one extreme, Rousseau's description is on the other. To Hobbes, it was a state of warfare; to Rousseau, it was one of divine happiness.
   If to one, man was selfish, to the other, man was noble savage. These are two extremes unjustifiable by history or logic or psychology.
3. Rousseau is as much illogical as the other contractualists are. How could the noble savage, not familiar with civil society, think of creating one and that too by contract?
4. The conception of General Will is vague, indefinite and abstract.
   It is difficult to find out the general will in practice. It can be at the most the will of the majority or even an overwhelming majority but not of all the people.
5. Rousseau by denying rights to the individual, thus subjects him to the tyranny of the State which in actual practice is represented by a government controlling a majority in the legislature.
6. Even if Rousseau's theory is accepted, it cannot be applied to big states. At the most it could suit small city-states where people could come together and decide matters directly and make laws and elect officers. It cannot be possible in modern nation States.
7. Rousseau was hardly aware of the fact that the unrestrained power of the general will might result in an absolutism similar to that of old kingdoms and oligarchies.
8. It is interesting to note that Rousseau equates individual liberty with the obedience of laws made by the Sovereign. He emphasizes the fact that an individual is a part and parcel of the corporate

community expressive of General Will. As such, by obeying the General Will which is the 'goodwill' of the Sovereign Community, he obeys none but himself and remains as free as ever.

Rousseau's Contribution to Political Thought

Despite the numerous flaws and contradictions in Rousseau's political thought discussed above, it cannot be denied that his writings have exercised profound influence on the subsequent political thinkers. His works, particularly, Social Contract exercised profound influence on the French people and prepared them for the Great French Revolution. His contributions to the development of political thought can be summarized as follows:

1. Rousseau emphasized the importance of the state in the life of the individual and asserted that the fullest development of individual's personality was possible only within the state. However, he refused to treat state as an end in itself. It was retained as an instrument of general welfare of the individual.
2. His theory of popular sovereignty is another outstanding contribution. No doubt, other thinkers before Rousseau gave theory of sovereignty but none of them emphasized the doctrine of popular sovereignty. His influence is clear from the fact that in the later years it became a fashion to talk of popular sovereignty.
3. Rousseau developed the concept of Nation-State by laying emphasis on the principle of common good, common interest, general will as well as unity and solidarity of the people.
4. Rousseau left deep impact on the idealist school of thought. His concept of General Will greatly influence idealist thinkers like Kant and Hegel. The latter's Spirit of Nation was nothing but a reformed form of Rousseau's concept of General Will.
5. Rousseau gave the concept of common good which was subsequently developed by the utilitarian thinkers like Bentham and Mill into the concept of "the greatest good of the greatest number."

We may conclude this discussion with the following estimation of Rousseau's contribution to political theory by Prof. Hearns "He (Rousseau) displays the people as the ultimate source of political authority, he proclaims the common good to be the proper end of government, he stresses the view that the State is a social organism; he develops the idea that as an organism, it has a common conscience and a general will; he maintains the doctrine that the true basis of political obligation is consent; he maintains the doctrine that the true basis of political obligation is consent; he proclaims the possibility of the ultimate reconciliation of freedom and authority… He takes a high place among political idealists."

Hobbes, Locke and Rousseau Comparison

	Hobbes	*Locke*	*Rousseau*
State of Nature	The state of nature is a state of war. No morality exists. Everyone lives in constant fear. Because of this fear, no one is really free, but, since even the "weakest" could kill the "strongest" men are equal.	Men exist in the state of nature in perfect freedom to do what they want. The state of nature is not necessarily good or bad. It is chaotic. So, men do give it up to secure the advantages of civilized society.	Men in a state of nature are free and equal. In a state of nature, men are "Noble Savages." Civilization is what corrupted him.
Purpose of Government	To impose law and order to prevent the state of war.	To secure natural rights, namely man's property and liberty.	To bring people into harmony. To unite them under the "General Will."
Representation	Governments are designed to control, not necessarily represent.	Representation ensures that governments are responsive to the people. Representation is a safeguard against oppression.	Representation is not enough. Citizens cannot delegate their civic duties. They must be actively involved. Rousseau favours a more direct democracy to enact the general will.
Impact on Founders	Governments must be designed to protect the people from themselves.	1. Governments must be designed to protect the people from the government. 2. Natural Rights must be secured.	1. Governments must be responsive and aligned with the general will. 2. People make a nation, not institutions. 3. Individual wills are subordinate to the general (collective) will.

JOHN STUART MILL (1806-1873)

John Stuart Mill, (20 May, 1806–8 May, 1873) was a British philosopher, political economist and civil servant. He was an influential contributor to social theory, political theory, and political economy. He has been called "the most influential English-speaking philosopher of the nineteenth century." Mill's conception of liberty justified the freedom of the individual in opposition to unlimited state control. He was a proponent of utilitarianism, an ethical theory developed by Jeremy Bentham. Hoping to remedy the problems found in an inductive approach to science, such as confirmation bias, he clearly set forth the premises of falsification as the key component in the scientific method. Mill was also a Member of Parliament and an important figure in liberal political philosophy.

Early Years

Born in 1806, John Stuart Mill was the eldest son of James Mill and Harriet Barrow (whose influence on Mill was vastly overshadowed by that of his father). A struggling man of letters, James Mill wrote History of British India (1818), and the work landed him a coveted position in the East India Company, where he rose to the post of chief examiner. When not carrying out his administrative duties, James Mill spent considerable time educating his son John, who began to learn Greek at age three and Latin at age eight. By the age of 14, John was extremely well versed in the Greek and Latin classics; had studied world history, logic and mathematics; and had mastered the basics of economic theory, all of which was part of his father's plan to make John Stuart Mill a young proponent of the views of the philosophical radicals.

By his late teens, Mill spent many hours editing Jeremy Bentham's manuscripts, and he threw himself into the work of the philosophic radicals (still guided by his father). He also founded a number of intellectual societies and began to contribute to periodicals, including the *Westminster Review* (which was founded by Bentham and James Mill). In 1823, his father secured him a junior position in the East India Company, and he, like his father before him, rose in the ranks, eventually taking his father's position of chief examiner.

Crisis and Evolution of the Thinker

In 1826, John Stuart Mill experienced what he would later call in his autobiography a "mental crisis," during which he suffered a nervous breakdown marked by depression. It was likely triggered by the intense stress of his education, the continual influence of his domineering father, and other factors, but what emerged from this period is in the end more important than what caused it: Because of the depression, Mill started to rethink his entire life's work thus far and to reformulate theories he had previously wholly embraced.

Mill's new path began with a struggle to revise his father's and Bentham's work, which he suddenly saw as limited in a number of ways. This new drive was perhaps triggered by the poetry he had begun reading, most notably that of William Wordsworth. Mill found something of a mental balm in the verses of Wordsworth. Over the course of several months, his depression disappeared, and with it many of his former firmly held ideals.

Mill came to believe that he had been emotionally stunted by his father's demanding analytical training, that his ability to feel had been compromised by the constant cultivation of his intellect, and that this emotional component was lacking from what the radical philosophers had been espousing. He, therefore, sought a philosophy that could overcome the limits imposed by culture and history (e.g. natural rights) on any possible reform movement and would advance the roles of feeling and imagination.

Mill began to dismantle much of the negative (and therefore limited) polemic of Bentham and his father.

He understood that fighting the negativity against which he was rebelling with more negativity was futile, so he allowed himself to see the good and to view the defenders of the old ways not as reactionaries but as those who have always advanced the good aspects of their generally flawed ways of thinking.

Mill must have considered his own role in advancing his formerly held beliefs, as he did not abandon Bentham's utilitarianism entirely, but now cantered his thoughts on its "positive" elements instead of attacking it critically and destructively; he focused on how its best parts could be used constructively in the creation of a new society. He advanced in his endeavour by immersing himself in the writings of a wide variety of thinkers (and corresponding with many as well), including John Ruskin, Auguste Comte and Alexis de Tocqueville, and editing a new journal that he co-founded with his father and Charles Moles worth, the London Review.

Major Works

In 1832, Jeremy Bentham died, followed closely by James Mill in 1836. With the deaths of his two mentors, Mill discovered that he had even more intellectual freedom. He used that freedom to create a new philosophic radicalism incorporating the ideas of thinkers such as Coleridge and Thomas Carlyle. He also acknowledged that while he was breaking away from Bentham, there were aspects of his mentor's philosophy that he intended to preserve.

The major works started to appear in 1843 with A System of Logic, Mill's most comprehensive and systematic philosophical work, which presented Mills' thoughts on inductive logic and the shortcomings of the use of syllogisms (arguments derived from general principles, in which two premises are used to deduce a conclusion) to advance deductive logic.

The year 1859 marked the publication of *On Liberty*, Mills' landmark work on supporting individuals' moral and economic freedom from the government and society at large. In his autobiography, Mill wrote of "the importance, to man and society, of giving full freedom to human nature to expand itself in innumerable and conflicting directions," an idea fully fleshed out in *On Liberty*. In the work, Mill asserts that individuals' opinions and behaviour should enjoy free rein, whether in the face of the law or social pressure. Perhaps as a segue into Mill's *Utilitarianism*, which would follow four years later, Mill makes one concession: If a person's behaviour harms other people, that behaviour should be constrained. The essay has been criticized for various vagaries in its arguments, but it provides an impassioned defence of non-conformity, diversity and individuality.

In 1861, *Utilitarianism* first began appearing in serialized form in *Fraser's Magazine*. The work comes from Mill's association with, and partial break from, the moral philosophy of Jeremy Bentham and would go on to be Mill's most famous work. It bolsters support for Bentham's philosophy and refutes certain misconceptions about it. In sum, utilitarianism as a moral philosophy rests on a single sentence: "Actions are right in proportion as they tend to promote happiness, wrong as they tend to produce the reverse of happiness." In his book, Mill argues that utilitarianism stems from "natural" sentiments that exist organically within human beings' social nature. Therefore, if society were simply to embrace acts that minimize pain and maximize happiness, the standards created would form an easily and naturally internalized code of ethics. In his exploration of this issue, Mill transcends discussions of good and evil, and humanity's fascination with concepts of them, and posits a single criterion for a universal morality.

Mill's Writings

Mill wrote a large number of books, pamphlets and articles. Some of his important works include *System of Logic* (1843); *Principles of Political Economy* (1848); *Enfranchisement of Women* (1848); *On Liberty* (1859); *Considerations on Representative Government* (1860); *Utilitarianism* (1863); *Women Suffrage* (1873); *Subjection of Women* (1869); *Three Essays on Religion* (1874) etc.

On Liberty

The topic of justice received further treatment at Mill's hands in his famous 1859 book *On Liberty*. This work is the one, along with *A System of Logic*, that Mill thought would have the most longevity. It concerns civil and social liberty or, to look at it from the contrary point of view, the nature and limits of the power that can legitimately be exercised by society over the individual.

Mill begins by retelling the history of struggle between rulers and ruled and suggests that social rather than political tyranny is the greater danger for modern, commercial nations like Britain. This social "tyranny of the majority" (a phrase Mill takes from Tocqueville) arises from the enforcement of rules of conduct that are both arbitrary and strongly adhered to. The practical principle that guides the majority "to their opinions on the regulation of human conduct, is the feeling in each person's mind that everybody should be required to act as he, and those with whom he sympathizes, would like them to act." Such a feeling is particularly dangerous because it is taken to be self-justifying and self-evident.

There is a need, therefore, for a rationally grounded principle which governs a society's dealings with individuals. This "one very simple principle"—often called the "harm principle"—entails that:

The sole end for which mankind are warranted, individually or collectively, in interfering with the liberty of action of any of their number, is self-protection. That the only purpose for which power can be rightfully exercised over any member of a civilized community, against his will, is to prevent harm to others. His own good, either physical or moral, is not a sufficient warrant. He cannot rightfully be compelled to do or forbear because it will be better for him to do so, because it will make him happier, because, in the opinion of others, to do so would be wise, or even right. These are good reasons for remonstrating with him, or reasoning with him, or persuading him, or entreating him, but not for compelling him, or visiting him with any evil in case he do otherwise.

This anti-paternalistic principle identifies three basic regions of human liberty: the "inward domain of consciousness," liberty of tastes and pursuits (i.e. of framing our own life plan), and the freedom to unite with others.

Mill, unlike other liberal theorists, makes no appeal to "abstract right" in order to justify the harm principle. The reason for accepting the freedom of individuals to act as they choose, so long as they cause minimal or no harm to others, is that it would promote "utility in the largest sense, grounded on the permanent interests of man as a progressive being." In other words, abiding by the harm principle is desirable because it promotes what Mill calls the "free development of individuality" or the development of our humanity.

Behind this rests the idea that humanity is capable of progress—that latent or underdeveloped abilities and virtues can be actualized under the right conditions. Human nature is not static. It is not merely re-expressed in generations and individuals. It is "not a machine to be built after a model, and set to do exactly the work prescribed for it, but a tree, which requires growing and developing itself on all sides, according to the tendency of the inward forces which make it a living thing." Though human nature can be thought of as something living, it is also, like an English garden, something amenable to improvement through effort. "Among the works of man, which human life is rightly employed in perfecting and beautifying, the first in importance surely is man himself." The two conditions that promote development of our humanity are freedom and variety of situation, both of which the harm principle encourages.

A basic philosophical problem presented by the work is what counts as "harm to others." Where should we mark the boundary between conduct that is principally self-regarding versus conduct that involves others? Does drug-use cause harm to others sufficient to be prevented? Does prostitution? Pornography? Should polygamy be allowed? How about public nudity? Though these are difficult questions, Mill provides the reader with a principled way of deliberating about them.

Mill and Utilitarianism

The canonical statement of Mill's utilitarianism can be found in Utilitarianism. This philosophy has a long tradition, although Mill's account is primarily influenced by Jeremy Bentham and Mill's father James Mill.

Utilitarianism is a theory in normative ethics holding that the proper course of action is the one that maximizes overall "happiness." It is now generally taken to be a form of consequentialism, although when Income first introduced that term it was to distinguish between 'old-fashioned Utilitarianism' and consequentialism. According to utilitarianism the moral worth of an action is determined only by its resulting outcome although there is debate over how much consideration should be given to actual consequences, foreseen consequences and intended consequences. Two influential contributors to this theory are Jeremy Bentham and John Stuart Mill. In A Fragment on Government Bentham says 'it is the greatest happiness of the greatest number that is the measure of right and wrong' and describes this as a fundamental axiom. In An Introduction to the Principles of Morals and Legislation he talks of "the principle of utility" but later prefers "the greatest happiness principle."

John Stuart Mill's book Utilitarianism is a philosophical defence of utilitarianism in ethics. The essay first appeared as a series of three articles published in Fraser's Magazine in 1861; the articles were collected and reprinted as a single book in 1863. It went through four editions during Mill's lifetime with minor additions and revisions.

Although Mill includes discussions of utilitarian ethical principles in other works such as On Liberty and The Subjection of Women, Utilitarianism contains Mill's only major discussion of the fundamental grounds for utilitarian ethical theory.

The essay is divided into five chapters, namely—

1. General Remarks;
2. What Utilitarianism Is;
3. Of the Ultimate Sanction of the Principle of Utility;
4. Of What Sort of Proof the Principle of Utility is Susceptible; and
5. On the Connection between Justice and Utility.

In the first two chapters, Mill aims to define precisely what utilitarianism claims in terms of the general moral principles that it uses to judge concrete actions, as well as in terms of the sort of evidence that is supposed to be given for such principles. He hopes thus to do away with some common misunderstandings of utilitarianism, as well as to defend it against philosophical criticisms, most notably those of Kant. In the first chapter, he distinguishes two broad schools of ethical theory—those whose principles are defended by appeals to intuition and those whose principles are defended by appeals to experience. He identifies utilitarianism as one of the empirical theories of ethics.

In the second chapter, Mill formulates a single ethical principle, from which he says all utilitarian ethical principles are derived:

The creed which accepts as the Foundation of Morals, Utility, or the Greatest-Happiness Principle, holds that actions are right in proportion as they tend to promote happiness, wrong as they tend to produce the reverse of happiness. By happiness are intended pleasure, and the absence of pain; by unhappiness, pain, and the privation of pleasure.

Most importantly, it is not the agent's own greatest happiness that matters "but the greatest amount of happiness altogether." Utilitarianism, therefore, can only attain its goal of greater happiness by cultivating the nobleness of individuals so that all can benefit from the honour of others. In fact, notes Mill, Utilitarianism is actually a "standard of morality" which uses happiness of the greater number of people as its ultimate goal.

The Greatest-Happiness Principle deals with doing the greatest good for the greatest number of people. With the famous words "it is better to be a human being dissatisfied than a pig satisfied; better to be Socrates dissatisfied than a fool satisfied," Mill touts the importance of being well brought up and knowledgeably curious about the world, and understanding higher pleasures such as art and music, than to be uneducated and complacent. One need not be personally satisfied with one's life to be able to contribute to the "total sum happiness" of a society.

Mill goes on to discuss what is meant by "pleasure" and "pain" in his formulation of the Greatest-Happiness Principle, to argue that it encompasses intellectual as well as sensual pleasures, and to offer a defence of intellectual pleasures as preferable not only in degree, but also in kind, to sensual pleasures. Throughout the volume, Mill writes mainly as if addressing opponents of utilitarianism, but here he is trying also to criticise and refine the understanding of the Greatest-Happiness Principle offered by earlier utilitarians, Jeremy Bentham in particular.

In the third chapter, Mill discusses questions concerning the motivation to follow utilitarian moral principles. He explores ways in which both external and internal sanctions—that is, the incentives provided by others and the inner feelings of sympathy and duty—encourage people to act in such a way as to promote general happiness.

The fourth chapter offers Mill's attempt at an inductive proof of the Greatest-Happiness Principle, on the grounds that happiness and happiness alone is desired as an end in itself.

The fifth chapter concludes the essay with a discussion of problems concerning utilitarianism, as well as the concept of justice. Critics of utilitarianism often claim that judging actions solely in terms of their consequences is incompatible with a foundational and universally-binding concept of justice. Mill sees this as the strongest objection to utilitarianism and sets out to argue:

1. that a binding concept of justice can be explained in strictly utilitarian terms; and
2. that the problems created by the utilitarian explanation are difficult problems for any concept of justice whatsoever, whether utilitarian or not.

Finally, in order to be truly happy, Mill believes that we must turn our attention away from our own happiness towards other objects and ends, such as doing well for others and such high pleasures in life as art and music.

We can clarify what Mill means by utilitarianism by comparing and contrasting it with Aristotle's classic position of Eudemonism or virtue ethics. Both Aristotle and Mill argue humans naturally seek the good life, which is happiness. Mill's principle of utility is natural because it is grounded in the psychological faculty of desiring pleasure and avoiding pain. In Chapter four of his text "Utilitarianism" Mill can claim that the proof for the principle of utility is the fact that it is human nature. Aristotle claims virtue is natural as the excellence of natural human function. But, for Aristotle, virtues are a means to the end of happiness. Virtues are chosen for the sake of happiness. According to Mill, this is an abstract philosophy separated from happiness. Means are, by definition, different from the end for which they are chosen. Mill seeks concrete happiness. The principle of utility establishes what is good because what is good brings about pleasure, while what is bad brings about pain. The principle of pleasure allows us to know what the best good is because it shows what contributes to the greatest good or happiness for the greatest many. As the principle of utility structures human nature it is present in every human action. Every human being desires happiness because everything a human being desires is desired for its pleasure. Mill shows that the principle of utility is necessary and that those things that are desired are parts of happiness and not a means to happiness. Because humans have parts of happiness, happiness is concrete and not abstract. Happiness remains abstract for Aristotle according to Mill. Mill wants concrete happiness so that people can be happy. For some proponents of Aristotle's Nichomachean Ethics, one only becomes happy after they die. Mill wants the living to be happy. According to Mill, the mistake of other moral theories, including Aristotle's, is that all systems are based on the principle of utility, but other moralists were blind to this fact. Mill's principle of utility is the true principle of morality and human nature and makes it possible for the greatest number to have the greatest happiness.

Mill's View on Liberty

Mill's On Liberty addresses the nature and limits of the power that can be legitimately exercised by society over the individual. One argument that Mill develops further than any previous philosopher is the harm principle. The harm principle holds that each individual has the right to act as he wants, so long as these actions do not harm others. If the action is self-regarding, that is, if it only directly affects the person undertaking the action, then society has no right to intervene, even if it feels the actor is harming himself. He does argue, however, that individuals are prevented from doing lasting, serious harm to themselves or their property by the harm principle. Because no one exists in isolation, harm done to oneself may also harm others, and destroying property deprives the community as well as oneself. Mill excuses those who are "incapable of self-government" from this principle, such as young children or those living in "backward states of society."

Mill argues that despotism is an acceptable form of government for those "societies that are "backward", as long as the despot has the best interests of the people at heart, because of the barriers to spontaneous progress. Though this principle seems clear, there are a number of complications. For example, Mill explicitly states that "harms" may include acts of omission as well as acts of commission. Thus, failing to rescue a drowning child counts as a harmful act, as does failing to pay taxes, or failing to appear as a witness in court. All such harmful omissions may be regulated, according to Mill. By contrast, it does not count as harming someone if—without force or fraud—the affected individual consents to assume the risk: thus one may permissibly offer unsafe employment to others, provided there is no deception involved. (Mill does, however, recognise one limit to consent: society should not permit people to sell themselves into slavery). In these and other cases, it is important to keep in mind that the arguments in On Liberty are grounded on the principle of Utility, and not on appeals to natural rights.

The question of what counts as a self-regarding action and what actions, whether of omission or commission, constitute harmful actions subject to regulation, continues to exercise interpreters of Mill. It is important to emphasise that Mill did not consider giving offence to constitute "harm"; an action could not be restricted because it violated the conventions or morals of a given society.

On Liberty involves an impassioned defence of free speech. Mill argues that free discourse is a necessary condition for intellectual and social progress. We can never be sure, he contends, that a silenced opinion does not contain some element of the truth. He also argues that allowing people to air false opinions is productive for two reasons. First, individuals are more likely to abandon erroneous beliefs if they are engaged in an open exchange of ideas. Second, by forcing other individuals to re-examine and re-affirm their beliefs in the process of debate, these beliefs are kept from declining into mere dogma. It is not enough for Mill that one simply has an unexamined belief that happens to be true; one must understand why the belief in question is the true one.

John Stuart Mill's view on liberty, which was influenced by Joseph Priestley and Josiah Warren, is that the individual ought to be free to do as he wishes unless he harms others. Individuals are rational enough to make decisions about their good being and choose any religion they want to. Government should interfere when it is for the protection of society. Mill explains,

"The sole end for which mankind are warranted, individually or collectively, in interfering with the liberty of action of any of their number, is self-protection. That the only purpose for which power can be rightfully exercised over any member of a civilized community, against his will, is to prevent harm to others. His own good, either physical or moral, is not sufficient warrant. He cannot rightfully be compelled to do or forbear because it will be better for him to do so, because it will make him happier, because, in the opinion of others, to do so would be wise, or even right. The only part of the conduct of anyone, for which he is amenable to society, is that which concerns others. In the part which merely concerns him, his independence is, of right, absolute. Over himself, over his own body and mind, the individual is sovereign." And yet immediately prior to the above referenced paragraph, Mill also explains, "There is, in fact, no recognised principle by which the propriety or impropriety of government interference is customarily tested. People decide according to their personal preferences. Some, whenever they see any good to be done, or evil to be remedied, would willingly instigate the government to undertake the business; while others prefer to bear almost any amount of social evil, rather than add one to the departments of human interests amenable to governmental control", thus, highlighting the highly contestable nature of liberty in the sense of its relationship to conceptions of both positive and negative rights.

Mill believed that "the struggle between Liberty and Authority is the most conspicuous feature in the portions of history." For him, liberty in antiquity was a "contest between subjects, or some classes of subjects, and the government." Mill defined "social liberty" as protection from "the tyranny of political rulers." He introduced a number of different tyrannies, including social tyranny, and also the tyranny of the majority.

Social liberty for Mill meant putting limits on the ruler's power so that he would not be able to use his power on his own wishes and make decisions which could harm society; in other words, people should have the right to have a say in the government's decisions. He said that social liberty was "the nature and limits of the power which can be legitimately exercised by society over the individual." It was attempted in two ways: first, by obtaining recognition of certain immunities, called political liberties or rights; second, by establishment of a system of "constitutional checks."

However, in Mill's view, limiting the power of government was not enough. He stated, "Society can and does execute its own mandates; and if it issues wrong mandates instead of right, or any mandates at all in things with which it ought not to meddle, it practices a social tyranny more formidable than many kinds of political oppression, since, though not usually upheld by such extreme penalties, it leaves fewer means of escape, penetrating much more deeply into the details of life, and enslaving the soul itself."

Mills views on liberty have met with severe criticism at the hands of scholars like Barker, who described him as the prophet of empty liberty. This charge is levelled against Mill chiefly because he hedged his doctrine of liberty with many restrictions. Some of the restrictions which Mill envisaged on individual liberty were as follows:

In the *first* place, his doctrine applies only to human beings in the maturity of the faculties and to the children or to young persons below a certain age. The validity of this exception cannot be refuted. However, it is difficult to agree with Mill when he refuses to give the benefits of liberty to the backward peoples or races. This point was fully exploited by the Imperialist powers to defend or justify their despotic rule over the colonies.

Secondly, though Mill considers absolute and unfettered freedom of thought and expression as necessary for the development of civilization, he does not favour grant of absolute liberty in the field of action. Thirdly, the free play of individual is likely to give rise to inequality among men.

Mill's View on Social Liberty and Tyranny of Majority

Mill believed that "the struggle between Liberty and Authority is the most conspicuous feature in the portions of history." For him, liberty in antiquity was a "contest between subjects, or some classes of subjects, and the government." Mill defined "social liberty" as protection from "the tyranny of political rulers." He introduced a number of different tyrannies, including social tyranny, and also the tyranny of the majority.

Social liberty for Mill meant putting limits on the ruler's power so that he would not be able to use his power on his own wishes and make decisions which could harm society; in other words, people should have the right to have a say in the government's decisions. He said that social liberty was "the nature and limits of the power which can be legitimately exercised by society over the individual." It was attempted in two ways: first, by obtaining recognition of certain immunities, called political liberties or rights; second, by establishment of a system of "constitutional checks."

However, in Mill's view, limiting the power of government was not enough. He stated, "Society can and does execute its own mandates; and if it issues wrong mandates instead of right, or any mandates at all in things with which it ought not to meddle, it practices a social tyranny more formidable than many kinds of political oppression, since, though not usually upheld by such extreme penalties, it leaves fewer means of escape, penetrating much more deeply into the details of life, and enslaving the soul itself."

Mill on Representative Government

According to Mill: "The ideally best form of government is that in which the sovereignty, or supreme controlling power in the last resort, is vested in the entire aggregate of the community; each citizen not only having a voice in the exercise of that ultimate sovereignty, but being, at least occasionally, called on to take an actual part in the government, by the personal discharge of some public function, local or general." Mill has recognized in representative government the ideal type of the most perfect polity, for which, in consequence, any portion of mankind are better adapted in proportion to their degree of general improvement. As they range lower and lower in development, that form of government will be, generally speaking, less suitable to them; though this is not true universally: for the adaptation of a people to representative government does not depend so much upon the place they occupy in the general scale of humanity as upon the degree in which they possess certain special requisites; requisites, however, so closely connected with their degree of general advancement, that any variation between the two is rather the exception than the rule. Let us examine at what point in the descending series representative government ceases altogether to be admissible, either through its own unfitness, or the superior fitness of some other regimen.

First, then, representative, like any other government, must be unsuitable in any case in which it cannot permanently subsist, i.e. in which it does not fulfil the three fundamental conditions enumerated in the first chapter. These were: (1) That the people should be willing to receive it. (2) That they should be willing and able to do what is necessary for its preservation. (3) That they should be willing and able to fulfil the duties and discharge the functions which it imposes on them.

The willingness of the people to accept representative government only becomes a practical question when an enlightened ruler, or a foreign nation or nations who have gained power over the country, are disposed to offer it the boon. To individual reformers the question is almost irrelevant, since, if no other objection can be made to their enterprise than that the opinion of the nation is not yet on their side, they have the ready and proper answer, that to bring it over to their side is the very end they aim at. When opinion is really adverse, its hostility is usually to the fact of change, rather than to representative government in itself. The contrary case is not indeed unexampled; there has sometimes been a religious repugnance to any limitation of the power of a particular line of rulers; but, in general, the doctrine of passive obedience meant only submission to the will of the powers that be, whether monarchical or popular. In any case in which the attempt to introduce representative government is at all likely to be made, indifference to it, and inability to understand its processes and requirements, rather than positive opposition, are the obstacles to be expected. These, however, are as fatal, and may be as hard to be got rid of, as actual aversion; it being easier, in most cases, to change the direction of an active feeling, than to create one in a state previously passive. When a people have no sufficient value for, and attachment to, a representative constitution, they have next to no chance of retaining it. In every country, the executive is the branch of the government which wields the immediate power, and is in direct contact with the public; to it, principally, the hopes and fears of individuals are directed, and by it both the benefits, and the terrors and prestige, of government are mainly represented to the public eye. Unless, therefore, the authorities whose office it is to check the executive are backed by an effective opinion and feeling in the country, the executive has always the means of setting them aside, or compelling them to subservience, and is sure to be well supported in doing so. Representative institutions necessarily depend for permanence upon the readiness of the people to fight for them in case of their being endangered. If too little valued for this, they seldom obtain a footing at all, and if they do, are almost sure to be overthrown, as soon as the head of the government, or any party leader who can muster force for a *coup de main*, is willing to run some small risk for absolute power.

The supposition is that absolute power, in the hands of an eminent individual, would ensure a virtuous and intelligent performance of all the duties of government. Good laws would be established and enforced, bad laws would be reformed; the best men would be placed in all situations of trust; justice would be as well administered, the public burdens would be as light and as judiciously imposed, every branch of administration would be as purely and as intelligently conducted, as the circumstances of the country and its degree of intellectual and moral cultivation would admit. I am willing, for the sake of the argument, to concede all this; but I must point out how great the concession is; how much more is needed to produce even an approximation to these results than is conveyed in the simple expression, a good despot. Their realisation would in fact imply, not merely a good monarch, but an all-seeing one. He must be at all times informed correctly, in considerable detail, of the conduct and working of every branch of administration, in every district of the country, and must be able, in the twenty-four hours per day which are all that is granted to a king as to the humblest labourer, to give an effective share of attention and superintendence to all parts of this vast field; or he must at least be capable of discerning and choosing out, from among the mass of his subjects, not only a large abundance of honest and able men, fit to conduct every branch of public administration under supervision and control, but also the small number of men of eminent virtues and talents who can be trusted not only to do without that supervision, but to exercise it themselves over others. So extraordinary are the faculties and energies required for performing this task in any supportable manner, that the good despot whom we are supposing can hardly be imagined as consenting to undertake it, unless as a refuge from intolerable evils, and a transitional preparation for something beyond. But the argument can do without even this immense item in the account. Suppose the difficulty vanquished. What should we then have? One man of superhuman mental activity managing the entire affairs of a mentally passive people. Their passivity is implied in the very idea of absolute power. The nation as a whole, and every individual composing it, are without any potential voice in their own destiny. They exercise no will in respect to their collective interests. All is decided for them by a will not their own, which it is legally a crime for them to disobey.

Mill on State

When we fuse Mill's insight with that of the modern ecologists, we have an understanding of the way in which Western society is going to change its form. "Mill turns to the question of what society is for to improve the lot of mankind. In the burst of the age of technology with its accompanying vast increase in population Mill saw that the problem of satisfying the human necessities was not to be solved by technology alone." "The decline of a philosophy based upon human relationships left the peoples of the world defenceless before the advance of industrialism. A renaissance of philosophy is essential, if we are to overcome the dehumanisation of unrestrained industrialism" (Waller 133, 135, 139). John Stuart Mill represented the high watermark of classical political economy, applying the insights of Smith and Ricardo in the nineteenth century. A free trade liberal who extolled the virtues of market economics, Mill was also extremely critical of the social and economic features of Victorian capitalism. This, in many respects, is the more enduring part of Mill's legacy. His thought is particularly relevant with respect to the urban ills of over scale, excess and endless growth. Mill's argument presupposed the productive achievements of capitalism. To Mill, the economic problem had been solved; the key question in the advanced capitalist economies was no longer production but distribution. Mill, therefore, sought to place the emphasis upon the end of the capitalist economy rather than the means. In the process, he rediscovered the Greek principle of limitation to define a stationary state in which human growth replaces material growth. The emphasis is placed upon exploiting the margins for freedom that capitalism has achieved for human self-realisation away from the world of necessity. Mill's stationary state defines a sense of scale, proportion and balance. Mill defends a classical notion of citizenship against the prevailing atomistic or market model of politics. Mill sharply attacked the market conception of society as "a society only held together by the relations and feelings arising out of pecuniary interests." Against the egoistic and destructive forces which characterise market society, Mill looked to transform existing social institutions so as to realise a more integrated community. This integrated, harmonious community, overcoming the distinctions which set individuals above, below and against each other, seemed a realistic prospect. "Every step in political improvement renders it more so, by removing the sources of opposition of interest, and levelling those inequalities of legal privilege between individuals or classes, owing to which there are large portions of mankind whose happiness is still practical to disregard." The socially divisive, iniquitous and destructive forms of differentiation were in the process of being overcome by legislative improvement, individual prudence, fair opportunity, education, extended participation in the political process. These advances would issue in a stable, harmonious, progressive state.

Mill's View on Religion

Mill's criticism of traditional religious doctrines and institutions and his promotion of the "Religion of Humanity," also depended largely on concerns about human cultivation and education. Though the Benthamite "philosophic radicals," including Mill, took Christianity to be a particularly pernicious superstition that fostered indifference or hostility to human happiness (the keystone of utilitarian morality), Mill also thought that religion could potentially serve important ethical needs by supplying us with "ideal conceptions grander and more beautiful than we see realized in the prose of human life." In so doing, religion elevates our feelings, cultivates sympathy with others, and imbues even our smallest activities with a sense of purpose.

The posthumously published three *Essays on Religion* (1874)—on "Nature," the "Utility of Religion," and "Theism"—criticized traditional religious views and formulated an alternative in the guise of the Religion of Humanity. Along with the criticism of religion's moral effects that he shared with the Benthamites, Mill was also critical of the intellectual laziness that permitted belief in an omnipotent and benevolent God. He felt, following his father, that the world as we find it could not possibly have come from such a God given the evils rampant in it; either his power is limited or he is not wholly benevolent.

Beyond attacking arguments concerning the *essence* of God, Mill undermines a variety of arguments for his *existence* including all *a priori* arguments. He concludes that the only legitimate proof of God is an *a posterior* and probabilistic argument from the design of the universe—the traditional argument (stemming from Aristotle) that complex features of the world, like the eye, are unlikely to have arisen by chance, hence there must be a designer. (Mill acknowledges the possibility that Darwin, in his 1859 *The Origin of Species*, has provided a wholly naturalistic explanation of such features, but he suggests that it is too early to judge of Darwin's success).

Inspired by Comte, Mill finds an alternative to traditional religion in the Religion of Humanity, in which an idealized humanity becomes an object of reverence and the morally useful features of traditional religion are supposedly purified and accentuated. Humanity becomes an inspiration by being placed imaginatively within the drama of human history, which has a destination or point, namely the victory of good over evil. As Mill puts it, history should be seen as "the unfolding of a great epic or dramatic action," which terminates "in the happiness or misery, the elevation or degradation, of the human race." It is "an unremitting conflict between good and evil powers, of which every act done by any of us, insignificant as we are, forms one of the incidents." As we begin to see ourselves as participants in this Manichean drama, as fighting alongside people like Socrates, Newton, and Jesus to secure the ultimate victory of good over evil, we become capable of greater sympathy, moral feeling, and an ennobled sense of the meaning of our own lives. The Religion of Humanity thereby acts as an instrument of human cultivation.

Mill's View on Freedom of Speech

An influential advocate of freedom of speech, Mill objected to censorship. He says: "I choose, by preference the cases which are least favourable to me—In which the argument against freedom of opinion, both on truth and that of utility, is considered the strongest. Let the opinions impugned be the belief of God and in a future state, or any of the commonly received doctrines of morality. But, I must be permitted to observe that it is not the feeling sure of a doctrine (be it what it may) which I call an assumption of infallibility. It is the undertaking to decide that question *for others*, without allowing them to hear what can be said on the contrary side. And I denounce and reprobate this pretension not the less if it is put forth on the side of my most solemn convictions. However, positive anyone's persuasion may be, not only of the faculty but of the pernicious consequences, but (to adopt expressions which I altogether condemn) the immorality and impiety of opinion.—Yet if, in pursuance of that private judgement, though backed by the public judgement of his country or contemporaries, he prevents the opinion from being heard in its defence, he assumes infallibility. And so far from the assumption being less objectionable or less dangerous because the opinion is called immoral or impious, this is the case of all others in which it is most fatal."

Mill outlines the benefits of "searching for and discovering the truth" as a way to further knowledge. He argued that even if an opinion is false, the truth can be better understood by refuting the error. And as most opinions are neither completely true nor completely false, he points out that allowing free expression allows the airing of competing views as a way to preserve partial truth in various opinions. Worried about minority views being suppressed, Mills also argued in support of freedom of speech on political grounds, stating that it is a critical component for a representative government to have in order to empower debate over public policy. Mill also eloquently argued that freedom of expression allows for personal growth and self-realization. He said that freedom of speech was a vital way to develop talents and realise a person's potential and creativity. He repeatedly said that eccentricity was preferable to uniformity and stagnation.

Mill's View on Human Right and Slavery

In 1850, Mill sent an anonymous letter (which came to be known under the title "The Negro Question"), in rebuttal to Thomas Carlyle's anonymous letter to *Fraser's Magazine for Town and Country*. Carlyle had defended slavery on grounds of genetic inferiority and claimed that the West Indies development was due to British ingenuity alone and dismissed any notion that there was a debtedness to imported slaves for building the economy there. Mill's rebuttal and references to the ongoing debate in the US at the time regarding slavery were emphatic and eloquent. The full text, as well as a link to the Carlyle letter that prompted it, is available only.

Mill's View on Economic Development

Mill regarded economic development as a function of land, labour and capital. While land and labour are the two original factors of production, capital is "a stock, previously accumulated of the products of former labour." Increase in wealth is possible only if land and capital help to increase production faster than the labour force. It is productive labour that is productive of wealth and capital accumulation. "The rate of capital accumulation is the function of the proportion of the labour force employed 'productively'. Profits earned by employing unproductive labours are merely transfers of income; unproductive labour does not generate wealth or income." It is productive labourers who do productive consumption. Productive consumption is that "which maintains and increase the productive capacity of the community." It implies that productive consumption is an input necessary to maintain productive labourers.

Mill's View on Women

Many volumes of Mill's writings deal with topics of social and political concern. These include writings on specific political problems in India, America, Ireland, France, and England, on the nature of democracy (Considerations on Representative Government) and civilization, on slavery, on law and jurisprudence, on the workplace, and on the family and the status of women. The last subject was the topic of Mill's well-known The Subjection of Women, an important work in the history of feminism.

The radical nature of Mill's call for women's equality is often lost to us after over a century of protest and changing social attitudes. Yet the subordination of women to men when Mill was writing remains striking. Among other indicators of this subordination are the following: (1) British women had fewer grounds for divorce than men until 1923; (2) Husbands controlled their wives personal property (with the occasional exception of land) until the Married Women's Property Acts of 1870 and 1882; (3) Children were the husband's; (4) Rape was impossible within a marriage; and (5) Wives lacked crucial features of legal personhood, since the husband was taken as the representative of the family (thereby eliminating the need for women's suffrage). This gives some indication of how disturbing and/or ridiculous the idea of a marriage between equals could appear to Victorians.

The object of the essay was to show "that the principle which regulates the existing social relations between the two sexes—the legal subordination of one sex to the other—is wrong in itself, and now one of the chief hindrances to human improvement; and that it ought to be replaced by a principle of perfect equality, admitting no power or privilege on the one side, nor disability on the other." This shows how Mill appeals to both the patent injustice of contemporary familial arrangements and to the negative moral impact of those arrangements on the people within them. In particular, he discusses the ways in which the subordination of women negatively affects not only the women, but also the men and children in the family. This subordination stunts the moral and intellectual development of women by restricting their field of activities, pushing them either into self-sacrifice or into selfishness and pettiness. Men, alternatively, either become brutal through their relationships with women or turn away from projects of self-improvement to pursue the social "consideration" that women desire.

It is important to note that Mill's concern for the status of women dovetails with the rest of his thought—it is not a disconnected issue. For example, his support for women's equality was buttressed by associationism, which claims that minds are created by associative laws operating on experience. This implies that if we change the experiences and upbringing of women, then their minds will change. This enabled Mill to argue against those who tried to suggest that the subordination of women to men reflected a natural order that women were by nature incapable of equality with men. If many women were incapable of true friendship with noble men, says Mill that is not a result of their natures, but of their faulty environments.

Evaluation of J.S. Mill

J.S. Mill was one of the most enlightened political thinkers of his times. He was a prophet of individualism and liberalism. His individualism occupies definitely a place of pride in political thought. He was the champion of individual liberty and champion of women's right. His various proposals for reform constituted an important contribution to the political theory. Mill humanised utilitarianism. It is interesting to observe that Mill was a utilitarian and at the same time he was a real democrat who understood fully the value of human personality. He stood for universal franchise and especially for the political rights of women.

Mill advocated qualitative pleasure for quantitative pleasure. The concept of quantitative pleasure had debased and degraded utilitarianism. By giving it a qualitative concept, the utilitarian concepts were made worthy. He contributed to utilitarianism in such a way as to make it convincing and acceptable. Mill was a very sensitive man with complex mind. He always demonstrated a spirit of inquiry, love of knowledge and readiness to learn. Mill must rank high. As logician, economist and political philosopher he was regarded as a prophet in his own age.

Conclusion

Mill's intellect engaged with the world rather than fled from it. His was not an ivory tower philosophy, even when dealing with the most abstract of philosophical topics. His work is of enduring interest because it reflects how a fine mind struggled with and attempted to synthesize important intellectual and cultural movements. He stands at the intersections of conflicts between enlightenment and romanticism, liberalism and conservatism, and historicism and rationalism. In each case, as someone interested in conversation rather than pronouncement, he makes sincere efforts to move beyond polemic into sustained and thoughtful analysis. That analysis produced challenging answers to problems that still remain. Whether or not one agrees with his answers, Mill serves as a model for thinking about human problems in a serious and civilized way.

KARL MARX (1818-1883)

The German philosopher, revolutionary economist (one who studies the use of money and other material funds), and leader Karl Marx founded modern "scientific" socialism (a system of society in which no property is held as private). His basic ideas—known as Marxism—form the foundation of Socialist and Communist (an economic and government system characterized by citizens holding all property and goods in common) movements throughout the world.

Early Life

Karl Heinreich Marx was born in Trier, Rhenish Prussia (present-day Germany), on May 5, 1818, the son of Heinrich Marx, a lawyer, and Henriette Presburg Marx, a Dutchwoman. Both Heinrich and Henriette were descendants of a long line of rabbis (masters or teachers of Jewish religion). Barred from the practice of law because he was Jewish, Heinrich Marx converted to Lutheranism about 1817. Karl was baptized in the same church in 1824 at the age of six. Karl attended a Lutheran elementary school but later became an atheist (one who does not believe in the existence of God) and a materialist (one who believes that physical matter is all that is real), rejecting both the Christian and Jewish religions. It was he who coined the saying "Religion is the opium (drug that deadens pain, is today illegal, and comes from the poppy flower) of the people," a basic principle in modern communism.

Karl attended the Friedrich Wilhelm Gymnasium in Trier for five years, graduating in 1835 at the age of seventeen. The gymnasium's programme was the usual classical one—history, mathematics, literature, and languages, particularly Greek and Latin. Karl became very skilful in French and Latin, both of which he learned to read and write fluently. In later years he taught himself other languages, so that as a mature scholar he could also read Spanish, Italian, Dutch, Scandinavian, Russian, and English. As his articles in the *New York Daily Tribune* show, he came to handle the English language masterfully [he loved Shakespeare (1564–1616), whose works he knew by heart], although he never lost his heavy German accent when speaking.

Young and Adult Years

In October 1835 Marx enrolled in Bonn University in Bonn, Germany, where he attended courses primarily in law, as it was his father's desire that he become a lawyer. Marx, however, was more interested in philosophy (the study of knowledge) and literature than in law. He wanted to be a poet and dramatist (one who writes plays). In his student days he wrote a great deal of poetry—most of it preserved—that in his mature years he rightly recognized as imitative.

Marx's dismayed father took him out of Bonn and had him enter the University of Berlin, then a centre of intellectual discussion. In Berlin a circle of brilliant thinkers was challenging existing institutions and ideas, including religion, philosophy, ethics (the study of good and bad involving morals), and politics. Marx joined this group of radical (extreme in opinion) thinkers wholeheartedly. He spent more than four years in Berlin, completing his studies with a doctoral degree in March 1841.

Forced to Move on

Marx then turned to writing and journalism to support himself. In 1842 he became editor of the liberal (open to new ideas) Cologne newspaper *Rheinische Zeitung,* but the Berlin government prohibited it from being published the following year. In January 1845 Marx was expelled from France "at the instigation (order) of the Prussian government," as he said. He moved to Brussels, Belgium, where he founded the German Workers' Party and was active in the Communist League. Here he wrote the famous *Manifesto of the Communist Party* (known as the *Communist Manifesto).* Expelled (forced out) by the Belgian government, Marx moved back to Cologne, where he became editor of the *Neue Rheinische Zeitung* in June 1848. Less than a year later, the Prussian government stopped the paper, and Marx himself was exiled (forced to leave). He went to Paris, but in September the French government expelled him again. Marx finally settled in London, England, where he lived as a stateless exile (Britain denied him citizenship and Prussia refused to take him back as a citizen) for the rest of his life.

In London Marx's sole means of support was journalism. He wrote for both German—and English—language publications. From August 1852 to March 1862 he was correspondent for the *New York Daily Tribune,* contributing a total of about 355 articles. Journalism, however, paid very poorly; Marx was literally saved from starvation by the financial support of friend and fellow writer, Friedrich Engels (1820–1895). In London in 1864 Marx helped to found the International Workingmen's Association (known as the First International), for which he wrote the inaugural (opening) address. Thereafter Marx's political activities were limited mainly to exchanging letters with radicals in Europe and America, offering advice, and helping to shape the socialist and labour movements.

Personal Life

Marx was married to his childhood sweetheart, Jenny von Westphalen, who was known as the "most beautiful girl in Trier," on June 19, 1843. She was totally devoted to him. She died of cancer on December 2, 1881, at the age of sixty-seven. For Marx it was a blow from which he never recovered.

The Marxes had seven children, four of whom died in infancy or childhood. He deeply loved his daughters, who, in turn, adored him. Of the three surviving daughters—Jenny, Laura, and Eleanor—two married Frenchmen. Both of Marx's sons-in-law became prominent French socialists and members of Parliament. Eleanor was active as a British labour organizer.

Marx spent most of his working time in the British Museum, doing research both for his newspaper articles and his books. In preparation for Das Kapital, he read every available work in economic and financial theory and practice.

Marx's excessive smoking, wine drinking, and love of heavily spiced foods may have been contributing causes to his illnesses. In the final dozen years of his life, he could no longer do any continuous intellectual work. He died in his armchair in London on March 14, 1883, about two months before his sixty-fifth birthday. He lies buried in London's Highgate Cemetery, where his grave is marked by a bust (sculpture of a person's head and shoulders) of him.

His Works

Marxism achieved its first great triumph in the Russian Revolution (1917–

21; when the lower class overthrew three hundred years of czar rule), when its successful leader, Vladimir Ilich Lenin (1870–1924), a lifelong follower of Marx, organized the Soviet Union as a proletarian dictatorship (country ruled by the lower class). Lenin based the new government on Marx's philosophy as Lenin interpreted it. Thus, Marx became a world figure and his theories became a subject of universal attention and controversy (open to dispute). Marx wrote hundreds of articles, brochures, and reports, but only five books.

Writings of Marx

Marx wrote extensively, but his most important writings include Economic and Philosophic Manuscripts (1844); *The Poverty of Philosophy* (1847); *The Communist Manifesto* (in collaboration with Engels) (1848); *The Critique of Political Economy* (1859); *Inaugural Address of the International Workmen's Association* (1864); *Value, Price, and Profit* (1865); Das Kapital (1867); and *The Civil War in France* (1870-71).

His Ideas

Marx's universal appeal lies in his moral approach to socio-economic problems, in his insights into the relationships between institutions and values, and in his ideas about the salvation (to save from destruction) of mankind. Hence, Marx is best understood if one studies not only his economics, but also his theory of history and politics. The central idea in Marx's thought, involves two basic notions: that the economic system at any given time determines the current ideas; and that history is an ongoing process keeping up with the economic institutions that change in regular stages.

To Marx, capitalism (an economic system characterized by private or corporate ownership of goods) was the last stage of historical development before communism. The lowest social or economic class of a community, when produced by capitalism, is the last historical class. The two are fated to be in conflict—the class struggle, which Marx wrote of in the Communist Manifesto—until the lower class inevitably wins. The proletarian dictatorship, in turn, develops into communism, in which there are no classes and no inequalities. The logical suggestion is that with the final establishment of communism, history comes to a sudden end. This Marxist interpretation has been criticized in the non-Communist world as historically inaccurate, scientifically weak, and logically ridiculous. Nevertheless, Marx's message of an earthly paradise (a classless society) has provided millions with hope and a new meaning of life. From this point of view, one may agree with the Austrian Economist Joseph A. Schumpeter that "Marxism is a religion" and Marx is its "prophet."

Inspirations

Marx's thought demonstrates influences from many thinkers, including but not limited to:

- Georg Wilhelm Friedrich Hegel's philosophy;
- The classical political economy (economics) of Adam Smith and David Ricardo;
- French socialist thought, in particular the thought of Jean-Jacques Rousseau, Henri de Saint-Simon, Pierre-Joseph Proudhon, and Charles Fourier;
- Earlier German philosophical materialism, particularly that of Ludwig Feuerbach; and
- The working class analysis by Friedrich Engels.

Marx's view of history, which came to be called historical materialism (controversially adapted as the philosophy of dialectical materialism by Engels and Lenin) certainly shows the influence of Hegel's claim that one should view reality (and history) dialectically. However, Hegel had thought in idealist terms, putting ideas in the forefront, whereas Marx sought to rewrite dialectics in materialist terms, arguing for the primacy of matter over idea. Where Hegel saw the "spirit" as driving history, Marx saw this as an unnecessary mystification, obscuring the reality of humanity and its physical actions shaping the world. He wrote that Hegelianism stood the movement of reality on its head, and that one needed to set it upon its feet.

Though inspired by French socialist and sociological thought, Marx criticised utopian socialists, arguing that their favoured small scale socialistic communities would be bound to marginalisation and poverty, and that only a large scale change in the economic system can bring about real change.

The other important contribution to Marx's revision of Hegelianism came from Engels' book, The Condition of the Working Class in England in 1844, which led Marx to conceive of the historical dialectic in terms of class conflict and to see the modern working class as the most progressive force for revolution.

Marx believed that he could study history and society scientifically and discern tendencies of history and the resulting outcome of social conflicts. Some followers of Marx concluded, therefore, that a communist revolution would inevitably occur. However, Marx famously asserted in the eleventh of his Theses on Feuerbach that "philosophers have only interpreted the world, in various ways; the point however is to change it", and he clearly dedicated himself to trying to alter the world.

Marxism

Followers of Marx have drawn on his work to propose grand, cohesive theoretical outlooks dubbed "Marxism." This body of works has had significant influence on both politics and science. Nevertheless, Marxists have frequently debated amongst themselves over how to interpret Marx's writings and apply his concepts to the modern world. The legacy of Marx's thought has become contested between numerous tendencies, each of which sees itself as Marx's most accurate interpreter. These tendencies include Leninism, Stalinism, Trotskyism, Maoism, Luxemburgism, and Marxism. Various currents have also developed in academic Marxism, often under influence of other views, resulting in structuralism Marxism, historical Marxism, phenomenological Marxism, Analytical Marxism and Hegelian Marxism. The Marxist revolutionary Chef Guevara summed up his own appeal to Marxism by stating that Marx produced "a qualitative change in the history of social thought. He interprets history, understands its dynamic, predicts the future, but in addition to predicting it, he expresses a revolutionary concept: the world must not only be interpreted, it must be transformed."

There is a distinction between "Marxism" and "what Marx believed"; for example, shortly before he died in 1883, Marx wrote a letter to the French workers' leader Jules Guesde, and to his own son-in-law Paul Lafarge, accusing them of "revolutionary phrase-mongering" and of lack of faith in the working class. After the French party split into a reformist and revolutionary party, some accused Guesde (leader of the latter) of taking orders from Marx; Marx remarked to Lafarge, "What is certain to me is [that, if this is Marxism, then] I myself am not [a] Marxist" (in a letter to Engels, Marx later accused Guesde of being a "Bakunin's").

The Communist Manifesto

The Communist Manifesto (Das Kommunistische Manifest), originally titled Manifesto of the Communist Party (German: Manifest der Kommunistischen Partei) is a short 1848 publication written by the German Marxist political theorists Karl Marx and Friedrich Engels. It has since been recognized as one of the world's most influential political manuscripts.

Commissioned by the Communist League, it laid out the League's purposes and programme. It presents an analytical approach to the class struggle (historical and present) and the problems of capitalism, rather than a prediction of communism's potential future forms.

The book contains Marx and Engels' Marxist theories about the nature of society and politics, that in their own words, "The history of all hitherto existing society is the history of class struggles." It also briefly features their ideas for how the capitalist society of the time would eventually be replaced by socialism, and then eventually communism.

Contents

The Manifesto is divided into an introduction, three substantive sections, and a conclusion.

Introduction

The preamble to the main text of the Manifesto states that the continent of Europe fears the "spectre of communism", and the powers of old Europe are uniting in "a holy alliance [intended to] exorcise this spectre." Marx refers here to not only the houses of power and landed gentry of old Europe—the bourgeoisie—but diverse factions such as the papacy and the emerging corporate world as well. Marx declares that "It is high time that Communists should openly, in the face of the whole world, publish their views, their aims, their tendencies, and meet this nursery tale of the spectre of communism with a manifesto of the party itself."

I. Bourgeois and Proletarians

The first chapter of the Manifesto, "Bourgeois and Proletarians", examines the Marxist conception of history, with the initial idea asserting that "The history of all hitherto existing society is the history of class struggles." It goes on to say that in capitalism, the working class, proletariat, are fighting in the class struggle against the owners of the means of production, the bourgeois, and that past class struggle ended either with revolution that restructured society, or "common ruin of the contending classes."

It continues by adding that the bourgeois exploits the proletariat through the "constant revolutionising of production and uninterrupted disturbance of all social conditions."

The Manifesto explains that the reason the bourgeois exist and exploit the proletariat with low wages is private property, "the accumulation of wealth in private hands, the formation and increase of capital", and that competition amongst the proletariat creates wage-labour, which rests entirely on the competition among the workers.

This section further explains that the proletarians will eventually rise to power through class struggle: the bourgeoisie constantly exploits the proletariat for its manual labour and cheap wages, ultimately to create profit for the bourgeois; the proletariat rise to power through revolution against the bourgeoisie such as riots or creation of unions. The Communist Manifesto states that while there is still class struggle amongst society, capitalism will be overthrown by the proletariat only to start again in the near future; ultimately communism is the key to class equality amongst the citizens of Europe.

II. Proletarians and Communists

The second section, "Proletarians and Communists", starts by stating the relationship of conscious communists to the rest of the working class, declaring that they will not form a separate party that opposes other working-class parties, will express the interests and general will of the proletariat as a whole, and will distinguish themselves from other working-class parties by always expressing the common interest of the entire proletariat independently of all nationalities and representing the interests of the movement as a whole.

The section goes on to defend communism from various objections, such as the claim that communists advocate "free love", and the claim that people will not perform labour in a communist society because they have no incentive to work. The section ends by outlining a set of short-term demands:

1. Abolition of property in land and application of all rents of land to public purposes.
2. A heavy progressive or graduated income tax.
3. Abolition of all right of inheritance.
4. Confiscation of the property of all emigrants and rebels.
5. Centralization of credit in the hands of the State, by means of a national bank with State capital and an exclusive monopoly.
6. Centralization of the means of communication and transport in the hands of the State.
7. Extension of factories and instruments of production owned by the State; the bringing into cultivation of waste-lands, and the improvement of the soil generally in accordance with a common plan.
8. Equal liability of all to labour. Establishment of industrial armies, especially for agriculture.

9. Combination of agriculture with manufacturing industries; gradual abolition of the distinction between town and country, by a more equitable distribution of the population over the country.
10. Free education for all children in public schools. Abolition of children's factory labour in its present form and combination of education with industrial production.

The implementation of these policies would, as believed by Marx and Engels, be a precursor to the stateless and classless society. In a controversial passage they suggested that the "proletariat" might in competition with the bourgeoisie be compelled to organise as a class, form a revolution, make itself a ruling class, sweep away the old conditions of production, and in that step have abolished its own supremacy as a class. This account of the transition from socialism to communism was criticised particularly during and after the Soviet era.

III. Socialist and Communist Literature

The third section, "Socialist and Communist Literature," distinguishes communism from other socialist doctrines prevalent at the time the *Manifesto* was written. While the degree of reproach of Marx and Engels toward rival perspectives varies, all are dismissed for advocating reformism and failing to recognise the preeminent role of the working class.

IV. Position of the Communists in Relation to the Various Opposition Parties

The concluding section, "Position of the Communists in Relation to the Various Opposition Parties", briefly discusses the communist position on struggles in specific countries in the mid-nineteenth century such as France, Switzerland, Poland, and Germany, and declares that Germany "is on the eve of a bourgeois revolution", and predicts that a world revolution will soon follow. It then ends by declaring an alliance with the social democrats, boldly supporting other communist revolutions, and calling the proletarians to action, ending with the rallying cry of communism, "Workers of the world, unite!".

Economic and Philosophical Manuscript

The *Economic and Philosophical Manuscripts* cover a wide range of topics, including much interesting material on private property and communism, and on money, as well as developing Marx's critique of Hegel. However, the manuscripts are best known for their account of alienated labour. Here

Marx famously depicts the worker under capitalism as suffering from four types of alienated labour. First, from the product, which as soon as it is created is taken away from its producer. Second, in productive activity (work) which is experienced as a torment. Third, from species-being, for humans produce blindly and not in accordance with their truly human powers. Finally, from other human beings, where the relation of exchange replaces the satisfaction of mutual need. That these categories overlap in some respects is not a surprise given Marx's remarkable methodological ambition in these writings. Essentially he attempts to apply a Hegelian deduction of categories to economics, trying to demonstrate that all the categories of bourgeois economics–wages, rent, exchange, profit etc.–are ultimately derived from an analysis of the concept of alienation. Consequently each category of alienated labour is supposed to be deducible from the previous one. However, Marx gets no further than deducing categories of alienated labour from each other. Quite possibly in the course of writing he came to understand that a different methodology is required for approaching economic issues. Nevertheless we are left with a very rich text on the nature of alienated labour. The idea of non-alienation has to be inferred from the negative, with the assistance of one short passage at the end of the text 'On James Mill' in which non-alienated labour is briefly described in terms which emphasise both the immediate producer's enjoyment of production as a confirmation of his or her powers, and also the idea that production is to meet the needs of others, thus confirming for both parties our human essence as mutual dependence. Both sides of our species essence are revealed here: our individual human powers and our membership in the human community.

It is important to understand that for Marx alienation is not merely a matter of subjective feeling, or confusion. The bridge between Marx's early analysis of alienation and his later social theory is the idea that the alienated individual is 'a plaything of alien forces', albeit alien forces which are themselves a product of human action. In our daily lives we take decisions that have unintended consequences, which then combine to create large-scale social forces which may have an utterly unpredicted effect. In Marx's view the institutions of capitalism—themselves the consequences of human behaviour—come back to structure our future behaviour, determining the possibilities of our action. For example, for as long as a capitalist intends to stay in business he must exploit his workers to the legal limit. Whether or not wracked by guilt the capitalist must act as a ruthless exploiter. Similarly, the worker must take the best job on offer; there is simply no other sane option. But by doing this we reinforce the very structures that oppress us. The urge to transcend this condition, and to take collective control of our destiny—whatever that would mean in practice—is one of the motivating and sustaining elements of Marx's social analysis.

Main Ideas of Marx's Political Philosophy

On the basis of the study of Communist Manifesto and other writings of Marx, we find the following main ideas in the political thought of Karl Marx.

1. Dialectical Materialism

Dialectical materialism is a strand of Marxism, synthesizing Hegel's dialectics, which proposes that every economic order grows to a state of maximum efficiency, while simultaneously developing internal contradictions and weaknesses that contribute to its systemic decay. Philosophically, dialectical materialism—that Man originates History through active consciousness—was originated by Moses Hess, and developed by Karl Marx and Friedrich Engels. Moreover, Joseph Dietzgen developed the hypotheses of dialectical materialism independent of Marx, Engels, and Hess.

The term dialectical materialism was coined in 1887, by Joseph Dietzgen, a socialist tanner who corresponded with Karl Marx, during and after the failed 1848 German Revolution. As a philosopher, Dietzgen had constructed the theory of dialectical materialism independently of Marx and Friedrich Engels. Casual mention of the term is also found in the biography Frederick Engels, by Karl Kautsky, written in the same year. Marx himself had talked about the "materialist conception of history", which was later referred to as "historical materialism" by Engels. Engels further exposed the "materialist dialectic"—not "dialectical materialism"—in his Dialectics of Nature in 1883. Georgi Plekhanov, the father of Russian Marxism, later introduced the term dialectical materialism to Marxist literature. Joseph Stalin further delineated and defined dialectical and historical materialism as the world outlook of Marxism-Leninism, and as a method to study society and its history.

The exact term was not used by Marx in any of his works, and the actual presence of "dialectical materialism" within his thought remains the subject of significant controversy, particularly regarding the relationship between dialectics, ontology and nature. For scholars working on these issues from a variety of perspectives see the works of Bertell Ollman, Roger Albritton, and Roy Bhaskar.

Dialectical materialism originates from two major aspects of Marx's philosophy. One is his transformation of Georg Wilhelm Friedrich Hegel's idealistic understanding of dialectics into a materialist one, an act commonly said to have "put Hegel's dialectics back on its feet." Marx's materialism developed through his engagement with Ludwig Feuerbach. Marx sought to base human social organization within the context of the material reproduction of their daily lives, which he calls sensuous practice in his early works (Marx, 1844, 1845). From this material context men and women develop certain ideas about their world, thereby leading to the core materialist conception that social being determines social consciousness. The dialectical aspect retains the Hegelian method within this materialist framework, and emphasizes the process of historical change arising from contradiction and class struggle based in a particular social context.

Dialectics as represented in dialectical materialism is a theory of the general and abstract factors that govern the development of nature, society, and thought. Its principal features are:

- The universe is an integral whole in which things are interdependent, rather than a mixture of things isolated from each other.
- The natural world or cosmos is in a state of constant motion:

  > "All nature, from the smallest thing to the biggest, from a grain of sand to the sun, from the protista to man, is in a constant state of coming into being and going out of being, in a constant flux, in a ceaseless state of movement and change."—Friedrich Engels, Dialectics of Nature.
- Development is a process whereby insignificant and imperceptible quantitative changes lead to fundamental, qualitative changes. Qualitative changes occur not gradually, but rapidly and abruptly, as leaps from one state to another. A simple example from the physical world is the heating of water: a one degree increase in temperature is a quantitative change, but between water of 100 degrees and steam of 100 degrees (the effect latent heat) there is a qualitative change.
- All things contain within themselves internal dialectical contradictions, which are the primary cause of motion, change, and development in the world. It is important to note that 'dialectical contradiction' is not about simple 'opposites' or 'negation'. For formal approaches, the core message of 'dialectical opposition/contradiction' must be understood as 'some sense' opposition between the objects involved in a directly associated context.

2. Historical Materialism

Historical materialism is a methodological approach to the study of society, economics, and history, first articulated by Karl Marx (1818–1883) as "the materialist conception of history." Historical materialism looks for the causes of developments and changes in human society in the means by which humans collectively produce the necessities of life. Social classes and the relationship between them, plus the political structures and ways of thinking in society, are founded on and reflect economic activity.

Historical materialism started from a fundamental underlying reality of human existence: that in order for human beings to survive and continue existence from generation to generation, it is necessary for them to produce and reproduce the material requirements of life. Marx then extended this premise by asserting the importance of the fact that, in order to carry out production and exchange, people have to enter into very definite social relations, most fundamentally "production relations."

However, production does not get carried out in the abstract, or by entering into arbitrary or random relations chosen at will. Human beings collectively work on nature but do not do the same work; there is a division of labour in which people not only do different jobs, but according to Marxist theory, some people live from the work of others by owning the means of production. How this is accomplished depends on the type of society. Production is carried out through very definite relations between people. And, in turn, these production relations are determined by the level and character of the productive forces that are present at any given time in history. For Marx, productive forces refer to the means of production such as the tools, instruments, technology, land, raw materials, and human knowledge and abilities in terms of using these means of production.

Writers who identify with historical materialism usually postulate that society has moved through a number of types or modes of production. That is, the character of the production relations is determined by the character of the productive forces; these could be the simple tools and instruments of early human existence, or the more developed machinery and technology of present age. The main modes of production Marx identified generally include primitive communism or tribal society (a pre-historic stage), ancient society, feudalism, and capitalism. In each of these social stages, people interact with nature and produce their living in different ways. Any surplus from that production is allotted in different ways. Ancient society was based on a ruling class of slave owners and a class of slaves; feudalism was based on landowners and serfs; and capitalism based on the capitalist class and the working class. The capitalist class privately owns the means of production, distribution and exchange (e.g. factories, mines, shops and banks) while the working class live by exchanging their socialized labour with the capitalist class for wages.

Marx identified the production relations of society (arising on the basis of given productive forces) as the economic base of society. He also explained that on the foundation of the economic base there arise certain political institutions, laws, customs, culture etc. and ideas, ways of thinking, morality etc. These constituted the political/ideological superstructure of society. This superstructure not only has its origin in the economic base, but its features also ultimately correspond to the character and development of that economic base, i.e. the way people organize society is determined by the economic base and the relations that arise from its mode of production.

Historical materialism can be seen to rest on the following principles:

1. The basis of human society is how humans work on nature to produce the means of subsistence.
2. There is a division of labour into social classes (relations of production) based on property ownership where some people live from the labour of others.
3. The system of class division is dependent on the mode of production.
4. The mode of production is based on the level of the productive forces.
5. Society moves from stage to stage when the dominant class is displaced by a new emerging class, by overthrowing the "political shell" that enforces the old relations of production no longer corresponding to the new productive forces. This takes place in the superstructure of society, the political arena in the form of revolution, whereby the underclass "liberates" the productive forces with new relations of production, and social relations, corresponding to it.

Marx's clearest formulation of his "Materialist Conception of History" was in the 1859 Preface to his book "*A Contribution to the Critique of Political Economy*," whose relevant passage is reproduced here:

> "In the social production of their existence, men inevitably enter into definite relations, which are independent of their will, namely relations of production appropriate to a given stage in the development of their material forces of production. The totality of these relations of production constitutes the economic structure of society, the real foundation, on which arises a legal and political superstructure and to which correspond definite forms of consciousness. The mode of production of material life conditions

the general process of social, political and intellectual life. It is not the consciousness of men that determines their existence, but their social existence that determines their consciousness. At a certain stage of development, the material productive forces of society come into conflict with the existing relations of production or—this merely expresses the same thing in legal terms—with the property relations within the framework of which they have operated hitherto. From forms of development of the productive forces these relations turn into their fetters. Then begins an era of social revolution. The changes in the economic foundation lead sooner or later to the transformation of the whole immense superstructure. In studying such transformations it is always necessary to distinguish between the material transformation of the economic conditions of production, which can be determined with the precision of natural science, and the legal, political, religious, artistic or philosophic—in short, ideological forms in which men become conscious of this conflict and fight it out. Just as one does not judge an individual by what he thinks about himself, so one cannot judge such a period of transformation by its consciousness, but, on the contrary, this consciousness must be explained from the contradictions of material life, from the conflict existing between the social forces of production and the relations of production."

3. Theory of Class Struggle

Marxian Class Theory is a broad range of social concepts related to the study of Marxism. It asserts that an individual's position within a class hierarchy is determined by his role in the production process, and argues that political and ideological consciousness is determined by class position (Parkin). Within Marxian Class Theory, the structure of the production process forms the basis of class construction.

Marxian Class Theory has been open to a range of alternate positions, most notably from scholars such as E.P. Thompson and Mario Tronti. Both Thompson and Tronti suggest class consciousness within the production process precedes the formation of productive relationships. In this sense, Marxian Class Theory often relates to discussion over pre-existing class struggles.

Marx's class theory derives from a range of philosophical schools of thought including left Hegelianism, Scottish Empiricism and Anglo-French Political-economics. Marx's view of class originated from a series of personal interests relating to social alienation and human struggle, whereby the formation of class structure relates to acute historical consciousness.

Political-economics also contributed to Marx's theories, centring around the concept of "origin of income" where society is divided into three sub-groups: Rentier, Capitalist, and Worker. This construction is based on Ricardo's theory of capitalism. Marx strengthened this with a discussion over verifiable class relationships.

Marx sought to define class as embedded in productive relations rather than social status. His political and economic thought developed towards an interest in production as opposed to distribution, and this henceforth became a central theme in his concept of class.

Marx distinguishes one class from another on the basis of two criteria: ownership of the means of production and control of the labour power of others. From this, he defines modern society as having three distinct classes:

(i) Capitalists, or bourgeoisie, own the means of production and purchase the labour power of others.
(ii) Workers, or proletariat, do not own any means of production or the ability to purchase the labour power of others. Rather, they sell their own labour power.
(iii) A small, transitional class known as the petite bourgeoisie own sufficient means of production but do not purchase labour power. Marx's Communist Manifesto fails to properly define the petite bourgeoisie beyond "smaller capitalists" (Marx and Engels, 1848: 25).

Class is thus determined by property relations not by income or status. These factors are determined by distribution and consumption, which mirror the production and power relations of classes.

> "The history of all hitherto existing society is the history of class struggles... Freeman and slave, patrician and plebeian, lord and serf, guild-master and journeyman, in a word, oppressor and oppressed, stood in constant opposition to one another, carried on an uninterrupted, now hidden, now open fight, a fight that each time ended, either in a revolutionary reconstruction of society at large, or in the common ruin of the contending classes. The modern bourgeois society that has sprouted from the ruins of feudal society has not done away with class antagonisms. It has but established new classes, new conditions of oppression, and new forms of struggle in place of the old ones. Our epoch, the epoch of the bourgeoisie, possesses, however, this distinctive feature: it has simplified class antagonisms. Society as a whole is more and more splitting up into two great hostile camps, into two great classes directly faces each other: Bourgeoisie and Proletariat." —*Communist Manifesto*.

Marx established conflict as the key driving force of history and the main determinant of social trajectories (Kingston). However, in order to understand the nature of "class conflict," we must first understand that such conflict arises from a unified class interest, also known as class consciousness. Class consciousness is an aspect of Marxist theory, referring to the self-awareness of social classes, the capacity to act in its own rational interests, or measuring the extent to which an individual is conscious of the historical tasks their class (or class allegiance) sets for them.

Moreover, by definition, the objective interests of classes are fundamentally in opposition; consequently, these opposing interests and consciousnesses eventually lead to class conflict.

Marx first saw the development of class conflict confined to individual factories and capitalists. However, given the maturation of capitalism, the life conditions of bourgeoisie and proletariat began to grow more disparate. This increased the homogenization within classes to foster the environment for individual struggles to become more generalized. When increasing class conflict is manifested at the societal level, class consciousness and common interests are also increased. Consequently, when class consciousness is augmented, policies are organized to ensure the duration of such interest for the ruling class. Here begins the use of the struggle for political power and classes become political forces.

Since the distribution of political power is determined by power over production, or power over capital, it is no surprise that the bourgeois class uses their wealth to legitimatize and protect their property and consequent social relations. Thus the ruling class is those who hold the economic power and make the decisions (Dahrendorf).

4. Theory of Surplus Value

Surplus value is a concept used famously by Karl Marx in his critique of political economy. Although Marx did not himself invent the term, he developed the concept. It refers roughly to the new value created by workers in excess of their own labour-cost, a value which Marx said was appropriated by the capitalist as gross profit, and which is the basis of capital accumulation.

For Marx, the gigantic increase in wealth and population from the nineteenth century onwards was mainly due to the competitive striving to obtain maximum surplus-value from the employment of labour, resulting in an equally gigantic increase of productivity and capital resources. To the extent that increasingly the economic surplus is convertible into money and expressed in money, the amassment of wealth is possible on a larger and larger scale (see capital accumulation and surplus product).

Marx's solution was to distinguish between labour-time worked and labour power. Marx's theory of surplus values was an extension of his labour theory. According to Marx, as the value of commodity was produced by the labour, labour, whole of the price should be paid to him. Bot in actual practice the capitalists give to the labour much less that what he produces by labour and pocket the rest of it. This difference between the exchange value of manufactured commodity and the amount paid to the workman for his labour is called surplus value. A worker who is sufficiently productive can produce an output value greater than what it costs to hire him. Although his wage seems to be based on hours worked, in an economic sense this wage does not reflect the full value of what the worker produces. Effectively it is not labour which the worker sells, but his capacity to work.

Imagine a worker who is hired for an hour and paid \$10. Once in the capitalist's employ, the capitalist can have him operate a boot-making machine using which the worker produces \$10 worth of work every fifteen minutes. Every hour, the capitalist receives \$40 worth of work and only pays the worker \$10, capturing the remaining \$30 as gross revenue. Once the capitalist has deducted fixed and variable operating costs of (say) \$20 (leather, depreciation of the machine etc.), he is left with \$10. Thus, for an outlay of capital of \$30, the capitalist obtains a surplus value of \$10; his capital has not only been replaced by the operation, but also has increased by \$10.

The worker cannot capture this benefit directly because he has no claim to the means of production (e.g. the boot-making machine) or to its products, and his capacity to bargain over wages is restricted by laws and the supply/demand for wage labour. Hence the rise of trade unions which aim to create a more favourable bargaining position through collective action by workers.

Surplus value may be viewed in five ways:

1. As a component of the new value product, which Marx himself defines as equal to the sum of labour costs in respect of capitalistically productive labour (variable capital) and surplus-value. In production, he argues, the workers produce a value equal to their wages plus an additional value, the surplus-value. They also transfer part of the value of fixed assets and materials to the new product, equal to economic depreciation (consumption of fixed capital) and intermediate goods used up (constant capital inputs). Labour costs and surplus-value are the monetary valuations of what Marx calls the necessary product and the surplus product, or paid labour and unpaid labour.

2. Surplus-value can also be viewed as a flow of net income

appropriated by the owners of capital in virtue of asset ownership, comprising both distributed personal income and undistributed business income. In the whole economy, this will include both income directly from production and property income.

3. Surplus-value can be viewed as the source of society's accumulation fund or investment fund; part of it is re-invested, but part is appropriated as personal income, and used for consumptive purposes by the owners of capital assets (see capital accumulation); in exceptional circumstances, part of it may also be hoarded in someway). In this context, surplus value can also be measured as the increase in the value of the stock of capital assets through an accounting period, prior to distribution.

4. Surplus-value can be viewed as a social relation of production, or as the monetary valuation of surplus-labour—a sort of "index" of the balance of power between social classes or nations in the process of the division of the social product.

5. Surplus-value can, in a developed capitalist economy, be viewed also as an indicator of the level of social productivity that has been reached by the working population, i.e. the net amount of value it can produce with its labour in excess of its own consumption requirements.

5. Dictatorship of Proletariat

Dictatorship of the proletariat, in Marxism, rule by the proletariat—the economic and social class consisting of industrial workers who derive income solely from their labour—during the transitional phase between the abolition of capitalism and the establishment of communism. During this transition, the proletariat is to suppress resistance to the socialist revolution by the bourgeoisie, destroy the social relations of production underlying the class system, and create a new, classless society.

The dictatorship of the proletariat originally was conceived by Karl Marx (1818–83) as a dictatorship by the majority class. Because Marx regarded all governments as class dictatorships, he viewed proletarian dictatorship as no worse than any other form of government. However, the Bolshevik Revolution in Russia in 1917 resulted in a dictatorship not of the majority class of proletarians but of a political party that claimed to represent proletarian interests. Contrary to Marx's vision and as George Orwell (1903–50), Mikhail Bakunin (1814–76), and others had foreseen, the proposed dictatorship of the proletariat eventually became a dictatorship of former proletarians.

In Marxist socio-political thought, the dictatorship of the proletariat refers to a socialist state in which the proletariat, or the working class, has control of political power. The term, coined by Joseph Weydemeyer, was adopted by the founders of Marxism, Karl Marx and Friedrich Engels, in the nineteenth century. The use of the term "dictatorship" does not refer to the Classical Roman concept of the *dictatura* (the governance of a state by a small group with no democratic process), but instead to the Marxist concept of dictatorship (that an entire societal class holds political and economic control, within a democratic system).

One of the issues most closely associated with the transition to socialism is "the dictatorship of the proletariat." In Marxist theory, the transition to socialism is meant to come about through the eruption of the struggle between the bourgeoisie and the working class, or proletariat, whereby state power would pass into the hands of the proletariat. The latter would exercise its dictatorship until it triumphs over all the other classes which remain in society even after the proletariat assumes power as residuals of a long, deep-rooted past. During that phase, all powers would be in the hands of the proletariat to enable it to accomplish its historic task, that of eliminating all classes antagonistic to the working class. Once it has accomplished its mission, its dictatorship will come to an end, since no other classes will exist and the state apparatus will fall, along with the entire system of laws, when all men (those who remain!) will have attained the highest stage of communism.

Briefly, that is the idea of the "dictatorship of the proletariat", its rationale, functions and fate. To show how basic this idea is to the whole structure of Marxist ideology, and to leave no room for the argument that its repudiation is a development within the framework of the Marxist theory itself and not a blatant contradiction of its very foundations, let us turn to the words of Marx himself.

Following on from the theories of Marx and Engels, Marxists believe that such a socialist state is an inevitable step in the evolution of human society. They argue that it is a transitional phase that emerges out of the "dictatorship of the bourgeoisie", or capitalist society, in which the private ownership of industry and resources leads to a monopoly of economic power (albeit sometimes within a democratic parliament) by the capitalist class. With an economy under democratic control, Marxists expect political power to be held by the majority working class. Whether or not capitalists are disenfranchised would depend upon the particular circumstances of a nation. In a period immediately after the Russian Revolution, the mode in which democracy was organised (elections within workplace 'soviets') automatically disenfranchised capitalists (who were not a part of the workforce); however, Marxists such as Lenin argued that other forms of a "dictatorship of the proletariat" in more developed countries would include capitalists among the electorate. However, as large-scale capitalism is phased out, future generations would not become capitalist owners, and class divisions would no longer exist within the electorate. As a result, the "dictatorship of the proletariat" would wither away, resulting in an entirely classless, stateless form of society known as *pure communism*.

In other words, the accession to power by these dictatorships did not proceed in the manner envisaged by Marx. Another glaring discrepancy between the theory he expounded and its application in practice is that not one of the dictatorships of the proletariat existing in countries of the socialist bloc can claim to have been established by the working class. In the Soviet Union, for example, the leaders of the Bolshevik party all came either from the middle or upper-middle class. Trotsky, Zinoviev, Kamenev, Kaganovitch and other Bolshevik leaders who laid the foundations of the dictatorship of the proletariat in the Soviet Union were all middle class intellectuals, many of them Russian Jews from professional and merchant families. The same applies to those who created dictatorships of the proletariat in the rest of the socialist countries, including those in the Third World. In Cuba, for example, the dictatorship of the proletariat was established by members of the upper middle class, by the sons of rich families who had been sent to European capitals for their studies, a great luxury in such poor societies.

Marx Theory of State

Karl Marx's ideas about the state can be divided into three subject areas: pre-capitalist states, states in the capitalist (i.e. present) era, and the state (or absence of one) in post-capitalist society. Overlaying this is the fact that his own ideas about the state changed as he grew older, differing in his early pre-communist phase, the "young Marx" phase which predates the unsuccessful 1848 uprisings in Europe, and in his mature, more nuanced work.

In Marx's 1843 Critique of Hegel's Philosophy of Right, his basic conception is that the state and civil society are separate; however, he already saw some limitations to that model: "The political state everywhere needs the guarantee of spheres lying outside it."

He as yet was saying nothing about the abolition of private property, does not express a developed theory of class, and "the solution to the problem of the state/civil society separation is a purely political solution, namely universal suffrage."

By the time he wrote *The German Ideology* (1846), Marx viewed the state as a creature of the bourgeois economic interest. Two years later that idea was expounded in *The Communist Manifesto*. The executive of the modern state is nothing but a committee for managing the common affairs of the whole bourgeoisie. his represents the high point of conformance of the state theory to a strict economic interpretation of history: The forces of production determine peoples' production relations; their production relations determine all other relations, including the political.("Determines" is the strong form of the claim, Marx also uses "conditions." Also, even "determination" is not causality, and some reciprocity of action is admitted.) The bourgeoisie control the economy, therefore, they control the state. The state, in this theory, is an instrument of class rule.

The Relation of State and the Law to Property

In the case of the nations which grew out of the Middle Ages, tribal property evolved through various stages—feudal landed property, corporative movable property, capital invested in manufacture—to modern capital, determined by big industry and universal competition, i.e. pure private property, which has cast off all semblance of a communal institution and has shut out the State from any influence on the development of property. To this modern private property corresponds the modern State, which, purchased gradually by the owners of property by means of taxation, has fallen entirely into their hands through the national debt, and its existence has become wholly dependent on the commercial credit which the owners of property, the bourgeois, extend to it, as reflected in the rise and fall of State funds on the stock exchange. By the mere fact that it is a class and no longer an estate, the bourgeoisie is forced to organise itself no longer locally, but nationally, and to give a general form to its mean average interest. Through the emancipation of private property from the community, the State has become a separate entity, beside and outside civil society; but it is nothing more than the form of organisation which the bourgeois necessarily adopt both for internal and external purposes, for the mutual guarantee of their property and interests. The independence of the State is only found now-a-days in those countries where the estates have not yet completely developed into classes, where the estates, done away with in more advanced countries, still have a part to play, and where there exists a mixture; countries, that is to say, in which no one section of the population can achieve dominance over the others. This is the case particularly in Germany. The most perfect example of the modern State is North America. The modern French, English and American writers all express the opinion that the State exists only for the sake of private property, so that this fact has penetrated into the consciousness of the normal man.

Economic Dependence of the State on the Bourgeoisie

With the development and accumulation of bourgeois property, i.e. with the development of commerce and industry, individuals grew richer and richer while the state fell ever more deeply into debt. This phenomenon was evident already in the first Italian commercial republics; later, since the last century, it showed itself to a marked degree in Holland, where the stock exchange speculator Pinto drew attention to it as early as 1750, and now it is again occurring in England. It is, therefore, obvious that as soon as the bourgeoisie has accumulated money, the state has to beg from the bourgeoisie and in the end it is actually bought up by the latter. This takes place in a period in which the bourgeoisie is still confronted by another class, and consequently the state can retain some appearance of independence in relation to both of them. Even after the state has been bought up, it still needs money and, therefore, continues to be dependent on the bourgeoisie; nevertheless, when the interests of the bourgeoisie demand it, the state can have at its disposal more funds than states which are less developed and, therefore, less burdened with debts. However, even the least developed states of Europe, those of the Holy Alliance, are inexorably approaching this fate, for they will be bought up by the bourgeoisie; then Stirner will be able to console them with the identity of private and state property, especially his own sovereign, who is trying in vain to postpone the hour when political power will be sold to the "burghers" who have become "angry."

Marx on Capitalism

According to Marx, capitalists are able to make profits only by exploiting their workers. Profits are made by the capitalist's appropriation of the surplus value created by the labour of his workers. In other words, profits are made by the workers producing for their capitalist employers sums of value greater than they are paid in wages. That sum of value which the workers receive in wages they pay back to the capitalist by working for the period of necessary labour. The sums of value that are created by workers during the period of surplus labour represent for the capitalist pure gain. It is a return for which they make no equivalent outlay. Marx called the rate of surplus value, therefore, "an exact expression for the degree of exploitation of labour-power by capital, or of the worker by the capitalist."

What exactly did Marx mean by 'exploitation'? What did he think was wrong with it? Was Marx correct to regard capitalism as a system involving the systematic exploitation of the workers? These are questions we shall not attempt to answer.

Broadly speaking, there are two schools of opinion on the question of what Marx meant by the term exploitation. Both schools agree that exploitation, for Marx, involves non-reciprocal benefit; that is, one person benefits another without the second benefiting the first in return. Further, both schools agree that non-reciprocal benefit is not a sufficient condition of exploitation for Marx. This is because both schools agree that Marx recognizes there to be cases of non-exploitative, non-reciprocal benefit of one party by another. The paradigm case of such non-exploitative non-reciprocal benefit is the deductions to earnings of the able-bodied that are to be made in socialism for provision of welfare for the disabled. As a result of these deductions, the disabled are benefited by the able-bodied without benefiting the able-bodied in return. Yet such welfare deductions to earnings are not regarded by Marx as instances of the disabled exploiting the able-bodied. Granted that such welfare provisions will be present in socialism and that welfare provisions involves the able-bodied benefiting the disabled, it follows that non-reciprocal benefit is not a sufficient condition of exploitation for Marx.

What more is needed for exploitation besides non-reciprocal benefit? According to the interpretation of one school, which I will call the justice interpretation, as well as there being non-reciprocal benefit, it must be unjust that the benefited party gain their benefit without reciprocating the benefit. In other words, proponents of the justice interpretation advance the following understanding of exploitation: A exploits B, if and only if: (1) B benefits A in some way without A benefiting B in return, and (2) A's failure to benefit B in return for B's benefiting A is unjust.

According to proponents of the justice interpretation, Marx believed that capitalism involves exploitation because he believed it was unjust that the capitalist appropriates the surplus value created by the worker without making a reciprocal return to the worker. On this view, Marx believed that a person was morally entitled to the full product of his labour, minus certain deductions that are necessary for replenishing and expanding means of production and for providing public goods and welfare for the disabled. Workers in socialism will receive such a product of their labour. In capitalism, workers receive less than this. Some surplus value that the worker produces which rightly ought to go to the worker goes to the capitalist. On this view, the deductions made from the product of the labour of the able-bodied for the provision of welfare for the disabled are not instances of exploitation because such deductions are not unjust. The disabled are morally entitled to them.

According to the coercion interpretation, the provision of welfare for the disabled by deductions from the product of the labour of the able-bodied is not exploitation because it is not the case that the disabled force the able-bodied to make such provision. Such contributions are either made voluntarily or, if forced, are forced by the state. In the case of capitalism, the provision of surplus value for the capitalist is a non-reciprocal benefit forced from the worker by the capitalist. It is, therefore, a case of exploitation. The worker in capitalism is not forced to engage in surplus labour in the same way that slaves and serfs were. In the case of the latter it was threat of punishment if they refused. Rather, what forces the wage-labourer in capitalism to engage in surplus labour is the fact that the capitalist owns the means of production. Lacking means of production of their own, the wage-labourers are forced to accept the wage offers of the capitalists to procure means of subsistence, and the wage contracts to which they are forced to agree bind them to perform surplus labour.

According to the coercion interpretation of exploitation, not only is injustice not part of the notion of exploitation, it is not implied by it. The foremost proponent of this interpretation, Allen Wood, claims that Marx did not regard exploitation as unjust. Wood's coercion interpretation is based upon a number of remarks of Marx's which are *prima facie* difficult to reconcile with the view that he took exploitation to be unjust. Wood takes these remarks to establish conclusively that Marx regards capitalist exploitation to be just. However, according to Wood, the fact that exploitation is just, for Marx, does not constitute any defence of it. According to Wood, justice, for Marx, is simply whatever conforms to and harmonizes with the prevailing mode of production. That an act or institution is just, therefore, does not justify or commend the act or institution in anyway. Wood writes: "[for Marx] it is not an analytic proposition or trivial truth to say that the just, the virtuous or the morally right thing is the thing which, all things considered, should be done. For Marx, in fact, it is sometimes a pernicious falsehood."

Such an account of Marx's view of morality as Wood offers squares with Marx's assertion that talk of 'fair distribution' by socialists constitute 'obsolete verbal rubbish.' It also squares with the fact that Marx nowhere says that capitalist exploitation is unjust, nor even says that socialism and communism will establish justice.

Despite the impressive *prima facie* case in support of the coercion interpretation of exploitation made out by Wood, the case is by no means conclusive. There is, in fact, considerable reason for preferring the justice interpretation to it. First, as G.A. Cohen has pointed out, coercion seems to be neither a necessary condition, nor—together with non-reciprocal benefit—a sufficient condition, of exploitation as Marx understands the term. That coercion is not a necessary condition of exploitation, for Marx, becomes evident from the following case. Imagine a rich capitalist B who has no need to work but who—for a bet or for amusement—finds employment as a wage-labourer with capitalist A. In this case, A would obtain surplus value through B's labour and B would accordingly be exploited by A. Yet, in the case as presented, B is not forced to work as, therefore, is not forced to provide surplus value for A. Accordingly, since he is exploited but not coerced, it follows that coercion is not a necessary condition of exploitation. As Cohen has pointed out, coercion seems also not to be, together with non-reciprocal benefit, a sufficient condition of exploitation. Cohen asks us to imagine involuntarily unemployed adults with many dependants who threatens violence in the streets unless welfare payments are made to them by those able to provide them. On Wood's definition, these people would be exploiters. Yet it is difficult to believe that would have been Marx's view of them. Accordingly, coercion and non-reciprocal benefit are not jointly a sufficient condition of exploitation. The role that coercion plays in capitalist exploitation is that the workers' lack of means of production forces them to suffer exploitation. So, coercion is a cause of exploitation but is not itself part of what exploitation consists in.

A second reason for preferring the justice interpretation of exploitation to the coercion interpretation is that Marx makes many assertions which are otherwise difficult to understand if he did not think exploitation to be a form of injustice. Thus, for instance, Marx talks of "the theft of alien labour-time on which the present wealth is based." He also speaks of "the learned dispute between the industrial capitalist and the wealthy landowning idler as to how the booty pumped out of the workers may most advantageously be divided for the purposes of accumulation." Why did Marx talk of 'theft' and 'booty' if he regarded exploitation as just?

Finally, it is possible to reconcile the justice interpretation of exploitation with Marx's assertion that talk of 'just distribution' is obsolete verbal rubbish. Allen Buchanan has argued that Marx thought capitalism unjust but did not wish to emphasize its injustice because he thought that the very need for justice was a shortcoming in society. A virtue of communism would be that it would dispense with the need for justice. Justice is necessary only where there is scarcity and an opposition of interests between members of society. In full communism, scarcity will have been abolished on Marx's view and there will be complete identification between people. The circumstances giving rise to the need for justice will thus no longer obtain. This view leads to a very interesting interpretation of Marx. A famous passage of Marx's is the following one from the Critique of the Gotha Programme: "In a more advanced phase of communist society, when the enslaving subjugation of the individual to the division of labour, and thereby the antithesis between intellectual and physical labour, have disappeared; when labour is no longer just a means of keeping alive but has itself become a vital need; when the all-round development of individuals has also increased their productive powers, and all the springs of cooperative wealth flow more abundantly—only then can society wholly cross the narrow horizon of bourgeois right and inscribe on its banners: From each according to his abilities, to each according to his needs."

It is Buchanan's view that Marx refrained from calling capitalism unjust (despite his speaking of the appropriation of surplus value as theft) because he believed that communism would be a society 'beyond justice.' The principle 'From each according to his abilities, to each according to his need' is not, says Buchanan, a communist principle of distributive justice. Rather it is a description of how things will in fact be in communism. Thus, Marx refrained from calling the capitalist's exploitation unjust, because this would have obscured the fact that what Marx thought special about communism was not that it would be a just society, but that it would dispense with the need for justice by abolishing the circumstances that give rise to it.

Marx's View on Socialism

Socialists adhere to a diverse range of philosophical views. Marxian socialism is philosophically materialist as well as having at its centre a commitment to historical materialism. Many forms of socialist theory hold that human behaviour is largely shaped by the social environment. In particular, Marxism and socialists inspired by Marxist theory, holds that social mores, values, cultural traits and economic practices are social creations, and are not the result of an immutable natural law. The ultimate goal for Marxist socialists is the emancipation of labour from alienating work. Marxists argue that freeing the individual from the necessity of performing alienating work in order to receive goods would allow people to pursue their own interests and develop their own talents without being coerced into performing labour for others. For Marxists, the stage of economic development in which this is possible is contingent upon advances in the productive capabilities of society.

Socialists generally argue that capitalism concentrates power and wealth within a small segment of society that controls the means of production and derives its wealth through a system of exploitation. This creates a stratified society based on unequal social relations that fails to provide equal opportunities for every individual to maximise their potential, and does not utilise available technology and resources to their maximum potential in the interests of the public.

Socialists hold that capitalism is an illegitimate economic system, since it largely serves the interests of the owners of capital and involves the exploitation of other economic classes. As such, they wish to replace it completely or at least make substantial modifications to it, in order to create a more just society that would guarantee a certain basic standard of living.

In the most influential of all socialist theories, Karl Marx and Friedrich Engels believed the consciousness of those who earn a wage or salary (the "working class" in the broadest Marxist sense) would be moulded by their "conditions" of "wage-slavery", leading to a tendency to seek their freedom or "emancipation" by overthrowing ownership of the means of production by capitalists. For Marx and Engels, conditions determine consciousness and ending the role of the capitalist class leads eventually to a classless society in which the state would wither away.

Marx wrote: "It is not the consciousness of [people] that determines their existence, but their social existence that determines their consciousness."

The Marxist conception of socialism is that of a specific historical phase that will displace capitalism and precede communism. The major characteristics of socialism (particularly as conceived by Marx and Engels after the Paris Commune of 1871) are that the proletariat will control the means of production through a workers' state erected by the workers in their interests. Economic activity would still be organised through the use of incentive systems and social classes would still exist, but to a lesser and diminishing extent than under capitalism.

For orthodox Marxists, socialism is the lower stage of communism based on the principle of "from each according to his ability, to each according to his contribution" while upper stage communism is based on the principle of "from each according to his ability, to each according to his need"; the upper stage becoming possible only after the socialist stage further develops economic efficiency and the automation of production has led to a superabundance of goods and services.

Marx argued that the material productive forces (in industry and commerce) brought into existence by capitalism predicated a cooperative society since production had become a mass social, collective activity of the working class to create commodities but with private ownership (the relations of production or property relations). This conflict between collective effort in large factories and private ownership would bring about a conscious desire in the working class to establish collective ownership commensurate with the collective efforts their daily experience.

"At a certain stage of development, the material productive forces of society come into conflict with the existing relations of production or—this merely expresses the same thing in legal terms—with the property relations within the framework of which they have operated hitherto. Then begins an era of social revolution. The changes in the economic foundation lead sooner or later to the transformation of the whole immense superstructure."

Che Guevara sought socialism based on the rural peasantry rather than the urban working class, attempting to inspire the peasants of Bolivia by his own example into a change of consciousness. Guevara said in 1965:

> "Socialism cannot exist without a change in consciousness resulting in a new fraternal attitude toward humanity, both at an individual level, within the societies where socialism is being built or has been built, and on a world scale, with regard to all peoples suffering from imperialist oppression."

Marx's Theory of Religion

It is vital to understand the meaning of Marx to grasp his ideas in relation to his development. In this connection, his conception of religion is one of the most important aspects of his notions. It was quite easy to deal with religion by just being against it, but that was not good enough. 'Everybody knows' that Marx wrote about religion being the opium of the people, so we shall look at the entire passage from which this comes. 'Everybody' thinks that Marx was saying that religion was dope manufactured by the ruling class to keep the masses happy. The real Marx, however, was concerned with much more weighty problems. Among other things, he was thinking about how an abstract human being could exist. He concludes that one could not. 'Man is the world of man, state, society', and the conception of God was a necessary conception in an 'inverted world'. Once the world was right side up, the idea would not be needed. Meanwhile we should pay attention to it. Marx brings together his views on religion and his historical view of the communist revolution and the growth of production generally. He relates religion to the effort to unite human beings without really understanding the sweeping historical forces which have separated them. Marx said, "The religious reflections of the real world can, in any case, vanish only when the practical relations of everyday life between man and man, and man and nature, generally present themselves to him in a transparent and rational form. The veil is not removed from the countenance of the social life-process, i.e. the process of material production, until it becomes production by freely associated men, and stands under their conscious and planned control. This, however, requires that society possess a material foundation, or a series of material conditions of existence, which in their turn are the natural and spontaneous product of a long and tormented historical development."

Here, Marx has set out his conception of religion in the light of his notion of the stages of history as a whole. First, humans see themselves as a local community, with their local gods. Then, in the era of money and exploitation, God Almighty rules over all. Finally, there is no use for Him, as humans freely govern their own lives.

Marx's View on Alienation

Karl Marx's Theory of Alienation, which describes the separation of things that naturally belong together; and the placement of antagonism between things that are properly in harmony. Theoretically, *Entfremdung* describes the social alienation (estrangement) of people from aspects of their human nature (*Gattungswesen*, "species-essence") as a consequence of living in a society stratified into social classes; Marx had earlier expressed the *entfremdung* theory in the *Economic and Philosophic Manuscripts of 1844* (1927). Philosophically, the *Entfremdung* theory relies upon *The Essence of Christianity* (1841), by Ludwig Feuerbach, which argues that the supernatural idea of "God" has alienated the natural characteristics of the human being. Moreover, in *The Ego and its Own* (1845), Max Stirner extends the Feurbach analysis by arguing that even the idea of "humanity" is an alienating concept for the individual man and woman to intellectually consider; Marx and Engels responded to these philosophic propositions in *The German Ideology* (1845).

Alienation is the systemic result of living in a socially stratified society, because being a *mechanistic part* of a social class alienates a person from his or her humanity. The theoretic basis of alienation within the capitalist mode of production is that the worker invariably loses the ability to determine his or her life and destiny, when deprived of the right to think (conceive) of himself as the director of his actions; to determine the character of said actions; to define his relationship with other people; and to own the things and use the value of the goods and services, produced with his labour. Although the worker is an autonomous, self-realised human being, as an economic entity, he or she is directed to goals and diverted to activities that are dictated by the bourgeoisie, who own the means of production, in order to extract from the worker the maximal amount of surplus value, in the course of business competition among industrialists.

In a capitalist society, the worker's alienation from his and her humanity occurs because the worker can only express *labour*—a fundamental social aspect of personal individuality—through a privately-owned system of industrial production in which each worker is an instrument, a thing, not a person.

Types of Alienation

In the *Economic and Philosophic Manuscripts of 1844* (1927), Karl Marx identified four types of alienation that occur to the worker labouring under a capitalist system of industrial production.

The four types of Alienation are as follows:

(I) Alienation of the Worker from the Work—from the Product of his Labour

The design of the product and how it is produced are determined, not by the producers who make it (the workers), nor by the consumers of the product (the buyers), but by the Capitalist class, who, besides appropriating the worker's manual labour, also appropriate the intellectual labour of the engineer and the industrial designer who create the product, in order to shape the taste of the consumer to buy the goods and services at a price that yields a maximal profit. Aside from the workers having no control over the design-and-production protocol, alienation (*Entfremdung*) broadly describes the conversion of labour (work as an activity), which is performed to generate a use value (the product) into a commodity, which—like products—can be assigned an exchange value. That is, the Capitalist gains control of the manual and intellectual workers, and the benefits of their labour, with a system of industrial production that converts said labour into concrete products (goods and services) that benefit the consumer. Moreover, the capitalist production system also reifies labour into the "concrete" concept of "work" (a job), for which the worker is paid wages—at the lowest possible rate—that maintain a maximum rate of return on the Capitalist's investment capital; this is an aspect of exploitation. Furthermore, with such a reified system of industrial production, the profit (exchange value) generated by the sale of the goods and services (products) that could be paid to the workers, instead is paid to the capitalist classes: the functional capitalist, who manages the means of production, and the rentier capitalist, who owns the means of production.

(II) Alienation of the Worker from Working—From the Act of Producing

In the Capitalist Mode of Production, the generation of products (goods and services) is accomplished with an endless sequence of discrete, repetitive, motions that offer the worker little psychological satisfaction for "a job well done." By means of commodification, the labour power of the worker is reduced to wages (an exchange value); the psychological estrangement (*Entfremdung*) of the worker results from the unmediated relation between his productive labour and the wages paid him for the labour. That division of labour, within the capitalist mode of production, further exploits the worker by limiting his or her *Gattungswesen* (species-essence)—the human being's power to determine the purpose to which the product (goods and services) shall be applied; the human nature (species-essence) of the worker is fulfilled when he or she controls the "subject of labour." Hence does capitalism remove from the worker the right to exercise control upon the value and the effects of his and her labour, which, in turn, robs the worker of the ability to either buy (consume) the goods and services, or to receive the full value from the sale of the product. The alienation of the worker from the act of producing renders the worker unable to specialize in a type of productive labour, which is a psychologically satisfying condition; within an industrial system of production, social alienation reduces the worker to an instrument, to an object, and thus cannot productively apply every aspect of his or her human nature.

(III) Alienation of the Worker From Himself, as a Producer

The *Gattungswesen* (species-essence), the human nature of a man and of a woman is not discrete (separate and apart) from his or her activity as a worker; as such, *species-essence* also comprises all of his and her innate human potential as a person. Conceptually, in the term "species-essence", the word "species" describes the intrinsic human mental essence that is characterised by a "plurality of interests" and "psychological dynamism", whereby every man and woman has the desire and the tendency to engage in many activities that promote mutual human survival and psychological well-being, by means of emotional connections with other people, with society. The psychic value of a man consists in being able to conceive (think) of the ends of his actions as purposeful ideas, which are distinct from the actions required to realise a given idea. That is, man is able to objectify his intentions, by means of an idea of himself, as "the subject", and an idea of the thing that he produces, "the object." Conversely, unlike a human being, an animal does not objectify itself, as "the subject", nor its products as ideas, "the object", because an animal engages in directly self-sustaining actions that have neither a future intention, nor a conscious intention. Whereas a person's *Gattungswesen* (human nature) does not exist independent of specific, historically-conditioned activities, the essential nature of a human being is actualized when a man—within his given historical circumstance—is free to subordinate his will to the external demands he has imposed upon himself, by his imagination, and not the external demands imposed upon him by other people.

(IV) Alienation of the Worker from Other Workers

Capitalism reduces the labour of the worker to a commercial commodity that can be traded in the competitive labour-market, rather than as a constructive socio-economic activity that is part of the collective common effort performed for personal survival and the betterment of society. In a capitalist economy, the businessmen who own the means of production establish a competitive labour-market meant to extract from the worker as much labour (value) as possible, in the form of capital. The capitalist economy's arrangement of the relations of production provokes social conflict by pitting worker against worker, in a competition for "higher wages", thereby alienating them from their mutual economic interests; the effect is a false consciousness, which is a form of ideologic control exercised by the capitalist bourgeoisie. (*See*: Cultural hegemony) Furthermore, in the capitalist mode of production, the philosophic collusion of religion in justifying the relations of production facilitates the realisation, and then worsens, the alienation (*Entfremdung*) of the worker from his and her humanity; it is a socio-economic role independent of religion being "the opiate of the masses."

Marx and Internationalism

Proletarian internationalism, sometimes referred to as **international socialism**, is a Marxist social class concept based on the view that capitalism is now a global system, and therefore, the working class must act as a global class if it is to defeat it. Workers should struggle in solidarity with their fellow workers in other countries on the basis of a common class interest.

Proletarian internationalism is closely linked to Marxist goals of world revolution, to be achieved through successive or simultaneous communist revolutions in all nations. Marxist theory is that world revolution would lead to world communism, and later still, stateless communism.

Marxists regard proletarian internationalism as the antonym of bourgeois nationalism but the term has been subjected to different interpretations by various currents of Marxist thought.

Proletarian internationalism is summed up in the slogan coined by Marx and Engels, *Workers of all countries, unite!*, the last line of The Communist Manifesto, published in 1848. However, Marx and Engels' approach to the national question was also shaped by tactical considerations in their pursuit of a long-term revolutionary strategy. In 1848, the proletariat was a small minority in all but a handful of countries. Political and economic conditions needed to ripen in order to advance the possibility of proletarian revolution.

Thus, for example, Marx and Engels supported the emergence of an independent and democratic Poland, which at the time was divided between Germany, Russia and Austria-Hungary. Rosa Luxemburg's biographer Peter Nettl writes, "In general, Marx and Engels' conception of the national-geographical rearrangement of Europe was based on four criteria: the development of progress, the creation of large-scale economic units, the weighting of approval and disapproval in accordance with revolutionary possibilities, and their specific enmity to Russia." Russia was seen as the heartland of European reaction at the time.

Shortcomings of Marx

Democratic socialists and social democrats reject the idea that socialism can be accomplished only through class conflict and a proletarian revolution. Many anarchists reject the need for a transitory state phase. Some thinkers have rejected the fundamentals of Marxist theory, such as historical materialism and the labour theory of value, and gone on to criticize capitalism—and advocate socialism—using other arguments.

Some contemporary supporters of Marxism argue that many aspects of Marxist thought are viable, but that the corpus is incomplete or somewhat outdated in regards to certain aspects of economic, political or social theory. They may, therefore, combine some Marxist concepts with the ideas of other theorists such as Max Weber: the Frankfurt school is one example.

V.K. Dmitriev, writing in 1898, Ladislaus von Bortkiewicz, writing in 1906-07, and subsequent critics have alleged that Marx's value theory and law of the tendency of the rate of profit to fall are internally inconsistent. In other words, the critics allege that Marx drew conclusions that actually do not follow from his theoretical premises. Once these alleged errors are corrected, his conclusion that aggregate price and profit are determined by, and equal to, aggregate value and surplus value no longer holds true. This result calls into question his theory that the exploitation of workers is the sole source of profit.

Whether the rate of profit in capitalism has, as Marx predicted, tended to fall is a subject of debate. N. Okishio, in 1961, devised a theorem (Okishio's theorem) showing that if capitalists pursue cost-cutting techniques and if the real wage does not rise, the rate of profit must rise Real wages have risen, however, making this theorem indecisive to the real case.

The inconsistency allegations have been a prominent feature of Marxian economics and the debate surrounding it since the 1970s. Andrew Kliman argues that, since internally inconsistent theories cannot possibly be right, the inconsistency charges serve to legitimate the suppression of Marx's critique of political economy and current-day research based upon it, as well as the correction of Marx's alleged inconsistencies.

Critics who have alleged that Marx has been proved internally inconsistent include former and current Marxian and/or Sraffian economists, such as Paul Sweezy, Nobuo Okishio, Ian Steedman, John Roemer, Gary Mongiovi, and David Laibman, who propose that the field be grounded in their correct versions of Marxian economics instead of in Marx's critique of political economy in the original form in which he presented and developed it in Capital.

Proponents of the Temporal Single System Interpretation (TSSI) of Marx's value theory claim that the supposed inconsistencies are actually the result of misinterpretation; they argue that when Marx's theory is understood as "temporal" and "single-system," the alleged internal inconsistencies disappear. In a recent survey of the debate, a proponent of the TSSI concludes that "the proofs of inconsistency are no longer defended; the entire case against Marx has been reduced to the interpretive issue." Some other key points of criticism of Marx are as follows:

1. In the first place it is alleged that Marx is a dogmatic philosopher who completely relaxed the logical rigidity of the theory. All his propositions are neither supported by logic not by historical evidence.
2. Marx wrongly emphasised that the economic forces operate independent of the will of man, and the economic factor is the only factor which moves the whole world.
3. Marx's theory of class and class struggle is basically wrong. His thesis that the economic position always determines the social eminence is not supported even by the history of Western civilization.
4. Marx had assumed that in course of time the capitalists and the proletariat shall be pitched in opposition camps, but this has not happened.
5. Marx believed that the state will ultimately wither away. This prophecy of Marx has not come true. In fact the state with the passage of time has assumed more and more powers.
6. Marx believed that social change can be effected only through revolution. But in actual practice we find that great many changes

have been brought about through non-violent methods and by change of mind.

7. Marx assumed that the establishment of the classless society will be marked by an end to all violence. It is difficult to accept this contention of Marx. It is indeed difficult to understand how a party coming to power through violence will at once abandon violence.
8. Marx's distribution of history into four periods is arbitrary. He probably accepted it because it was demanded by his dialectic.
9. Finally, Marx completely ignored the psychological aspect of politics and did not give adequate treatment to the concept of power.

Estimate of Marx

The above noted shortcomings and limitations in Marx's political thought do not in anyway undermine his contributions to political thought. He made numerous valuable contributions to the political thoughts which have greatly changed the face of the world.

Marx had a special concern with how people relate to that most fundamental resource of all, their own labour power. He wrote extensively about this in terms of the problem of alienation. As with the dialectic, Marx began with a Hegelian notion of alienation but developed a more materialist conception. Capitalism mediates social relationships of production (such as among workers or between workers and capitalists) through commodities, including labour, that are bought and sold on the market. For Marx, the possibility that one may give up ownership of one's own labour—one's capacity to transform the world—is tantamount to being alienated from one's own nature; it is a spiritual loss. Marx described this loss as commodity fetishism, in which the things that people produce, commodities, appear to have a life and movement of their own to which humans and their behavior merely adapt.

Commodity fetishism provides an example of what Engels called "false consciousness", which relates closely to the understanding of ideology. By "ideology", Marx and Engels meant ideas that reflect the interests of a particular class at a particular time in history, but which contemporaries see as universal and eternal. Marx and Engels' point was not only that such beliefs are at best half-truths; they serve an important political function. Put another way, the control that one class exercises over the means of production includes not only the production of food or manufactured goods; it includes the production of ideas as well (this provides one possible explanation for why members of a subordinate class may hold ideas contrary to their own interests). An example of this sort of analysis is Marx's understanding of religion, summed up in a passage from the preface to his 1843 Contribution to the Critique of Hegel's Philosophy of Right:

> Religious suffering is, at one and the same time, the expression of real suffering and a protest against real suffering. Religion is the sigh of the oppressed creature, the heart of a heartless world, and the soul of soulless conditions. It is the opium of the people. The abolition of religion as the illusory happiness of the people is the demand for their real happiness. To call on them to give up their illusions about their condition is to call on them to give up a condition that requires illusions.

Marx's thoughts on labour were related to the primacy he gave to the economic relation in determining the society's past, present and future (see also economic determinism). Accumulation of capital shapes the social system. Social change, for Marx, was about conflict between opposing interests, driven, in the background, by economic forces. This became the inspiration for the body of works known as the conflict theory. In his evolutionary model of history, he argued that human history began with free, productive and creative work that was over time coerced and dehumanised, a trend most apparent under capitalism. Marx noted that this was not an intentional process; rather, no individual or even no state can go against the forces of economy.

The organisation of society depends on means of production. Literally those things, like land, natural resources, and technology, necessary for the production of material goods and the relations of production, in other words, the social relationships people enter into as they acquire and use the means of production. Together these compose the mode of production, and Marx distinguished historical eras in terms of distinct modes of production. Marx differentiated between base and superstructure, with the base (or substructure) referring to the economic system, and superstructure, to the cultural and political system. Marx regarded this mismatch between (economic) base and (social) superstructure as a major source of social disruption and conflict.

Despite Marx's stress on critique of capitalism and discussion of the new communist society that should replace it, his explicit critique of capitalism is guarded, as he saw it as an improved society compared to the past ones (slavery and feudal). Marx also never clearly discusses issues of morality and justice, although scholars agree that his work contained implicit discussion of those concepts.

Marx's view of capitalism was two sided. On one hand, Marx, in the nineteenth century's deepest critique of the dehumanising aspects of this system, noted that defining features of capitalism include alienation, exploitation and recurring, cyclical depressions leading to mass unemployment; on the other hand capitalism is also characterised by "revolutionizing, industrializing and universalizing qualities of development, growth and progressivity" (by which Marx meant industrialisation, urbanisation, technological progress, increased productivity and growth, rationality and scientific revolution), that are responsible for progress. Marx considered the capitalist class to be one of the most revolutionary in history, because it constantly improved the means of production, more so than any other class in history, and was responsible for the overthrow of feudalism and its transition to capitalism. Capitalism can stimulate considerable growth because the capitalist can, and has an incentive to, reinvest profits in new technologies and capital equipment.

According to Marx capitalists take advantage of the difference between the labour market and the market for whatever commodity the capitalist can produce. Marx observed that in practically every successful industry input unit-costs are lower than output unit-prices. Marx called the difference "surplus value" and argued that this surplus value had its source in surplus labour, the difference between what it costs to keep workers alive and what they can produce. Marx's dual view of capitalism can be seen in his description of the capitalists: he refers to them as to vampires sucking worker's blood, but at the same time, he notes that drawing profit is "by no means an injustice" and that capitalists simply cannot go against the system. The true problem lies with the "cancerous cell" of capital, understood not as property or equipment, but the relations between workers and owners—the economic system in general.

At the same time, Marx stressed that capitalism was unstable, and prone to periodic crises. He suggested that over time, capitalists would invest more and more in new technologies, and less and less in labour. Since Marx believed that surplus value appropriated from labour is the source of profits, he concluded that the rate of profit would fall even as the economy grew. Marx believed that increasingly severe crises would punctuate this cycle of growth, collapse, and more growth. Moreover, he believed that in the long-term this process would necessarily enrich and empower the capitalist class and impoverish the proletariat. In section one of The Communist Manifesto, Marx describes feudalism, capitalism, and the role internal social contradictions play in the historical process.

We see then: the means of production and of exchange, on whose foundation the bourgeoisie built itself up, were generated in feudal society. At a certain stage in the development of these means of production and of exchange, the conditions under which feudal society produced and exchanged the feudal relations of property became no longer compatible with the already developed productive forces; they became so many fetters. They had to be burst asunder; they were burst asunder. Into their place stepped free competition, accompanied by a social and political constitution adapted in it, and the economic and political sway of the bourgeois class. A similar movement is going on before our own eyes. The productive forces at the disposal of society no longer tend to further the development of the conditions of bourgeois property; on the contrary, they have become too powerful for these conditions, by which they are fettered, and so soon as they overcome these fetters, they bring order into the whole of bourgeois society, endanger the existence of bourgeois property.

In this new society the self-alienation would end, and humans would be free to act without being bound by the labour market. It would be a democratic society, enfranchising the entire population. In such a utopian world there would also be little if any need for a state, which goal was to enforce the alienation. He theorized that between capitalism and the establishment of a socialist/communist system, a dictatorship of the proletariat—a period where the working class holds political power and forcibly socializes the means of production—would exist. As he wrote in his "Critique of the Gotha Programme", between capitalist and communist society there lies the period of the revolutionary transformation of the one into the other. Corresponding to this is also a political transition period in which the state can be nothing but the revolutionary dictatorship of the proletariat. "While he allowed for the possibility of peaceful transition in some countries with strong democratic institutional structures (such as Britain, the US and the Netherlands), he suggested that in other countries with strong centralized state-oriented traditions, like France and Germany, the "lever of our revolution must be force."